The Problem with "Problem-Solving Skills"

CASE STUDIES IN COMPUTER SCIENCE
VOLUME 0

"Somebody has to do the hard jobs."
– Mark Weaver in *The Wreck of the* Phosploion

Computing is an Experimental Science.
– James M. Waclawik

I revert to the doctrinal methods of the thirteenth century, inspired by the general hope of getting something done.
– G. K. Chesterton
Heretics, CW1:46

"I often stare at windows."
– G. K. Chesterton
"The Crime of Gabriel Gale" in
The Poet and the Lunatics

* * *

A beginning should be a basis; and a basis should be something accepted... Not only the physical basis of life, but the mathematical basis of physics, is being questioned. The professors really believe that they have found the window wider than the wall; and that they must widen their minds till there is no such thing as width.
– G. K. Chesterton
Illustrated London News
December 13, 1919, CW31:57

* * *

For more information, visit
`http://DeBellisStellarum/CSCS/cscs.htm`

* * *

Case Studies in Computer Science

Volume	Title
0	The Problem with "Problem-Solving Skills" (or, Base Two Basics)
planned	Free the Monoid! (or, Wildcards, Signatures and other String Stuff)
planned	Out, Damned Spot! (or, How the Pope Helped with Local Ad Insertion)
planned	Sometimes... (or, CNC Punch Press Optimization and Related Problems)

The Problem with "Problem-Solving Skills"

Peter J. Floriani, Ph.D.

CASE STUDIES IN COMPUTER SCIENCE
VOLUME 0

Penn Street Productions
Reading, PA

Dedication

Ad Majorem Dei Gloriam

Εστω δε 'ο λογος 'υμων **ναι ναι, ου ου**:
το δε περισσον τουτων εκ του πονηρου εσην.
Let your speech be **yes, yes: no, no**:
and that which is over and above these is of evil.

Matthew 5:37, emphasis added

With special thanks to
Jim Waclawik
Nancy Carpentier Brown
Joseph Romano, Ph.D.
and my co-workers of the past 30-plus years.

In Memoriam
my parents
Sr. Miriam, O.S.B.
Sr. Jean Anthony, O.S.B.
Sr. Jude Ellen, O.S.B.
Sr. Mary Joy, O.S.B.
Sr. Kathryn Mary, O.S.F.
Eugene Paolini, M.S.
Samuel L. Gulden, M.S.
Samuel R. Frankel, M.S., P.E.
Charles H. Blouch
E. Thomas Sheetz

Produced by
⌐ 📖 ⌐
Penn Street Productions,
Reading, PA

ISBN-13 978-1494245863
ISBN-10 1494245868

Table of Contents
(the asterisk (*) indicates a Case Study)

Preface
(A Comment from a Friend of the Author)

I met Peter in 1990 at graduate school. He is a lunatic, but given our experiences together I must refrain from any further revelations – and so I will limit my comment to the following four ASCII characters:

/**/

James M. Waclawik

Series Foreword

This series of monographs is my attempt to enrich your own personal collection of previously solved problems – which is, in the end, the only "problem-solving skill" worthy of the name.

The "monograph" format is not the one usually expected in the modern academic world. People expect journal articles, or perhaps FACEBOOK postings. However, the monograph is a traditional approach to exotic topics for many disciplines: even Sherlock Holmes said (in *The Sign of the Four*) he was "guilty of several monographs." Besides, it is gratifying to explore such fascinating topics by this means, thereby aiding in the advance of Science writ large, and in the pursuit of Wisdom.

I can imagine Sherlock Holmes remarking, in a light allusive fashion, that he himself had written a little monograph on the subject of cows' tails; with diagrams and tables solving the great traditional problem of how many cows' tails would reach the moon; a subject of extraordinary interest to moonlighters. And I can still more easily imagine him saying afterwards, having resumed the pipe and dressing-gown of Baker Street, "A remarkable little problem, Watson. In some of its features it was perhaps more singular than any you have been good enough to report. I do not think that even the Tooting Trouser-Stretching Mystery, or the singular little affair of the Radium Toothpick, offered more strange and sensational developments."

GKC, *Irish Impressions* CW20

* * *

At the Ambrosian, we are constantly striving to synthesize – that is to unite – the various disparate topics and subjects of knowledge – indeed, we strive to see, and therefore to carry out all that is implicit in seeing, that most scientific phrase in the Creed: *Per quem omnia facta sunt* = "through Him all things were made."

We desire to be Christians first: followers of Jesus Christ, and therefore will arm ourselves with every possible weapon in the war we must wage until our deaths. That means we call upon science and literature, upon mathematics and philosophy, upon history, language, engineering... it is said in many ways, and shall be said in many ways, but for us, there is no such thing as a different subject, simply because we wish to say with St. Paul, we have resolved to know nothing but Jesus Christ and Him crucified. (1 Cor 2:2)

However, that does not mean we are locked into some sort of a morbid perpetual Good Friday asceticism. What it means is that we try to always be conscious of what it is we are doing. We have our Final End in mind, whether we are studying or reading or lecturing or working in a laboratory or playing a game or an instrument, or even walking across the campus. That is why our bells ring every hour: to remind us how little time is left to us.

– from the introduction to the Course Catalog of the Ambrosian University

Foreword for This Volume

Everyone talks about problem-solving skills, but no one seems to be able to name what any of those skills are. That's annoying, since most of the thirty-odd years I've been in computer science I have been using my skills to solve problems, so when I hear people talking about this, I always wonder what they could possibly mean.

Well... I'm not going to attempt to solve *that* problem. Instead, I am going to examine another problem: what are some of the skills I have been using to solve problems? It's not an easy thing to do, but being a Catholic and a Chestertonian have helped me with such a bizarre intellectual and self-critical question.

This study, like GKC's *Orthodoxy*, is unavoidably autobiographical, at least in part, but that may help rescue this book from being very dry and dull. It may be fun for you to see the horrible challenges someone else has faced, and thrilling to see how these puzzles were solved – or weren't solved.

Peter J. Floriani, Ph.D.

Things to Have on Hand

1. A computer, with some sort of compiler/interpreter and development tools, since there will be some experiments you ought to perform

2. Your choice of writing implement [1] and a notebook (I mean a real, tactile, paper one) for taking notes, for working out puzzles, and other assignments. Probably some scrap paper will also be handy.

3. Other items will be mentioned at the appropriate time, as there will be some "show and tell" projects which require other materials.

Don't forget:

The programming examples can be found on the website:

```
http://www.DeBellisStellarum/cscs/cscs.htm
```

---

[1] Preferably a pencil: the "magic wand" given to Milo by the Mathemagician. With it and the bag full of words given to him by King Azaz, Milo fought the terrible Demons of Ignorance. Yes, I am referring to Juster's *The Phantom Tollbooth*, but lest you think that "bag of words" is imaginary, in computer science it is quite real, and we call it A*. See the second volume of this series for details.

The Pedagogy of Computer Science

*It is as if the whole life of the mind were animated from within
by a natural desire for the fullest possible unification...*
Gilson, *The Spirit of Medieval Philosophy*, 260

Chapter 1
Getting to the Root of the Subject

Incipe nunc philosophiae, non pecuniae, studere.
"Begin now to study philosophy, not money."
– Seneca, *Epistulae* 17.5.

This study had its germination in an odd occurrence from the early 1990s, at the time when I was working on my Ph.D. A certain "talking doll" appeared, causing consternation and discussion because one of its sayings was: "Math is hard!" This prompted a fascinating but mostly fruitless discussion among the graduate students in the computer science department: *Well, is Math really hard, or isn't it?*

I found the answer in a book called *The Division and Methods of the Sciences* which is a commentary by St. Thomas Aquinas on *De Trinitate* by Boethius (who also wrote *The Consolation of Philosophy*).

Aquinas answered that mathematics considered as a subject is *easy*: it is a simpler subject than "natural philosophy" (which includes physics), which in turn is simpler than "divine science" (or theology).

In fact, the subject is called "Mathematics" which is Greek for "the Learning" because it is *learned* – someone can teach it to you, and then you know it! And, though any given aspect of mathematics may be "easier" or "harder" for any given student, it is still possible for a dedicated teacher and a diligent student to work together – and for the student to acquire a complete understanding of that topic or principle. (Providing, of course, they are both enthusiastic about it.)

As I continued my exploration of mathematics and the larger question of the division and method of the sciences, I slowly became more and more aware of *philosophy*: the old Greek word which means the love of wisdom. Not the dull and sterile modern kind – Kant and Nietzsche and Marx and Darwin, the hilarious Copenhagen version of the Uncertainty Principle, the goofy and absolutely hypocritical Relativists – and so on. All empty and sterile. No: I mean the rich, sound, eminently reasonable *and fruitful* system of the High Middle Ages, the Scholastic Philosophy. And as I explored I began to find all the missing words – words for tools I was already using – words like

teleology – the science of Ends, that is, of purposes,
epistemology – the science of Knowledge in itself,
etiology – the science of Causes,
pedagogy – the science of Teaching.[2]

There were also: dramatic cautions against things like "equivocation" – using the same word to mean two different things; powerful epigrams like *Nemo dat quod non habet* = "Nobody gives what he does not have" or *Quidquid recipitur secundum*

---

[2] Note, this is not "how" to teach, but the study of the act of Teaching which is the propagation of knowledge. (Yeah, that sounds recursive as well as complex, which is why it's a branch of philosophy.)

modum recipientis recipitur = "Whatever is received is received according to the mode of the receiver"; and wonderful insights like: "A thing is more perfect as it is more perfectly one." Awesome.

Somewhat later, during my wanderings through the great realm of Wisdom while hunting for clues to use in my fictional writing, I encountered a fascinating diagram known as the Tree of Virtues. This huge diagram [3] of some 200 nodes with dozens of annotated branches appeared in the *Cursus Theologicus* of the University of Salamanca; it shows the interrelations of dozens of "virtues" including under that term a diverse number of human occupations and fields of study. It is quite intricate, on a par with the amazing "Chart of the Metabolic Processes."[4]

Why a *tree*? The tree as a method of organization is very ancient, suggested to Moses by his father-in-law.[5] Almost anyone who deals with computers in the present age will know about the hierarchical system of directories, subdirectories, and files with its root called either "\" or "/" depending on the conventions of the operating system. It is a powerful tool, and so is the wonderful scheme in Biology called Taxonomy – which is itself a tree, organizing the millions of types of living creatures into their kingdoms and phylums, classes, orders, families, genuses, and species. These words are merely the titles of the various levels in the tree, providing terms to specify the degree of similarity or difference between two forms of life.

While such "trees" may not meet all the formal requirements of the "tree" in graph theory (a branch of discrete mathematics), the concept is a convenient one, aiding with the organization of otherwise difficult collections of material – and it is traditional as well. For example, here is the "Tree of Sciences" from the work of Henry of Langenstein [6] in the late 1300s, drawn by software from the early 2000s:

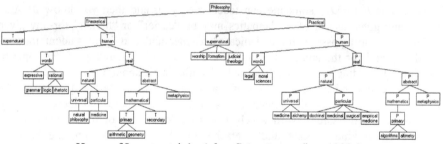

Henry of Langenstein's *Arbor Scientiarum* (late 1300s).

---

[3] It occupies an entire page in an "elephant folio," the very large form of book like those atlases you can see in libraries. I received a photo of it from my friend Andrew Poole; unfortunately it is not suitable for re-printing here.

[4] For some time now I have wanted a wall-size copy of that Tree, but even more I want an *updated* one to include all the fields and subdivisions one finds at a typical university. This idea of an updated Tree of Virtues has made so strong an impression on me that I have made it the identifying symbol of my imaginary Ambrosian University, an important place in my fictional Saga, and the cover and organizing principle of its course catalog. In keeping with the "Little Red Hen" principle, I have been collecting data in preparation for such a diagram, and this book includes the subtree which applies to Computer Science.

[5] See Exodus 18:13-26; this is also the foundation of the principle of Subsidiarity.

[6] Drawn by my software from data given in Steneck, "A Late Medieval *Arbor Scientiarum*" in *Speculum*, Vol. 50, No.2 (Apr. 1975) pp. 245-269. Note that in computer science, we always draw our trees with the root at the *top*.

It may also be instructive to consider Henry's original data in the usual outline form:

Philosophy:
1. Theoretical
    1.a. supernatural
        1.a.1. supernatural
    1.b. human
        1.a.1. words
            1.a.1.a. expressive
                1.a.1.a.1. grammar
            1.a.1.b. rational
                1.a.1.b.1. logic
                1.a.1.b.2. rhetoric
        1.a.2. real
            1.a.2.a. natural (physics)
                1.a.2.a.1. universal
                      1.a.2.a.1.a. natural philosophy
                1.a.2.a.2. particular
                      1.a.2.a.2.a. medicine
            1.a.2.b. abstract
                1.a.2.b.1. mathematical
                      1.a.2.b.1.a. primary
                          1.a.2.b.1.a.1 arithmetic
                          1.a.2.b.1.a.2 geometry
                      1.a.2.b.1.b. secondary
                          1.a.2.b.1.b.1. music
                          1.a.2.b.1.b.2. astronomy
                          1.a.2.b.1.b.3. perspective
                          1.a.2.b.1.b.4. weights
                          1.a.2.b.1.b.5. latitudes
                1.a.2.b.2. metaphysics
2. Practical
    2.a. supernatural
        2.a.1 worship
        2.a.2 formation
        2.a.3 judicial theology
    2.b. human
        2.b.1. words
            2.b.1.a. legal
            2.b.1.b. moral sciences
        2.b.2. real
            2.b.2.a. natural
                2.b.2.a.1. universal
                      2.b.2.a.1.a medicine
                      2.b.2.a.1.b alchemy
                2.b.2.a.2. particular
                      2.b.2.a.2.a. doctrinal
                      2.b.2.a.2.b. medicinal
                      2.b.2.a.2.c. surgical
                      2.b.2.a.2.d. empirical medicine
            2.b.2.b. abstract
                2.b.2.b.1. mathematical
                      2.b.2.b.1.a. primary
                          2.b.2.b.1.a.1. algorithms
                          2.b.2.b.1.a.2. altimetry
                      2.b.2.b.1.b. secondary
                          2.b.2.b.1.b.1. practical music
                          2.b.2.b.1.b.2, astronomy
                2.b.2.b.2. metaphysics

This particular issue in epistemology – the organization of Knowledge according to the various fields of study and work – was a major topic during the ages of Scholastic Philosophy. Besides the above arrangement Henry of Langenstein also used the "six days" of Genesis 1 as a sort of index.[7] There is also Aquinas' version in the above-mentioned commentary on Boethius, and the topic is dealt with at length in *The Didascalicon of Hugh of St. Victor*.[8] Then there is the Tree of Virtues from the *Cursus* of Salamanca. Five different schemes, each providing distinct insights.

Why do I turn to such ancient materials in my attempt to discuss the pedagogy of this modern discipline called Computer Science?

Simply because in order to talk rationally about a subject, one must organize it. This is a fundamental rule of software development: defining one's problem, organizing its components, the data structures and algorithms one needs, and so on. Though I know this technique and have applied it many times, it is not easy to apply it to such an abstract matter, partly because I have had a relatively brief time (only 30-odd years) in the field, and a relatively narrow perspective despite all my varied experiences in academics and companies both small and large. Also, the topic is of limited interest, except perhaps to faculty committees who are trying to decide on what courses to include – or exclude. Moreover, even in those long-past days when this matter of pedagogy was seriously studied, there were multiple approaches used, and debates about what to include – or exclude.

So, in my usual bread-boarding, experimental, industrial "let's get it done" style, I am only making an attempt at starting an implementation. It is a fascinating project, and worth further exploration. One challenge I have noted is to segregate several important related topics from the more fundamental one of pure taxonomy: I wish to specifically mention (1) the history of these branches and how they arose, and (2) the proper pedagogy for this field, that is, the order in which the branches are best taught, with a view to what many colleges call "prerequisites." History will get mentioned occasionally, but for the most part I hope to defer that topic to a separate treatment. The matter of pedagogy, however, will be considered shortly.

In order to begin properly, it may be advisable to start with a key principle from another ancient work, *The Consolation of Philosophy* by Boethius. This interesting book (which, among other things has a very relevant discussion of the philosophy of "chance" which ought to be studied by anyone hoping to understand so-called random-number generators) starts with the author in prison awaiting execution. Suddenly the personification of Philosophy appears to him: she has the form of a majestic woman wearing a robe which is described in this detail:

> On the border below was inwoven the symbol Π, on that above was to be read a Θ. And between the two letters there could be marked degrees, by which, as by the rungs of a ladder, ascent might be made from the lower principle to the higher.[9]

A footnote in the translation explains: "Π and Θ are the first letters of the Greek words [10] denoting Practical and Theoretical, the two divisions of Philosophy."

---

[7] See Steneck, *Science and Creation in the Middle Ages*.

[8] Translated and annotated by Jerome Taylor.

[9] Boethius, *The Consolation of Philosophy*, translated by W. V. Cooper.

[10] Πραξις (*praxis*) = practice; Θεωρια (*theôria*) = theory. These words, and that even most mystical ladder, deserve a far larger treatment than I dare attempt here, but regardless of its antiquity, this is indeed fundamental to our work.

This quote (or something like it) ought to be blazoned upon an arch over the entrance to every institute of higher learning. Here we have the great key to the field of Philosophy, the Love of Wisdom, which comprises all the manifold branches of human thought, both intellectual and active: while those two great realms are separated, and Θ is indeed higher than Π, yet the key is that link, that ladder or staircase enabling contact between them. A powerful and mystical truth.

All too often I have seen these two realms at war: one might say that the *theory* side is somehow represented by academics, and the *practice* side is industry – I have spent long years in both realms, and after considerable frustration I have taken the view: "I sit squarely on the fence." Or, perhaps I should say, on that staircase. Such an attitude is part of the Medieval way, the "doctrinal methods of the thirteenth century" by which things actually get done.[11] In reality, the one realm aids the other; they provide mutual assistance even in their own special tasks, and so it is fitting that we computer scientists also spend our time on that staircase, whether we are in industry or academics, especially since our discipline is so young, and hence so clearly an alliance of theory and practice. For other branches of the Tree of Virtues, there may be somewhat more profound divisions, as in the case of the branch of Physics called mechanics and its corresponding branch of Engineering called mechanical engineering – but there due regard is paid by one to the other. There are many places where computing has taken on a truly engineering character, yet even those are still in the ever-altering turmoils of growth and – let us hope – improvement. But there are other places where the division of theory and practice occurs almost naturally, and in a far more amicable manner, since the staircase seems to be burgeoning with fruit for both ends, and the work of organization has barely begun.

Let us, then, begin our organization by making a start at a design of the Tree by which we might order the branches of our discipline.

---

[11] Cf. Chesterton speaking about Aquinas, the great scholar of many books who also composed poetry: "His double function rather recalls the double activity of some great Renaissance craftsman, like Michelangelo or Leonardo da Vinci, who would work on the outer wall, planning and building the fortifications of the city; and then retire into the inner chamber to carve or model some cup or casket for a reliquary." GKC *St. Thomas Aquinas* CW2:509. One need not be a genius to practice the disciplines of a genius. Or, perhaps, that is the secret to getting things done.

Chapter 2
Where To Start?

Lignum quod plantatum est secus decursus aquarum
quod fructum suum dabit in tempore suo
et folium eius non defluet et omnia quaecumque faciet prosperabuntur.

Those Latin words form the elegant border of the diagram called "the Tree of Virtues" in the *Cursus Theologicus* of Salamanca. In case you do not know Latin, it is from the Psalms: "And he shall be like a tree which is planted near the running waters, which shall bring forth its fruit, in due season. And his leaf shall not fall off: and all whatsoever he shall do shall prosper." [Ps 1:3]

It may annoy some to think that the start of computing is found in the Hebrew Psalms, which gave rise to the long history of the monastic discipline called the Divine Office: a regular schedule of praying seven times each day:

Seven times a day I have given praise to Thee, for the judgments of Thy justice. [12]

While timekeeping has driven Man's curiosity in Science and Engineering for millennia, the real mechanics of time began in the Middle Ages, when the first mechanical clocks were devised.[13] (I leave musical instruments for another study, especially the complexities of the pipe organ and its automatic version.) But perhaps such allegorical hints of the origin of computing are not appropriate here, which is why I ask: *Where are we to start our list of what's important for computer science?*

It is a daunting task, at least at first glimpse. However, it is a famous paradigm from adventure-stories: the shipwrecked hero has to recover sufficient gear to rebuild his life, at least enough to survive, but especially to achieve his eventual rescue. It is so important to us that I will recommend several books, partly for your reading pleasure, but also for the sake of pedagogy:

1. Defoe, *Robinson Crusoe*. The classic tale of this paradigm.

2. Wyss, *Swiss Family Robinson*. The other classic tale.

3. Williams and Abrashkin. *Danny Dunn on a Desert Island*. A science adventure for young people.

4. Smith. *Spacehounds of IPC*. An old science fiction "spacewreck" tale.

But especially you should consult Chesterton. You may not expect such things from a literary man, but then you might consider his very engineer-like response when asked the classic question "What book would you want if you were wrecked on a desert island?" He replied: "Thomas's Guide To Practical Shipbuilding."[14] But he also observed that *Robinson Crusoe*

...owes its eternal vivacity to the fact that it celebrates the poetry of limits, nay, even the wild romance of prudence. Crusoe is a man on a small rock with a few comforts just snatched from the sea: the best thing in the book is simply the list of things saved from the wreck. The greatest of poems is an inventory. Every kitchen

---

[12] Ps 118:164. Prayer, it appears, is a 24/7 operation.

[13] "I should not be at all surprised if, when you counted the scientific investigations and discoveries since the fall of Rome, you found that a great mass of them had been made by monks." in GKC, *The Ball and the Cross*. Those may be debating words, but for facts see Jaki's essay, "Medieval Creativity in Science and Technology" in *Patterns or Principles and Other Essays*, 63-83, and elsewhere, especially "The Sighting of New Horizons," chapter 10 of his *Science and Creation*.

[14] Reported in Ward, *Gilbert Keith Chesterton*, 204.

tool becomes ideal because Crusoe might have dropped it in the sea. It is a good exercise, in empty or ugly hours of the day, to look at anything, the coal-scuttle or the bookcase, and think how happy one could be to have brought it out of the sinking ship on to the solitary island. But it is a better exercise still to remember how all things have had this hair-breadth escape: everything has been saved from a wreck.[15]

Indeed – so it is very adventurous for me to try to write that "greatest of poems" called an inventory. I will tabulate that inventory using what some call an "outline" but computer scientists call a "tree."

Why a tree? Even though "tree" is a very important idea in computer science, whether we are speaking of a special kind of graph (in the discrete math sense), a data structure, or a scheme for the directories of disk files, I am referring to the far more ancient usage of the Scholastics who, as we discussed in the last section, organized the many kinds of knowledge, disciplines, trades, crafts, and human occupations which make up the realm of Wisdom by means of a Tree.[16]

Organization of such a varied discipline as computer science – and such a *young* discipline – is by no means an easy task. It requires the very odd skill of self-reflective analysis, which might best be described by an odd little assignment:

Assignment: Draw a picture of yourself drawing a picture of yourself in a mirror. We'll talk more about this later, so don't hurry off for your drawing kit now.

Yeah, it's not easy – and I am not talking about the mere challenge of good draftsmanship. It's the idea of simultaneously being inside *and outside*, being both subject and object... trying to use the tool to deal with the tool-in-itself. (And this is why one of my particular interests in computing is the making of tools for the use of making tools.)

There are, moreover, a multitude of distractions to such a task, and like another sort of self-reflective problem we shall mention later, it begs the question: where to begin?

This, then, is a good time to poke at least a little into history and the related concepts of precedence and parenthood. Our discipline has a number of curious predecessors among the existing fields, some of which we might call its "godparents." In particular I wish to single out music, because of its mystic character of representing the instructions for its art by traditional symbols; the supreme art which is cooking does the same in its recipes. We must not fail to mention the special craft of mechanical musical instruments, and other mechanical self-moving devices. But all these are only at best avuncular to our field; to find our roots we must go very deep into human culture itself, while not forgetting its recent advances.

Extremely ancient skills play a role in the genesis of computing: writing in its literal sense (that is, the representation of speech by carved or printed symbol), speech in itself (the representation of thought by sound), and even weaving (the interlacing of series of orthogonal threads to make fabric). Indeed, punch cards (a derivative of the old musical scrolls for automatic instruments) were first used in 1801 on the famous Jacquard Loom. The modern sciences, especially the branch of physics which deals with electricity, and those branches of engineering dealing with electricity and electronics are intimately involved, given the form of our present-day computers – but as Babbage showed in the early 1800s [17] there are mechanical alternatives.

---

[15] GKC, *Orthodoxy*, CW1:267.

[16] And yes, the tree has a richer symbolism, but that belongs to another sort of treatise.

[17] In the early 1300s Raymund Llull proposed his rotating disks of the *Ars Magna*. In 1621 William Oughtred made a slide rule which multiplied. In 1639 the 16-year-old Pascal built an

But here the medieval scholar would exclaim (perhaps with a blow of his fist on the table): *Distinguo!*

(That is, *I distinguish!* This word is one of the classic responses in the old formal Argument of the Scholastics: it is said when the proposed idea must be divided into distinct aspects, each of which are treated independently.)

All that is *history*, and we need to know *geography*. Where in the vast realm of Wisdom does Computer Science truly arise in the intellectual sense? Where does it fit among history and mathematics, geography and science, literature and music, theology and engineering, trades and crafts and philosophy? In what field, what class of studies, is its authentic and rational origin? We must root it somewhere, at its most elementary level. But where?

As should be obvious to anyone who has entered computing or mathematics, Computer Science is a hybrid discipline comprising both abstract theoretical and concrete practical components, that is, it is both a Science and an Engineering.

And, once one delves deep enough, one will find that it is rooted in that branch of Mathematics known as Discrete Mathematics. So we shall start there, in Mathematics, which E. T. Bell called the "Queen and Servant of Science," and try to draw ourselves in a mirror, watching our activity with careful attention...

---

adding machine. See Jaki, *Brain, Mind, and Computers*, 22. There is also a curious device of gears found in 1900 near the Greek island of Anti-Kythera dating to 87 BC and conjectured to compute astronomical dates. See Cardwell, *The Norton History of Technology*, 22-3.

Chapter 3
The Tree of Computer Science

Disce ubi sit prudentia, ubi sit virtus, ubi sit intellectus...
ubi sit lumen oculorum et pax.
Learn where is wisdom, where is strength, where is understanding...
where is the light of the eyes, and peace. [18]

We root our tree in the classic Trivium of Grammar, Logic, and Rhetoric.

A§'. Logic
A§1'. Fundamentals (precision in the use of words)
A§2'. Propositional Calculus: TRUE, FALSE; terms combined with AND, OR, NOT.
A§3'. Predicate Calculus: statements of the forms "ALL x IS y," "ALL x IS NOT y," "SOME x IS y," "SOME x IS NOT y" and their combinations; the syllogism.
A§4'. Other topics in logic, etc.

Deriving from **A§2'.** we have the formal notation of Propositional Calculus

A§2. Boolean Algebra: the mathematics of only two values (TRUE and FALSE) and operations upon them (AND, OR, NOT, XOR, IF, IF-AND-ONLY-IF).
A§2.a. Boolean functions: the functions which can be computed by such operations
A§2.a.1. Physical representation of Boolean functions (machines without memory)
A§2.b. Add "time" (memory) to Boolean functions giving "state automata"
A§2.b.1. Logic machines with finite memory: finite state machines/automata (FSAs)
    A§2.b.1.a. The grammar of FSAs: regular expressions

A§2.b.2. Automata with infinite memory, and their corresponding grammars
    A§2.b.2.a. stack machines
    A§2.b.2.a.1. context-free grammars
    A§2.b.2.b. length-increasing machines (stacks with extensions)
    A§2.b.2.b.1. context-sensitive grammars
    A§2.b.2.c. unbounded automata (Turing machines)
    A§2.b.2.c.1. general (unrestricted) grammars
All these infinite automata of course cannot be implemented in real components, hence they remain abstractions, though approximations are possible. [19]

Let us consider **A§2.b.1.** again – logic machines with finite memory – and add a new node to specify these when implemented by electronics:

A§2.b.1.b. Electronic Logic Machines with Finite Memory (electronic FSAs)

We shall establish this node as a new subtree, and rename it "machine architecture." This very special subbranch **A§2.b.1.b.** deriving from Logic is the working root of our discipline:

---

[18] Baruch 3:14. Latin quoted on the "Tree" of the *Cursus Theologicus* of Salamanca.
[19] "We approximate infinity by a terabyte." Dr. E. Kaltofen, in class, Sept. 4, 1990.

A§2.b.1.b. ⇒ **B§** Machine architecture

This node is the master-foundation upon which the remainder of all subsequent matters in computer science are based. We note that it is simply, and always, a finite state machine comprised of elementary logic gates, the state of which perform the effect of "logic," along with flip-flops capable of retaining their states in time, thus having the effect of "memory." It is worth mentioning here that not all circuits built of logic gates and memory are properly "computers"; such things have their own purposes and indeed are useful as supporting components, both in CPUs or in other uses such as peripheral cards or devices.

And then we add one further attribute:

We augment FSAs with a novel idea, the Von Neumann Principle: **"Code is Data"** thus enabling the concept of a "machine instruction" which is represented by certain of the machine's states themselves. This is now true "computer architecture" which is a sub-discipline in itself:

B§1. Computer Architecture

At this point such an augmented machine can be considered a "computer" as the term is commonly understood, since it is "programmable": that is, it can be loaded with "instructions" which control its operation, yet these instructions are not inherent parts of the machine itself, but have been placed ("loaded") into it, just as any sort of musical roll can be placed into a player piano or other automatic instrument.

We note here that such devices may have their own restrictions (again for use in special purposes) by which the device (though programmable) fails to be a "general" computer – some of these may be distinguished by the title "Programmable Logic Controller." We further note that no distinction needs to be made at this point as to whether these devices contain a single processor or multiple processors.

There are formal ways of describing these machines, called Hardware Description Languages (HDLs); such tools permit condensed representations of the actual circuits, and may be studied and simulated; they may even provide the template by which the solid-state device is produced.

B§2. Control of the machine in itself. The various possible operations which this machine may perform are organized based on their function and other details. While the codes for each instruction are literally binary (a series of zero and one), they are typically represented in octal or hexadecimal for the sake of brevity. These operations are described in detail in a reference document using HDLs or another representation, showing what effect they have on the other parts of the machine.[20]

B§2.a Assembly Language. We symbolize such instructions by mnemonics, and augment this new "language" with other simplifying notations. This language is a symbolic convenience for handling the underlying numerical representations of the actual instructions

B§2.b Programming Languages. This concept of language is simplified and extended to yield various "programming languages." In 2013 there are a large array of such things, which may be classed into

---

[20] We note that such instructions may possess their own reality, but do not thereby demand that their machine *exist*, either in the real world or in some simulation.

B§2.b.1. imperative nonstructured (FORTRAN, BASIC, APL, COBOL &c)

B§2.b.2. imperative structured (ALGOL/PASCAL/C/ADA, &c)

B§2.b.3. functional (LISP, PROLOG, &c)

B§2.b.4. other (SNOBOL, RPG, SMALLTALK, &c).

B§3. Control of the machine according to its place in a larger environment:
Operating systems – the management and coordination of the use of the machine. Its subdivisions include

B§3.a. Control of the machine in itself [21]

B§3.a.1 startup and maintenance functions

B§3.a.2 protection of itself

B§3.a.3 direct use (command interpretor)

B§3.a.4 facility for the execution of applications

B§3.a.5 facility to arrange production of executable programs
- linker
- run-time libraries
- other service mechanisms (background processes, etc.)

B§3.b. Control of internal facilities of the system

B§3.b.1 memory management, addressing, "virtual memory" etc.

B§3.b.2 time (including concurrency and related matters)

B§3.b.3 other utility functions (clock, calendar, etc.)

B§3.c. System-managed control of external facilities

B§3.c.1. Disk drives
- system use (swapping, free space, directory management)
- files (disk space considered as storage for user data)
- databases (typically more than a specialized class of file)

B§3.c.2. Special user input and output devices
- keyboard
- mouse, trackball, light-pen, etc.
- video display
- audio (sound generation and control)

B§3.c.3. Media-effecting devices
- printers
- plotters
- others

B§3.c.4. Backup devices
- magnetic tape and floppy disks
- CDs, DVDs, and relatives
- removable storage devices

B§3.c.5. Networking
- low-level uses (system applications)
- file transport
- web-page support
- other forms of network activities

B§3.d. Special Topics

B§3.d.1. Comparative Studies of Operating Systems
- basics of classic systems (IBM OS, UNIX, CP/M, DOS, WINDOWS)

---

[21] It must be noted that most typical computers of the present time are *not* intended as single-program machines as some early models were, such as the CDC 160, PDP-8, and HP 2116, which we shall see later.

        – advantages & shortcomings of various systems
    B§3.d.2. Implementation issues in Operating System Design
        – queues; concurrency; memory management; etc.

We have considered the machine itself, its auxiliary components, and its place in the larger scene – but we have not yet considered how it might be brought to the aid of other disciplines. We therefore now come to another branch which has multiple ramifications, the branch by which all the above subdivisions are known and unified into a consistent skill. For **it is required that every program associate with and be served by the System.**[22]

B§4. Programming – that is, the use of the computer as a *Tool* to solve a problem or accomplish a task.

B§5. Other Aspects of the Discipline
B§5.a. History
        – when and how the various branches of Computer Science arose
        – major milestones in its chronology
        – its important workers
B§5.b. Interrelations with Other Disciplines. To some extent this will be covered under a subsequent branch, but there are various larger matters to be examined, especially relating to mathematics, philosophy, and (to some extent) neurology and those aspects of biology which deal with the human organism and its behavior. Other important topics besides its involvement with math and philosophy, science and engineering are its contributions to communication, to the arts, and particularly to work involving the printed word.
B§5.c. (For future expansion)

With the mention of Programming we again find it necessary to segregate a node as a distinct sub-branch for finer analysis:

B§4. $\Rightarrow$ **C§. Programming**
From this primary node arise the specific disciplines of "programming" either as a general tool of expression, or according to the requirements of a given language.[23] Portions of such study may proceed in an non-specific form, but generally we must designate some specific language, preferably one existing in the real world.

---

[22] This statement is a formal corollary of the Great Truth which is the ontological principle of every Program: "It was the function of every program to contact and serve its User." (Daley, *TRON*, 125.) In that very important allegory, the MCP was corrupted by a wicked man, echoing the *Non Serviam* ("I will not serve") Lucifer threw in the face of the Great Programmer. Indeed, the Operating System, as the "authority" within the Computer, must abide by the rule given by the Great Programmer: "Even as the Son of Man is not come to be served, but to serve, and to give his life a redemption for many." (see Matthew 20:28) Yes, it is paradoxical, and may even be unsettling to some, but this fact gives an amazingly useful insight into the nature of Operating Systems and indeed of Programming. As GKC noted: "...henceforth the highest thing can only work from below." (*The Everlasting Man*, CW2:313)
[23] Such as one might distinguish a composition of music in its general sense from a composition arranged for a given instrument. Clearly there are compositions possible to score which cannot be performed on any existing instrument.

All these branches are, to some extent, in the realm of Theory, since their results remain abstract unless one goes to the computer and proceeds with actual development – which drops the work into the realm of Practice. Furthermore these branches have other relatives in that realm, derivatives in the sense of applying programming to various fields including this discipline in itself, which gives rise to its own special division of applications as we shall see shortly.

Moreover, programming is necessarily performed in a given "real" language, (which may not yet "exist" in the sense of having been implemented!) or merely sketched using less formal notations, even a natural (human) language. Such sketches are often known as "algorithms" – the formats by which they are presented are termed "pseudo-code." Such presentations are made with greater or lesser rigor depending upon the demands of the situation – a casual discussion or informal explanation, versus a formal lecture, paper, or journal article. Think of humming the main notes suggesting the theme of a symphony versus their actual notation in the score.

C§1. Programming – in itself (Theoretical), or in Specific Language "X" (Practical)

Programming is studied in itself in order to grasp the use of a programming language (even in a trivial way) but more importantly to understand its abilities and limitations.

    C§1.a. Syntax of its elements
    C§1.b. Data structures (types, variables, constants; "declarative" code)
    C§1.c. Control forms (statements or instructions; "executable" code)
    C§1.d. Organization (logical hierarchy of "routines" and relatives.)[24]

Such knowledge enables actual *use* of the language in the abstract, i.e. to solve "mathematical problems" – note, however these may truly be "solved" but their solution is *not* known outside of the machine![25] Hence we require more:

    C§1.e.   As that language is (or may be) constrained by a given implementation in a specific compiler and run-time environment. Which leads to this:

C§2. As that language contacts the rest of things
    C§2.a. As it is *used*: the tools which implement this language
        C§2.a.1. compiler
        C§2.a.2. development tools
        C§2.a.3. debugging tools
        C§2.a.4. development libraries
        C§2.a.5. run-time environment
    C§2.b. As it contacts the Operating System

---

[24] This is also the place to treat the so-called "object-oriented" style of programming. It is a "style" since it can be applied regardless of whether or not a language has special "object-oriented" elements. Like many other useful things (GOTOs, recursion, databases, and so on) it can become a fad; it can be abused; it can also be a handy tool. Regardless of matters of preference, however, one must learn to choose the appropriate tool for the job at hand.

[25] Cf. *In Defense of Philosophy*, in which Pieper considers how a philosopher must actually let others know what he has thought, etc. Science itself is like this: a discovery must be *published*. Also these grand words of St. Paul: "How then shall they call on him in whom they have not believed? Or how shall they believe him of whom they have not heard? And how shall they hear without a preacher?" (Romans 10:14).

C§2.b.1. memory use

C§2.b.2. concurrency (threads, mutex, waits, etc.)

C§2.b.2. utility functions

    – logs, error management

    – current date/time, halt, abort, etc.

    – larger package organization (composition of software, files, etc.)

C§2.c. prewritten stuff

C§2.c.1. libraries

    – mathematical functions

    – strings

    – date/time

    – searching

    – sorting

    – other utility routines

C§2.c.2. other development tools

C§2.d. Input and Output

C§2.d.1. disk files

    – directory structure and management

    – security and forms of access

    – sequential use

    – random use

    – pipes and other specialized forms

C§2.d.2. user output ("windows" organization, text, graphics, color, etc)

C§2.d.3. user input (text, graphics, other)

C§2.d.4. external devices [26]

C§2.d.5. networks

C§2.d.6. databases

C§3. As that language is applied to a specific purpose

Each of the following sub-trees (yes, even the first) requires specialized knowledge beyond that proper to this discipline. In particular, good design requires an awareness of the *user* and his needs. One must adopt the maxim "We Use What We Code," always keeping in mind that "the function of every program" is "to contact and serve its User."[27]

C§3.a. Applied to computer science itself

This is "programming for the sake of programmers"; we might call this self-directed purpose the "Middle Voice," from the grammatical form of a verb (such as in classical Greek) which is neither active nor passive, as its action applies to its own subject as object.

C§3.a.1. Tools for program development

C§3.a.2. Tools for system management and control

C§3.a.3. Tools for user convenience

C§3.b. Applied to engineering (too huge to detail here)

C§3.c. Applied to science (too huge to detail here)

C§3.d. Applied to arts

C§3.c.1. Writing: word processors, publishing tools, etc.

---

[26] Devices are almost always *sui generis*, each requiring its own consideration, but general guidelines may be provided along with specific examples.

[27] Daley, *TRON*, 125.

C§3.c.2. Music: composing, performance aids, playback, etc.

C§3.c.3. Fine arts: drafting, drawing, painting, image storage, etc

C§3.c.4. Animation: 2-d; 3-d; technical vs. entertainment, etc.

C§3.c.5. Weaving, sculpture, applications to other media

C§3.e. Applied to industry (too huge to detail here)

C§3.f. Applied to business (too huge to detail here)

C§3.g. Applied to casual (non-technical) users

       – email, browsers, word-processing, calculators, games

C§3.h. Applied to specialized (novel, unique) applications

C§4. Comparative Linguistics of Programming Languages

       – classification of programming languages

       – their shared characteristics, their unique oddities

       – their advantages and disadvantages (in the formal sense)

       – their advantages and disadvantages (in practical settings)

       – review of classical languages (list subject to debate and extension)

       – points to consider in developing a new language

C§5. Other Aspects of Programming

C§5.a. History of Languages (dialects, versions; pedigrees, familial relations)

C§5.b. The relations between a language and its development environment

C§5.c. Dialect issues in both formal and practical settings

C§5.d. For future expansion

* * *

A Disclaimer:

This Tree is but a proposed preliminary attempt at treating the matter. It is nothing new: the Scholastics were continually revising, reorganizing, and re-stating their own Trees. (I have two from Henry of Langenstein.) Indeed, in my fictional account of the Ambrosian, their famous Tree is revised annually for printing on the cover of their course catalog; they have arranged an interactive projection of a complete and annotated *but continually updated* diagram on a large bare wall in one of their main campus buildings. So it is entirely reasonable for you to suggest augmentations or alternative arrangements: we must apply the paradigm of Newton's Method for root-finding, and work by successive approximations to get ever closer to the desired *Root* – for where the Root is, there the Tree will be.

Chapter 4
Some Comments on the Tree

The primary and most immediate predecessor of this discipline must be Logic, which we must consider in two ways: in the classic way, where Logic is a branch of Philosophy, and in the modern way, considered as a branch of Discrete Mathematics.

Logic is a fundamental branch of learning, together with Grammar and Rhetoric, one of the three branches of the classic Trivium. (From Latin *tres* = three, and *via* = way, road, passage.) They are the three ways by which "a quick mind enters into the secret places of wisdom."[28] The Trivium instructs us on the use of language.

It is important to note that these three divisions were considered elementary materials, and had to be mastered before ascending to higher and more difficult materials, or specializing in a discipline – and though some might lump these together under names like Reading and Writing (or "Literature"), they still form the foundation of academic and intellectual development.

Logic specifically governs the use of language – which ought to be used accurately and consistently – more precisely we might say "Logic expresses thought accurately";[29] a Scholastic calls it "the science of right thinking."[30]

Whenever we speak of logic, however, we must always remember this profound dictum:

> Logic and truth, as a matter of fact, have very little to do with each other. Logic is concerned merely with the fidelity and accuracy with which a certain process is performed, a process which can be performed with any materials, with any assumption. You can be as logical about griffins and basilisks as about sheep and pigs. On the assumption that a man has two ears, it is good logic that three men have six ears, but on the assumption that a man has four ears, it is equally good logic that three men have twelve. And the power of seeing how many ears the average man, as a fact, possesses, the power of counting a gentleman's ears accurately and without mathematical confusion, is not a logical thing but a primary and direct experience, like a physical sense, like a religious vision. The power of counting ears may be limited by a blow on the head; it may be disturbed and even augmented by two bottles of champagne; but it cannot be affected by argument. Logic has again and again been expended, and expended most brilliantly and effectively, on things that do not exist at all. ... The relations of logic to truth depend, then, not upon its perfection as logic, but upon certain pre-logical faculties and certain pre-logical discoveries, upon the possession of those faculties, upon the power of making those discoveries. ... Logic, then, is not necessarily an instrument for finding truth; on the contrary, truth is necessarily an instrument for using logic – for using it, that is, for the discovery of further truth and for the profit of humanity. Briefly, **you can only find truth with logic if you have already found truth without it.**[31]

Let us, then, remember this truth about logic and proceed.

---

[28] Taylor, *The Didascalicon of Hugh of St. Victor*, 87.

[29] The other two might be phrased; "Grammar expresses thought validly, or understandably"; "Rhetoric expresses thought convincingly."

[30] Shallo, *Scholastic Philosophy*, 38.

[31] GKC, *Daily News* Feb 25, 1905 in Maycock 103-4; emphasis added. Strange to say, the concluding line seems to be an informal anticipation of Gödel's Incompleteness Theorem (1931).

There are two major divisions of Logic: (1) *Propositional Calculus*, which considers the validity of statements formed from terms (themselves either true or false) linked with the conjunctions AND, OR, NOT, IF, IF-AND-ONLY-IF, and more complex combinations. (2) *Predicate Calculus*, which considers statements with forms like: ALL x IS y, SOME x IS y, ALL x IS NOT y, SOME x IS NOT y, along with their combinations; the classic form called the *syllogism* contains three such statements.

All this goes far back in human intellectual work, as far back as the Greeks (Socrates, Plato, Aristotle); Scholastics and their disciples (or antagonists) such as Buridan, Bonaventure, Aquinas, Llull, and Ockham debated it; Peter of Spain [32] wrote a famous text on Logic, *Summulae Logicales*, which contains those grand mystic words BARBARA CELARENT DARII FERIO. (More on that another time.) Pascal, Descartes, Newton, De Morgan, and others continued its work, or more often, relied upon it without debate. It was in the mid-1800s that George Boole proposed his famous parabola:

$$y = x(1-x)$$

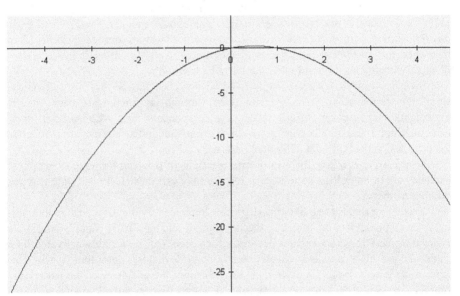

Thus he gave mathematical rigor to Propositional Calculus, and now the special branch of mathematics which applies to the exceedingly simple collection of two elements, ZERO and ONE, bears his name. It is here, in Boolean Algebra, we find the budding-off point of our own tree, and we see Logic given its place (be it only the grafting of a more mighty and ancient branch into a younger limb of the Tree of Virtues) in the formalisms of Discrete Mathematics.

An aside: that field generalizes the various properties and operations encountered in classical algebra to deal with finite collections of things ("sets, numbers") in simple

---

[32] Peter of Spain, Petrus Hispanus (1210s?-1277), a scholar, logician, eye-doctor, and scientist, became Pope John XXI and reigned 1276-7. His text on logic was the standard reference for almost 300 years. His book *Liber de oculo* on diseases of the eye was one of the first in Italian, and remarkably accurate for its day. He had a laboratory added to the papal apartments, and was fatally injured when its roof collapsed.

but orderly ways. (It is a distinct branch from Continuous or Real Algebra, which deals with the infinite sets of integers and of real numbers.) It is a powerful tool, able to handle certain difficult topics which arise in other branches of mathematics. Indeed it even provides a general concept [33] of "computation" which is nothing more than the mapping of "sets": that is, the production of a new collection which contains ordered pairs of items selected from two given collections. (Or from one, with elements taken twice.) While the education of a computer scientist ought to include a class on Discrete Math, our purpose here is to show the genesis or budding-off point of our discipline from the classical Tree of Virtues, and it seems most suitable to place it here.

Now there are Boolean Algebras of more than two items,[34] but they are rather esoteric, and most computer scientists think of ZERO and ONE as George Boole did: thus we shall root our sub-tree here, at the Boolean Algebra of exactly two items.

A study of this branch reveals that its major operators have the same properties as the conjunctions of the Propositional Calculus of Logic – which therefore is reduced to mathematical rigor, and provided with a convenient symbolic notation.

It is not hard to arrange simple machines (levers, gears, and springs) to perform these conjunctions or operations in an analogous manner, and very early experimentation with electricity revealed how easy it was to arrange switches (like those used for your house lights) to implement them. And it's not hard: I built a five-bit adder with switches when I was a junior in high school.

Switches moved by hand readily led to switches moved by electromagnets, which are called relays. These progressed through a number of ever smaller implementations in combinations of discrete components: first with vacuum tubes, then transistors, and finally the "solid-state" form: integrated circuits of ever more complex design (because the individual parts are ever more tiny).

So we arrive at a leaf, Physical Representations of Boolean formulas; when these machines are in one of the solid-state forms we may call these Gate or Logic Circuits (without memory).

Interesting issues arise like time-lag (how long does it take for a change in inputs for a series of devices to result in the appropriate change in the final output?), or power considerations (how many devices at one level can be reliably activated by a single device at a previous level?) Answers will require consultation with the appropriate engineering,[35] but one must also consider the character of the underlying formula, and whether it might be simplified, which will require knowledge of the properties of the underlying mathematics.

---

[33] But proposing this sort of formalism (as accurate as it may be) is unfairly trivializing the entire work of our discipline, and seems to grossly overlook the long list of topics listed in the previous chapter: one might as well shrug off one's checkbook with the term "algebra."

[34] Yes, there are such things, and the number must always be a power of two. We shall see an example in the second volume of this series, when we examine the DNA Wildcard Alphabet, which is a Boolean Algebra of 16 members.

[35] It's easy enough to think of an experiment by which a number of flashlight bulbs are powered by a single battery – but this is where I am glad to have studied the technology of organ-building. In the design of tracker organs (where keyboard action is mechanically transmitted to the pipes), one must keep in mind that the sole energy source is the organist's fingers: playing can become difficult when multiple manuals are coupled together.

Now, such devices are interesting, and it is worth pointing out that important operations like addition and subtraction can be performed in this manner.[36] What is more important is that rather annoying question about time, and the idea that when inputs change in time, a change in the output follows more or less directly.

What if we wanted to be able to control such changes? We would need a special kind of thing which "held" or "latched" its new input, until it was told to permit that value to register on its output. Such a thing is readily built from springs and levers, or from relays or tubes or solid-state devices, and is known as a flip-flop. Such an addition radically changes things, however, so we must now arrange a new way of handling this abstractly. We might say this is Boolean Algebra extended to handle "time" – that is, with some sort of memory added. We call this mathematical abstraction a Finite State Machine or Automaton (FSA). The implementation in solid-state devices of such abstractions forms a Logic Circuit With Memory.

Formally, the mathematics of FSAs is fascinating, and quite well-known. Associated with such things is a description of the possible values which they may compute: this "grammar" is known as a Regular Grammar, and its notation a Regular Expression. These are exceedingly useful and easy to implement.

What if the memory could somehow be "infinite?" Granted we cannot build such things, but mathematicians are used to handling unbounded and other so-called infinite items; they know the risks they run. Three additional classes of automata are distinguished, along with their corresponding grammars:

Automaton	Grammar
Stack machine	Context-free
Length-increasing	Context-sensitive
Turing machine	Unrestricted grammar

None of these can be built except in a limited sense – which of course only means we use finite-state machines to model the behavior of the others, which is fine as long as one does not go out of bounds of the large-but-finite approximation of the infinite abstractions. In particular, stack machines are very useful, as are certain context-free grammars.

---

[36] Subject, that is, to certain limitations; but this is not the time for such digressions. See e.g. Shiva, *Computer Design and Architecture*.

Chapter 5
The Pedagogy of Computer Science

He alone is capable of carrying out a rational work, who is able to give a complete account of the why and wherefore of every detail from its conception to its completion.

— Theobald Boehm, *The Flute and Flute-Playing*, p. xxv.

What do we mean by pedagogy? It means the "science" (which is simply an organized system of knowledge) of teaching: that is, the planning and organization of

- a systematic set of courses to cover all major branches with due regard
- for "prerequisites" (what topic must precede another),
- for the subject-in-itself,
- and for both adjacent and derivative subjects, as well as those it contacts.[37]

We might propose a kind of mnemonic, named for the following properties, with an eye to our parentage of mathematics:

1. Closure (a systematic set of courses to cover all major branches of the field)
2. Associativity (with due regard for "prerequisites")
3. Identity (for both the subject-in-itself)
4. Inverse (and for both adjacent and derivative subjects and its contacts.)

Not very satisfactory, but it is like the various tricks scholars have used over the centuries. Sometimes they use poetry, alliteration, or (horror of horrors) puns. The point is to try to cover everything relevant and make it capable of being remembered.

In the previous section we worked out our Tree [38] with the major branches and leaves of our discipline, and we have considered a handful of important skills which will aid in its work. This does not mean we have exhaustively listed every possible course which might be offered in our discipline: the most I will claim is to have given a reasonably comprehensive list to serve as a starting point for further discussion.

Some of the topics listed in our tree are structural, and can be covered sufficiently along with others: for example, some of the outer layers regarding Boolean Algebra, gates, and finite machines might be presented as part of a class on Machine Architecture. Note, however, the mere hierarchical ordering of our tree does not necessarily suggest the order in which such material is presented: our tree is organized according to *knowledge*, hence it belongs to epistemology rather than pedagogy. But we need such a thing to start with, and for reference: it is our map.

Just as with other systematic arrangements of classes, or even of sciences (think of Euclid's five axioms) we must start by assuming a certain amount of pre-existing knowledge. (This might amount to a kind of "closure" in the sense that the information about to be imparted by the teacher should become unified with the existing knowledge of the student.)

---

[37] Properly one ought to consider *all* other disciplines, but practicalities often place severe limits on such elegance. Newman, however, said: "I observe, then, that if you drop any science out of the circle of knowledge, you cannot keep its place vacant for it; that science is forgotten; the other sciences close up, or, in other words, they exceed their proper bounds, and intrude where they have no right." *The Idea of a University*, Discourse IV section 2.

[38] Well, a *graph*, to be accurate, since there are cross-links, but traditionally it's called a tree.

Moreover, even though "Grammar" appears as a primary in the Trivium, it cannot even be taught [39] unless there already exists some form of communication – which indeed assumes possession of *some* grammar by the student! Hence, we will not be remiss if we expect the student to have already encountered some form of programming, even if it was not presented in any rigorous manner. Nevertheless, we can't expect knowledge to be recursive.

Briefly, then: what preliminary training should we require of a student who embarks on a course of study in computer science?

1. Fluency with some natural language, along with a study of its grammar.

2. At least an introductory knowledge of a second language (which thus reveals the power of *distinguo*, I distinguish).

3. Satisfactory training in mathematics, including algebra, geometry, and set theory, preferably including trigonometry and calculus. Additional work ought to proceed contemporaneously with work in our discipline, and should cover linear algebra, combinatorics, probability and statistics, and group theory.

4. A reasonably diverse background in the sciences. Of particular value are :
    a. a solid foundation in measurement and dimensional analysis
    b. the chemical elements, formulas for inorganic and organic compounds
    c. experimental work with electricity (basics of series/parallel circuits)
    d. enough biology to grasp the astounding complexity and variety of
       living beings, and deep enough to appreciate its relation with chemistry.

5. Knowledge of musical notations, preferably including the ability to play some instrument, and some basic familiarity with the musical keyboard. After all, music provides a major analogy to many topics in computer science.

Then there are certain other characters we might expect of the prospective student – not that these are necessarily to be found in a transcript or offered by typical pre-college curricula, but they ought to be inculcated by any teacher:

1. a delight and love of reading

2. a desire to solve problems

3. a curiosity about how things work

4. a fascination with symbols: letters, numbers, musical notation, "codes," etc.

5. a fascination with intricacies: railroads, clocks, musical instruments, etc.

After letting all this stew for a while, here is my attempt at a summary:

A Proposed Course of Study Leading to the B.S. in Computer Science

Note: this is not so much a list of *courses* as usually described in college catalogs, but a collection of *topics* to be covered in classes.

1. Theory
    a. Automata Theory and Grammars
    b. Theory of Algorithms, Complexity
    c. Combinatorics

2. Practice
    a. Programming (with rigor, and with attention to larger details)

---

[39] I do not include the teaching of that tongue initially learned by a person, which occurs by a long process of training by the parents. That is another topic for another time, but lest I never get the chance, be sure to see the discussion in GKC's *Orthodoxy*, CW1:360 which begins "When your father told you..."

b. Machine Architecture
c. Assembly Language Programming
d. Data Structures and Algorithms
e. Compiler Design
f. Operating Systems
g. Introduction to Other Programming Languages (overview)
h. Applications for the real world
    1) files
    2) graphics
    3) networking
    4) errors & handling of practical issues (tracking, security, etc.)
    5) concurrency
    6) user-oriented issues (interfaces, report/display presentation, etc.)
i. History of the Discipline including chronology and famous people

3. What the student ought to know afterwards:
    a. The ability to implement *and also design* a program from specifications.
    b. A sound basis of formal standard problems through experience with:
        1) Data structures (arrays, lists, graphs, trees, stacks, queues, heaps, etc)
        2) String manipulation
        3) Sorting & merging
        4) Searching
        5) Basic numerical methods
        6) Basic graphics
        7) Basic user interaction
        8) Basic combinatorics
        9) Databases
        10) Networking
        11) Major OS features: files, special I/O, memory, concurrency, etc
        12) Novelties (exotic but practical issues such as using peripheral devices)
4. Other courses to be covered:
    a. Mathematics:
        1) calculus
        2) linear algebra & matrices
        3) number theory
        4) probability and statistics
        5) combinatorics
    b. Sciences: (*with* labs)
        1) An introductory class to cover
            a) measurement, units, dimensions, errors, dimensional analysis
            b) the senses and their limits
            c) illusions (sight, hearing, touch)
            d) experimental method
            e) keeping of proper lab notes
        2) Physics, including mechanics, electricity and magnetism, and light
        3) Chemistry, including the elements, compounds and symbolic formulae,
            reactions, organic nomenclature and structure.
        4) Biology, including taxonomy, anatomy, histology, cytology,
            and the basic molecular biology of DNA and proteins.
        5) Geology including basic terms and the 32 crystal classes

      6) Astronomy including stellar types and distances (parallax and cepheids)
  c. Some foreign language
  d. A writing course to cover
      1) abstracts
      2) white papers
      3) journal articles
      4) summaries & reviews
  e. A class in Media, covering especially
      1) Printing and its history (printing in the traditional sense; books)
      2) Basics of music, radio, and television.
      3) Some sense of performance such as theater and oratory
  f. Some awareness of the Arts:
      1) the Spoken Word
      2) Music (instrumental, singing, various groups)
      3) Presentation (stage, radio, TV, etc.)
      4) the Printed Word (fiction, essays, poetry, etc.)
      5) Fine Art (painting, sculpture, architecture, etc.)
  g. Some awareness of authentic Philosophy, including the basic topics of metaphysics and logic, glimpses of ontology, teleology, and related fields, and in particular the Scholastic form of Argument: a formal discussion made not to convince, but in the pursuit of Truth.

Upon review this course plan seems utterly unrealistic, but at such a very early stage of design, one tends to throw in all sorts of good ideas which will have to be sorted out (and sometimes restricted, or deferred) when it is finally time to begin implementation.

Still, it seems to make a suitable pattern, and once one realizes I do *not* intend that this Plan describes standard 3-credit 15-week per semester *courses*, and some topics may be unified in a single place, or covered by other means – well, then it begins to sound possible.

Eventually I may try to sketch out what comparable degrees at my fictional Ambrosian University will require. Like simulation using software, it is lots easier to play with an imaginary campus and see how things go. If we knew how to teach *curiosity* we might try that, but until then we have to go with a traditional shotgun approach, and hope to hit most rings of the target. Hmmm: *curiosity*.

A comment about Curiosity and Educational Saturation

In discussing the larger topic of pedagogy with some friends, we noted a curious question: "How do you know when to conclude one's formal education?" Certainly there is no doubt that everyone needs the typical training of elementary school: everyone needs the basics of communication, of reading and writing, of numbers and their operations, and an overview of the whole array of human studies from philosophy, geography and history through science, art, literature, and music. But what is really needed after that? What is the real point of high school, of a bachelor's degree, of graduate work, or of trade school? Sure, there's the matter of getting a job, and having a sufficient preparation for it, especially if one has some particular interest in a given field of work. But in the largest sense, what is the boundary, if there is one? What is the threshold where one reaches (as the chemists put it) "saturation" of the intellect? *Does such a thing even exist?*

Well, I was away from my references then, and I told them I expect Newman had something to say about this. He did. Here is one insight about what he calls "a seat of universal learning, considered as a place of education":

> An assemblage of learned men, zealous for their own sciences, and rivals of each other, are brought, by familiar intercourse and for the sake of intellectual peace, to adjust together the claims and relations of their respective subjects of investigation. They learn to respect, to consult, to aid each other. Thus is created a pure and clear atmosphere of thought, which the student also breathes, though in his own case he only pursues a few sciences out of the multitude. He profits by an intellectual tradition, which is independent of particular teachers, which guides him in his choice of subjects, and duly interprets for him those which he chooses. He apprehends the great outlines of knowledge, the principles on which it rests, the scale of its parts, its lights and its shades, its great points and its little, as he otherwise cannot apprehend them. Hence it is that his education is called "Liberal."
> A habit of mind is formed which lasts through life, of which the attributes are, freedom, equitableness, calmness, moderation, and wisdom; or what in a former Discourse I have ventured to call a philosophical habit.[40]

Later in that Discourse (§9) he says "Liberal Education, viewed in itself, is simply the cultivation of the intellect, as such, and its object is nothing more or less than intellectual excellence." Obviously, this *cultivation* never really concludes, or it would not truly be rooted in *colere*: to cultivate, cause to grow as a farmer.[41]

My reading of another masterly reference on Epistemology, *The Phantom Tollbooth*, seems to suggest another way of discerning the issue.

There is a boundary between two mental states: the first, younger, or untrained state is the one wherein the student is required to be nourished by the teacher – one might almost say "forcibly" nourished. At that age, the student has no reason to refuse to learn these basic facts and skills, since the possibility of making a choice can only come once those facts and skills have been imparted. The second, more mature, state is the one wherein the student wilfully seeks knowledge on his own: he will read books, perform experiments, pay attention to teachers – and these efforts are driven not from any mandate but from an honest longing *to know*. The threshold, then, might for our convenience be labelled CURIOSITY. It is the point when the student becomes sufficiently curious to self-educate: when the teachers are no longer intellectual placentas, providing nourishment without any taste, but are perceived as the Master Chefs, setting a rich and varied banquet, fruits of the harvest of five thousand years of human thought and labor. After that point is reached, the student must rely on himself if he is to learn anything more. Of course, as Newman suggests, learning will proceed throughout life; there are always new things to learn about, new situations to deal with... but the individual must deal with those situations using the tools he already has – or build his own new tools using his toolbox. (Recall our discussion of Robinson Crusoe salvaging items from the wreck?) This is why the student is first given those marvellous gifts of communication: of speaking and comprehending a language, and especially of *Reading*.

This is no criticism of those who have no formal education, nor of those who have left the formal modes of education to enter into their Life-Work. That is why I use the term "saturation" – some people find their intellectual toolbox full at an earlier time than others. But some people "catch" the curiosity-bug, and want to know more.

---

[40] Newman, *The Idea of a University*, Discourse V, "Knowledge: its Own End," §1.

[41] The Romans are always accused of their militancy with all their terms for killing and the actions of war. Yet it seems to me there are just as many words showing they were farmers.

Often this "more" is about a specific discipline, or field of study; sometimes it is more insatiable. But the desire to know is at the inner core of our being (we can explore that matter some other time) and even those who have left school "early" continue their learning in the School of the World.

Hence, the motive which underlies all Teaching beyond the merely elementary levels is to enkindle a fire in the students: a fire of Enthusiastic, Disciplined, and Diligent Curiosity:[42] a fire sufficient to bring them into that intellectual independence where they (on their own) want to know more, and are willing to pursue Knowledge.

The Greeks had a word for it, the Middle Voice of the verb παιδευω (*paideuô*) = "I educate, teach" which is παιδευομαι (*paideuomai*) = "I educate myself, or for my own sake" – and another ancient people gave us unforgettable eloquence:

> To know wisdom, and instruction: to understand the words of prudence: and to receive the instruction of doctrine, justice, and judgment, and equity: to give subtilty to little ones, to the young man knowledge and understanding. ... The fear of the Lord is the beginning of wisdom. Fools despise wisdom and instruction. My son, hear the instruction of thy father, and forsake not the law of thy mother. ... [Wisdom] is a tree of life to them that lay hold on her: and he that shall retain her is blessed. ... Get wisdom, get prudence: forget not, neither decline from the words of my mouth. Forsake her not, and she shall keep thee: love her, and she shall preserve thee. ... Take hold on instruction, leave it not: keep it, because it is thy life.
>
> Proverbs 1:2-4, 7-8; 3:18, 4:5-6, 13

---

[42] Enthusiasm comes from Greek terms meaning "having God within"; the equivalent Latin *inflammatio animi* means "the conflagration of the soul." Discipline means to work as a student does, in striving to learn. Diligence comes from the Latin verb meaning to prize, to love, to esteem highly, to choose in exclusion of others. Our goal is that Curiosity, that thirst for Knowledge, which is striven for as a student works, is esteemed highly to the exclusion of all other things, and which has God at its center.

Chapter 6
"Problem-Solving Skills" for Computer Science
Part a. About Real Tools for Solving Problems

> Compared with these materials, [uranium, radium, silver nitrate, etc.] almost ridiculous may be a reference to the material called beer, which, however, sparked Glaser's mind to think about the bubble chamber, a chief tool in fundamental particle research.
>
> Jaki, "The Relevance of Materials Science"
> in *Numbers Decide and Other Essays*, 187

Now that we have devised a Tree enumerating the various facets of our discipline and even devised a possible curriculum for introducing the field to sufficiently prepared students, let us consider the matter of "problem-solving skills" as they apply to our discipline. But what are these problem-solving skills, anyway? This is another sort of "draw-yourself-in-the-mirror" project, an attempt to witness *and describe* the motions of the mind as it is focussed on something quite different. It is for that reason I have recommended that little drawing project, or the more apt one of writing a program which prints itself out: indeed, this concept of recursion, of self-referential entities, and of the Von Neumann Principle, "Code is Data" is one of the problem-solving skills useful for computer science.[43]

Obviously it is hard (if not impossible) to solve problems if you don't know any solutions – and so, despite the apparent self-reference, the best way of learning how to solve problems is by solving problems. The long experience of many other fields have shown the need to give their students a healthy amount of experience in such things, with a knowledgeable guide to assist along the way – so it is easy enough to appeal to "Experience" writ large, and claim that solving plenty of problems is the most important problem-solving skill. Indeed, the idea of presenting a sample of curious problems was a major motivation for me to write this book.

But this does not mean letting kids drop eggs from helicopters, or build bridges with spaghetti – I have no idea what sort of problem those naive "educators" would recommend if their awareness ever reaches computer science, though I don't expect it ever will. Those other "problems" are fun, "crafts" which can be done without scrap paper, math, slide rules, or calculators... you just download a cute website and let the kids go – and they can "feel good" about "doing science" while they entertain themselves. But in the real world where I live, there are real problems waiting to be solved... and those real problems need real skills, which means serious efforts on the part of both teacher and student.

An aside: Just in case you think I have some sort of bone to pick with letting kids tackle tough things – I don't. But don't give them absurdities beyond their preparation – you might as well ask them to separate praseodymium from neodymium. I do *not* think it is worthwhile misleading them about handling such things when they have not yet gained the elementary knowledge about the field. That is not science, and it surely isn't "education." And if you want to hear more about possibilities of young people, I suggest you read the story about the ten-year-old Gauss which you will find in our study of recursion, or books like *Danny Dunn on a Desert Island*, or *Project: Genius,*

---

[43] The ultimate test of this power is to use a given language to develop a compiler for that language. It should be a lot of fun, but a major challenge. Maybe someday I'll try it.

or "Night Rescue" in *The Mad Scientists' Club*. There are countless tricks for introducing the heights of every discipline to young people, but they *must* have a sufficiently good basis of elementary knowledge to start with. This was covered with stunning clarity in the movie, "The Karate Kid," in which a young boy endures some traditional dull and seemingly pointless chores assigned by his wise mentor from the East – each of which happen to be steps in building his experience. But when the "educators" cast out all the traditional dull and seemingly pointless chores like LONG DIVISION... Alas! Is it that they fear the mighty intellectual powers which a wise mentor from the West [44] could be inculcating in the young? Well...this *is* an aside, and not relevant to our purpose here. But when you grimace at words like... like Purpose (writ large, of course!) or "Associative Property" or (horror of horrors) LONG DIVISION, think of that boy painting the fence, or standing on one foot, and realize that mental training comes in many forms.

Let us return to our discussion of these skills. I find it somehow misleading to call them *skills* – which too often are ultimately reduced to special gifts of an individual, or are too vague to characterize in any way. Rather I think such things might be better described as *tools*: specific intellectual devices which may be acquired through teaching and experience. Like any other kind of tools, be they mechanical, scientific, mathematical, or computational, they come in various kinds, since their purposes – their ends, or the problems which they can solve – come in various kinds.

Part b. Tools to Deal with Metaphysical Issues

Dic Cur Hic – Tell Why You Are Here

One might well wonder what sort of "metaphysical issues" might arise in problem-solving – but then these are far more important than the relatively trivial topics relating to algorithm selection or implementation. Then again, you might be surprised after you have sat and thought for a while about the problem of problem-solving...

Knowing the problem in itself ("What is to be solved? ")
It's obvious: if you can't state the problem, you can by no means find a solution. Hence the first and most important task in problem-solving is always to frame a statement of the problem in clear and unambiguous terms.

As you may recall from doing science labs in high school, it has ever been a classic requirement of lab writeups to begin by stating the problem to be examined in clear and unambiguous terms. This same policy is required in the scholarly papers of

---

[44] I mean no disrespect to the great cultures of the East: they have many virtues, their concern for Family and especially for the Aged is a great thing, and many of their arts are truly beautiful and inspiring. But it would be wrong for me to pretend that their philosophy is compatible with mine, or with that demanded by my field. It is not for me to argue this; you can find a dispassionate treatment in (for example) Jaki's *Science and Creation*, or in GKC's stunningly relevant words: "The Eastern says fate governs everything and he sits and looks pretty; we believe in Free-will and Predestination and we invent Babbage's Calculating Machine." (quoted in Ward, *Gilbert Keith Chesterton*, 268). I witnessed it for myself in graduate school: the East's world-view does not readily admit such things as Logic or Computers. And it is because the West's world-view is rapidly decaying – many are nearly to the point of believing that computers work by "magic" – that I bother to write, both fiction and non-fiction, in the hope of preserving some of our culture including technology.

academic journals: the abstract is to provide a succinct statement of the problem, the work done, and the result. As one professor advised us in grad school, these papers are *not* detective novels; one does not keep the conclusion secret until the end, but rather must state it at the very beginning – but then (by pure logic) we must recall that even detective stories have to state the premise (Lord Jones is alive) before concluding with the revelation that "Lord Jones was stabbed by Colonel Mustard in the Conservatory."[45]

But this statement of the problem needs to possess sufficient rigor – the terms must be as precise as possible. If the matter is specialized, you may need to devise your own glossary for the project; even more importantly, you may need to begin devising one or more mathematical objects to use in organizing the materials of the problem. One ought not, of course, think that these are going to turn into data structures, or files, or "tables" in a relational database; they ought to remain abstract as long as possible. (For an example, see our treatment of the local ad insertion project in a subsequent volume.)

Often, producing this clear statement of the problem is the hardest job of all, requiring the most intense contemplation of any of the following stages of the job: the mode of work which Sir Henry Merrivale [46] called "sittin'and thinkin'." Be sure to allow some time for this. There have been many cases where I have heard a puzzle presented, and I thought I could sit down at the computer and begin doodling up a program to solve it... only to find I was a bit premature. It's easy to get carried away, and early in my career I learned to put in strategic pauses to "let the pots simmer" while I pondered the matter. (That is a very important trick and I will talk about it again later.)

Here, more than at any other stage of the job, one must have humility and patience. In nearly every case in the real world, be it in industry or in academics, the person coming to you with a problem is an expert, or at least professionally skilled, in some field, and finds the matter at hand too challenging for him to solve himself. The popularization of computers has not increased the awareness of technology, so it is likely that this expert will not know anything about the working of computers, about the niceties of problem-statements in computing, the challenges of implementation, or the rest of our field – and it will *not* be your task to introduce him to all that.

At the same time, it is likely that *you* will not have a clue about *his* field, and there will be special issues which will require patient work for you to understand. It is a challenge in both directions.

Rather, you will need to interact to such an extent – enlarging your own field of knowledge when necessary – that you are able to grasp the problem and its related issues to a sufficient degree that you will be able to proceed. This suggests the analogy of the antibody: you, a computer scientist, must adapt yourself – yes, I will go so far as to say re-program yourself just as the cellular machinery re-programs its own DNA

---

[45] See GKC's "The Purple Wig" in *The Wisdom of Father Brown*: "I know it is the practice of journalists to put the end of the story at the beginning and call it a headline. I know that journalism largely consists in saying 'Lord Jones Dead' to people who never knew that Lord Jones was alive." There is also the dramatic opening of Dickens' *A Christmas Carol*: "Marley was dead: to begin with. ... There is no doubt that Marley was dead. This must be distinctly understood, or nothing wonderful can come of the story I am going to relate." Indeed, detection does play an important role in our field, but then "detection" is just the Latin for "uncovering" or "taking the roof off."

[46] Detective in the stories of Carter Dickson, pen name of John Dickson Carr.

– to fit the need, that is, according to the nature and character of the problem presented, in order to solve that problem.

Depending on the situation (be it a consultation, a research project, or a more casual encounter) this interaction may – and in many cases must – involve a complete re-statement of the problem by the computer scientist, augmented with comments regarding difficulties, limitations, and even opportunities for extension. The result of this interaction might well be a "white paper" giving your summary of the problem, along with relevant issues, comments about definitions, any mathematical objects you propose, and so on. (This is where to put your glossary of any special terms needed for the project.)

Humility also means having a willingness to seek assistance, which is the function of Subsidiarity: it means being ready to appeal to authority, whether it be an associate in the field or "the literature" (which may even include the "net").

Some auxiliary tools:
   a. Rigorous diction of lab writeups/journal abstracts
   b. Mathematical objects
   c. "Sittin' and thinkin' "
   d. White papers to summarize the problem
   e. Humility
   f. Patience
Antagonists:
   a. Vagueness
   b. Imprecision
   c. Careless/insufficient contemplation
   d. Wilful concealment
   e. Failure to admit your ignorance
   f. Failure to admit the other's abilities

Knowing the problem in its purpose ("Why is it to be solved?")
Purpose is a highly loaded word these days – but not for computer scientists, who understand the requirement of having a purpose: once one has spent hours, days, and weeks of effort, designing and implementing a system with a Purpose, that is, to perform a specific duty, it's a bit ridiculous to think that software happens by random chance. But this is not the place to examine that topic.[47] Nor is it sufficient to say "because I told you so" or "because it's your job" or the other glib "explanations" often given. (I am not talking about "why bother" as a motivational matter. That also deserves treatment, but not today.) I am talking about the *why* from the requester's perspective: why does this user desire a solution to this problem? Is it a casual sort of curiosity, a heavy demand, a requirement for accomplishing work, a burning need of humanity – *Why must this be solved?* There are many reasons which might be given, but it is the nature of the specific reason which will govern our work. Casual curiosity does not impose the same demand as questions underlying matters of human life. Moreover, if the computer scientist is typically handling a multitude of projects (as

---

[47] Often the discussion comes down to issues about Darwin and God. But as Whitehead pointed out, "Those who devote themselves to the purpose of proving that there is no purpose constitute an interesting subject for study." A. N. Whitehead, *The Function of Reason*, 12, quoted in Jaki, *The Purpose of It All*, 57. Also see my *Subsidiarity*.

was often the case in my own experience) this new project may need to be given a priority among them – and its *Why* must play a role in determining that priority.

Some auxiliary tools
    a. Teleology – the science of Ends (Purposes)
    b. *Dic cur hic* – "tell why you are here."
Antagonists
    a. Tennysonian cockiness: "Not to ask the reason why"
    b. Magisterial pomp
    c. Laziness
    d. Lack of consistency.

Knowing the tool at hand ("How is it to be solved?")
    With this question we are now on the frontier between Theta (theory) and Pi (practice): we begin to consider what sort of work we are actually to perform. There are cases, all too prevalent in academics, in which the problem to be solved is never "incarnated" in actual software, but comes to a completion by a formal algorithm. This is quite acceptable; I have rejoiced in such things as you will hear in another volume of this series. Perhaps the question at hand is so constrained you may be able to solve it by completely *ad hoc* programming, or by using existing tools without regard for efficiency or for ease of use. It may be that the requester wants an answer to a given problem, rather than a complete application ready for his own use; there are cases where it may be far more tractable to handle the work yourself than to build a tool for use by casual, technically unskilled users. Or, it may be that you are to develop a single-purpose tool, or a program, or a suite of applications, or an entire system of programs, to handle the matter, which may be used by anyone from extremely competent experts to barely trained temps – and you may need a computer, or a series of computers... it all depends on the nature and issues of the given problem.
    However, in every case you need to know the tool at hand, both its capabilities and its limitations: the machine (or collection of machines) itself, its operating system, the language(s), run-time environment, and development tools.

> "Were you ever an isosceles triangle? ... I wondered whether it would be a cramping sort of thing to be surrounded by straight lines, and whether being in a circle would be any better. ... I used to want a hammer to smash things with, but I've learnt to do something else with a hammer, which is what a hammer is meant for; and every now and then I manage to do it."
> "What do you mean by that?" inquired the doctor.
> "I can hit the right nail on the head," answered the poet.
>   GKC "The Yellow Bird" in *The Poet and the Lunatics*

Remember what it is you are doing, and what it is you are using. You are hopefully designing or implementing or supporting a piece of software: an implemented algorithm, a program (or component thereof) for an electronic digital computer. Such writing is very much like other kinds of writing, but it is especially like composing music, which must be played, unless you are as gifted as a Beethoven who was deaf when he composed his famous Ninth (Choral) Symphony. It is also like writing recipes for food, and there also you ought to test your recipe to verify not only the protocol but the overall flavor, texture, and so on. There are "artists" who can get away with flinging gobs of paint at a canvas; there are "writers" (if the term be not utterly distorted in this context) whose results seem to be what I call "Thesaurus in a

Blender" style: one shreds a thesaurus and sticks in a chunk of adhesive tape, then copies whatever words happen to be glued together that time. I won't attempt to speak further on their "art" (if that is the word). But we are engineers, who must perform the synthesis of theory and practice, of science and art, and it is only just that we listen to our own music, eat our own cooking, and test out our own software. Let the theory guys write nice juicy abstractions – providing they get sound results, you may find such things useful one of these years. (You'll hear about how this happened to me when we discuss signature strings.)

But don't misjudge your tool. Like Professor Harold Hill tells his "Boys' Band" in Willson's famous "The Music Man": you have to *know* your instrument. You should not even *touch* it... until you are READY.

Hopefully, this series of books will provide you with some guidance about knowing your instrument. But for now, just remember: that thing is a COMPUTER. It's a very special sort of tool. It's not Winthrop Paroo's "tholid gold thing" called a cornet; not a car, a bicycle, a hammer, a toaster, a weed-whacker, or a radio telescope... and especially it is not an intelligent and willing human being. It's an amazing piece of electronic equipment which can perform a small collection of simple instructions at an unbelievable speed. But it can do *nothing at all* unless it is given those instructions.

It is also important to remember that the computer is *not* a magic box. It is not a modern automobile with all its innards so beyond understanding that the hood might as well be welded closed. Sure, you cannot see "into" the CPU, or into the other chips; one of the greatest disappointments I have had over my years in computing is the almost total lack of *cool blinking lights* on most computers. That is a shame. Such a lack led me to writing a thesis on the animation of algorithms, and to some extent to the designs underlying my famous WATCHER monitor for the cable TV system I worked on.

It would be nice if more of the inner workings of modern computers were "visible" in some manner. But it is far more important for us to *know and understand* what is going on inside them, and that knowledge can be had, regardless of whether there are LEDs or other telltales on the exterior of the machine. We must understand the effective logical nature of the machine, even if we have little detailed knowledge of its precise electronic implementation. That means knowing Boolean Algebra, the formalisms of State Machines and Automata Theory, and the basics of computer architecture: in other words we need to know its abilities and its limits. This knowledge will protect us against overestimating, or underestimating, our instrument. Here is how Chesterton explains the matter:

> ...it is impossible to be an artist and not care for laws and limits. Art is limitation; the essence of every picture is the frame. If you draw a giraffe, you must draw him with a long neck. If, in your bold creative way, you hold yourself free to draw a giraffe with a short neck, you will really find that you are not free to draw a giraffe. The moment you step into the world of facts, you step into a world of limits. You can free things from alien or accidental laws, but not from the laws of their own nature. You may, if you like, free a tiger from his bars; but do not free him from his stripes. Do not free a camel of the burden of his hump: you may be freeing him from being a camel. Do not go about as a demagogue, encouraging triangles to break out of the prison of their three sides. If a triangle breaks out of its three sides, its life comes to a lamentable end. Somebody wrote a work called "The Loves of the Triangles"; I never read it, but I am sure that if triangles ever were loved, they were loved for being triangular. This is certainly the case with all artistic creation,

which is in some ways the most decisive example of pure will. The artist loves his limitations: they constitute the *thing* he is doing. The painter is glad that the canvas is flat. The sculptor is glad that the clay is colourless. [48]

It may sound odd to say this, but often those limits make it possible to have a solution – and the reason is that the *problem* also arises in this world of limits.
Some auxiliary tools.

    a. Study of the tool itself (read the manuals!)
    b. Readiness to contrive small tests to determine results
    c. Knowledge of both computing and the domain of the problem
    d. "Computing is an Experimental Science."
Antagonists

    a. overestimating the tool
    b. underestimating the tool
    c. marketing blurbs

Dealing with incomplete or nebulous specs.

Possibly this topic ought to come under one of the previous heads, but since it is a very common difficulty I decided to treat it separately. And, rather than trying to enumerate auxiliary tools, I will simply discuss two methods of approaching the problem.

(1) The first is a tool I call "Sitting on the fence." (This is a further argument in favor of writing preliminary or white papers, but I come at it from a different direction.)

How did I come to establish myself in such a ridiculous and precarious position? Partly because I am a Medievalist, and a Chestertonian; partly because I interleaved my academic experience with my industrial experience, and my colleagues never seemed to know where I fit:

When I was in industry, they groaned at me: "Peter, all you ever want to do is write technical papers."

When I was in academics, they groaned at me: "Peter, all you ever want to do is write programs."

And you, my reader, will wonder: *what is it I really do?*

I reply: "I sit squarely on the fence." I try to use the best of both worlds. When there is insufficient information in industry, I attempt to extract more by boiling down what is already available into a technical paper, hopefully indicating what I think the problem is, what resources we have and what is still lacking, and how to go about solving the problem. When an academic issue is raised, and there are loads of journal articles and plenty of input from colleagues, but nothing seems to help, I'll try to set up a demonstration program – a "breadboard" implementation as such things were once called in the days of actual (discrete) electronic components – in the hopes of finding guidance from the developmental effort and the results of its execution.

(2) The second tool is called "Lazy Evaluation," or, deferring commitments in development as long as possible.

This idea is related to the previous one; the term comes from the semantic trick in language/compiler design, whereby the success or failure of a compound

---

[48] GKC, *Orthodoxy* CW1:243-4.

conditional is decided as soon as possible, without evaluating *all* of its components.[49] In terms of design, this means I try to arrange things so that I can implement *enough* of a solution to test out a method, while leaving as much room as possible for future expansion to handle incompletely specified matters. This sounds dangerous, and can be if attempted without sufficient preparation, and without knowledge of the problem circumstances. Much depends upon the sophistication of the users or customers, and upon the degree of trust they place in the development team.

To be brutally honest, it also requires a certain fighter-pilot kind of programming skill, and ought not be attempted by the inexperienced – but I thought it should be included in our bag of tricks, ahem, I mean in our toolbox.

Part c. Tools to Deal with Practical Issues

"Computing is an Experimental Science."

– James Waclawik

We now enter the practical side of problem-solving. I had debated proposing a preliminary taxonomy, just for the sake of making a start at a very difficult study – but after further consideration, I am dissatisfied with it, and so I will merely list a number of points together with some discussion, hoping to make further progress on this matter for a future edition.

Humility

Perhaps, you think that humility, being a virtue, ought to come under the metaphysical head, but really it is a very practical tool. It should not surprise you that I mention humility in such a technical treatise. This does not mean letting Users trample us; it means a willingness to listen, and to work at understanding the disciplines of the Users, even disciplines remote from ours, in order to grasp the character and nuances of the problem at hand. It also means that, once we have enumerated the open or unresolved issues, asked all the questions needed to define the boundary conditions, and then cast the problem into a formal statement, we are willing to explain all this to our Users *without* any pomp or superiority.

Representation or Definition

If there is to be any hope of finding a solution to a given problem, that problem must be stated clearly and unambiguously. I mean no disrespect to other professionals, of whom I have met countless dozens over the years, to observe that few are capable of doing such a thing – and yes, I include computer scientists as well. Fortunately, we may rely on mathematics which provides powerful tools such as Sets, Relations, Functions, Operations, and other such things, sometimes collected under the term "Mathematical Objects."

In order to use them, of course, we must first find out what the User is talking about, and then reduce the relevant ideas to the most formal notation available.

---

[49] For example, in a conditional statement like

```
if (p≠NULL) AND (p→field=key) then Process(p)
```

a "lazy evaluation" of the AND means that when the variable p is NULL, the conditional can be known to fail from the falsehood of the left subexpression; the right subexpression does *not* need to be evaluated (thereby avoiding an erroneous indirection through a NULL pointer).

This forces us to pay attention to any subtle distinctions, and help us begin to organize the material in a rigorous manner. It is very likely that when we are able to bring the ideas to the level of Mathematical Objects (that is, a formal and symbolic list of the entities at hand: their sets, relations, operations, and functions) we will find that some of them will become files, or database tables, or some particular data structures in a program. However, *don't* try to start coding then. Collect data first, check it carefully, explain it to the User, revise it, and *think about it*. Make sure it's right. Such formalisms ought to be reviewed frequently as the project develops.

Abiding awareness of elementary tools

It is *so easy* to forget that you have learned all sorts of tools and tricks and methods of getting things done! Like reading, or adding, or the dozens of other simple intellectual activities of ordinary reading, writing, calculating or thinking. You become *so used* to doing them you think that they somehow belong to the "machine language" your body knows – and in some sense that is true. But they are not inherently so; they are just that way for you. You need to renew your awareness, not by – uh – a regression to childhood, but by bringing such things to your mature attention. You need to make them *visible*, at least to yourself. For example, you may know the various mathematical properties: associativity, commutativity, and so on; you no doubt know about binary trees, and may have already handled the semantic trees corresponding to algebraic expressions: you might envision these as *mobiles*, made of sticks and string and brightly colored cardboard, dangling from the ceiling, with the subtrees spinning in the breeze... and perhaps such a vision will aid in extending the concept of commutativity to things far beyond algebra.

Classification

Evolution is one of the most fighting of topics, and we are not going to open it for that purpose. It is remarkable, however, that it is founded upon the idea of a species, which is intended to be *specific*, that is, something to be distinguished from others, even if very similar – like Darwin's finches, but *not* like dogs! Ahem. And at the same time, there are those who seem to be arguing that Evolution shows that all those apparently distinct things are actually all the same... Rather than quarrel about that, let's hear something a bit more relevant. Chesterton was visiting Edinburgh, Scotland, and contemplating the Scott Monument, and beyond it the imposing mountain called "Arthur's Seat":

> They both show a dark and decisive outline; but I know the real difference between them, and the real difference is the whole difference between the handiwork and the image of God. The difference is that the outline of the mountain looks decisive, but the outline of the monument is decisive. If I went to the top of the mountain (which I have not the smallest intention of doing) I know that I should find vague curves of clay, vague masses of grass; everything which my contemporaries call evolutionary and I call without form and void. But if I were to climb up the face of the Scott Monument, I know that I should find lines of sculpture and masonry which were meant to be decisive and are decisive. In a word, I should find certainty, or conviction, or dogma, which is the thing that belongs to man only, and which, if you take it away from him, will not leave him even a man. For it is the whole business of humanity in this world to deny evolution, to make absolute distinctions, to take a pen and draw round certain actions a line that nature does not recognise; to take a pencil and draw round the human face a black line that is not there. I repeat, it is the business of the divine human reason to deny that evolutionary

appearance whereby all species melt into each other. This is probably what was meant by Adam naming the animals.[50]

Often, we need to "name the animals" which our Users bring to our attention. Sometimes we must see them as incredible anomalies, exotic special cases lurking in a swamp or jungle, to be dealt with as an *ad hoc* piece of software. (That is Latin, and in case you didn't know, it means, "To This Thing," implying that the thing built has just one single purpose, the purpose at hand.) Other times we will see the creatures as common and almost dull: the user-oriented tools and packages, domestic livestock of our software farms – and yet (as they *are* farm creatures) they require far more orderly treatment and care. There will be other classifications, dividing our work according to the disciplines or needs of the end-users: business, engineering, and so on.

There will also be other sorts of classifications needed: those which are the work-a-day kinds of software, requiring only the usual sound training in software development and design: such things account for the vast majority of all programming. There are also the special, "academically interesting" problems, which will require care in arranging them for practical uses by Users, but also in the correct selection of the appropriate solution. You may even find some riddle which will not be in the "literature," either because its lair has not yet been reached by the theoretical explorers, or because its presentation has not been recognized; then you may have to cobble the solution together for yourself.

Algorithms

You will need to have some faint sense of the nature of algorithms, that is, of a formal series of instructions. (I omit the qualifier often added to the formal definition: "together with a terminating condition," since that applies only to certain classes of algorithms, and not to others, such as operating systems and their kin.) One acquires this knowledge in three ways: by studying the thing abstractly using mathematics, by meticulous exploration of a single common and preferably elementary algorithm (like, say, LONG DIVISION), and by examining an array of examples.[51]

Classic Solution Methods

One will find dozens of classic examples for problem-solving in Euclid's books on Geometry, or indeed in any mathematics text. These are excellent guides for learning properties, and acquiring the skill of distinguishing and classifying problems. Three methods in particular deserve special mention:

(a) **Mathematical induction**: also called "divide and conquer."[52] This is the underlying trick necessary for correct use of recursion: it simply means one must devise a way of splitting up the main problem into subproblems which are easier to solve, along with a way of uniting those subsolutions to achieve the solution of the main problem. See the discussion of recursion later in this book.

(b) **Boolean Algebra**: it is all too easy to overlook this since it is so elementary, but since it is simply a formal symbolizing of Logic, it holds the keys to many locks.

---

[50] GKC "The Way to the Stars" in *Lunacy and Letters*; reference to Genesis 2:19-20.

[51] This suggests the medieval origin of hospitals, originally established for merely charitable and humanitarian reasons, but as physicians were thereby enabled to consider an array of cases (both similar and dissimilar) they rapidly progressed in medical knowledge. See e.g. Walsh, *The Popes and Science.*

[52] Originally, "Divide and Command," an ancient military maxim quoted by Machiavelli, according to *Bartlett's.*

(c) **Automata**: knowledge of this fundamental method of computation can provide insight into approaches for handing problems. It's not just for parsing: when one has a problem involving a number of distinct states, among which transitions are made based on events, one has an automaton.

Acquiring a rich toolbox

This simply means gaining as much experience as possible at handling a varied selection of problems, whether in class, in lab, or on one's own. We shall examine this in a separate chapter.

Climbing around in the Tree of Virtues

That's just an eye-catcher to suggest exploration of other disciplines to get new tricks. These arise in both natural and human settings, and I myself have found answers this way. For example, in history I found Subsidiarity, which I applied to file transport for local ad insertion in cable television, and in biology I found anastomosis which has its use in monitoring and debugging. You will be surprised at what you may find if you go tree-climbing. (But do be careful. You'll hear about my cast later.)

Over-the-shoulder debugging

This trick is getting rather specific, but I felt it should be mentioned. It's very simple, but it does work. Ask someone else to come and watch you run your test, or even perform the test according to your instructions. There may be something "too large to be seen" which is causing the problem.[53]

Solving by teaching

I learned this trick from a famous musical, and I have used it to advantage:

> It's a very ancient saying,
> But a true and honest thought:
> That if you become a teacher,
> By your pupils you'll be taught.[54]

Find a colleague or two, and explain the situation to them. It is quite possible that you will yourself solve the puzzle as you are explaining it. This is one reason why writing white papers is such a good idea: apparently the mind's light provided by "Describe this" is brighter than that provided by "Solve this."

Some Cautions.

Such a list might be considered the "inverse" of a problem-solving technique, but in some sense, it is simply *preventing* problems from arising. There are many, of course, but I wish to mention a few which seem especially relevant, and which will be treated in our Case Studies.

(1) Applying the wrong tool for the job.
(2) Not specifying the problem correctly.
(3) Pride, or thinking a problem is beneath one's dignity to work on.
(4) Forgetting to consult the record.

But the worst (and really the overall danger) is NOT USING COMMON SENSE.

---

[53] A famous Chesterton motif classically stated in this line:

"Perhaps the weapon was too big to be noticed," said the priest, with an odd little giggle.

See "The Three Tools of Death" in *The Innocence of Father Brown*, CW12:227.

[54] Rodgers and Hammerstein's "Getting to Know You" in *The King and I*.

Finally, I will suggest this rather surprising idea.

Case Study: Standard (Traditional) Lab Practices

No, I don't simply mean wearing a white lab coat, or chuckling in that sinister Mad Scientist tone they taught us when I was in grad school. I mean what my good friend wrote when he sent me an elegant and unused lab notebook for my work:

> Dr. Floriani,
>
> Remember it goes –
> (1) Date
> (2) Title
> (3) Materials
> (4) Methods
> (5) Results
> (6) Conclusions
>
> And remember it's for Posterity!
>
> Dr. Romano

This is probably as insightful and as useful a guide as one will find. But let us be clear about what is meant, especially when it comes to the "Title," which as I recall from my own lab work was often split into "Title" and "Purpose." The title is not just the "cool" nickname chosen for the sake of marketing, or because someone in management decided to churn out a new and goofy buzzword. We are speaking as formally as possible here, so the Title ought to convey, succinctly *yet accurately* what this particular experiment is intended to study: the Title must reveal the Purpose.

Nor are we writing a detective/mystery story, where we are forbidden to tell the "end" of the story at the start (or worse, on the back cover). Rather, in our work we *must* tell the "End" (which is really another word for "Purpose") as early as possible. The technical term for this is called "Teleology" which means the science of "Ends" or Purposes. This is just one of the powerful results of reverting to "the doctrinal methods of the thirteenth century": one gets things done when one knows the purpose towards which one is working.[55]

It is *essential* to know the Purpose. In my book on Subsidiarity, I recalled a Latin phrase my mother taught me: *Dic cur hic* = "Tell why you are here." One needs to know *why* – what is the Purpose of the project. All too often the pressures of management may attempt to induce work to begin without a clear statement of what it is one is working on: this is dangerous, and almost always counterproductive. I cannot say I have always succeeded in coaxing others to attend to the Purpose in advance, but there are ways of doing this in a professional way. The most cunning of these strategies is what I call "Fence-sitting," that is, the writing of white papers in which one attempts to define the problem at hand, extracting both the *known* as well as the

---

[55] "I revert to the doctrinal methods of the thirteenth century, inspired by the general hope of getting something done." GKC *Heretics* CW1:46.

unknown issues, proposing various approaches and indicating their requirements, advantages and disadvantages. (Management seems to enjoy seeing alternatives, especially when the plusses and minuses are included.)

There are other aspects of traditional lab practices (and lab write-ups) which need to be presented and discussed, and I hope to cover them in a future volume.

Topical Case Studies

The following chapters present a number of important topics, each of which might constitute a kind of "tool" for problem-solving. In order to bolster the discussion I have provided examples from my strange and fascinating experiences in the field.

Chapter 7
Gathering a Rich Collection of Samples

The greatest of poems is an inventory.

GKC *Orthodoxy*, CW1:267

It is inarguable that the primary problem-solving tool is to have a rich collection of *solved* problems available for consultation. It is not necessary that *you* have solved them; indeed, it is nearly impossible for any single individual to have solved even a small handful of problems. (Those thirty-odd years of my experience in computing, over a billion seconds of time, seem very long, even in this very young discipline, but I have gained such a very small taste of it!) Indeed, you should face some of them on your own for practice, and to gain confidence in your tools; this is part of the reason for requiring lab work in the sciences, and programming assignments in our discipline. It underscores the necessity of *trust* – which is a synonym of confidence – in Authority, as difficult as that may be for some philosophically:

> If I want to know the volume of a cylinder I can, if I know how, work the problem out either by mathematics or by experiment: or I can ask a competent person to tell me what its volume is. In the last case I proceed on the lines of authority, and, in doing so, I convince myself first of all by an act of reason that my authority is a reliable one. This is only doing what every man of business does time and again in the conduct of his affairs.[56]

Note Windle's words: *by mathematics or by experiment*. In some cases you can proceed to solve the problem according to the pure methods of mathematics; other times you may proceed by composing a "test" (using a suitable programming language) and trying it out. Except in odd cases where you require some sort of unique piece of equipment (such as a video playback card, or a cue-tone detection device, as I needed in my work in cable TV) you will almost always be able to work with the *original* subject matter – demonstrating the remarkable character Computer Science shares with Astronomy:

> Considered as a collector of rare and precious things, the amateur astronomer has a great advantage over amateurs in all other fields, who must content themselves with second and third rate specimens. ... [he] has access at all times to the original objects of his study; the masterworks of the heavens belong to him as much as to the great observatories of the world.[57]

You, no less than any of the greatest workers in computer science, also have access to the original objects of study, even if you do not have the same tools at your disposal.

Your challenge is to collect solutions, or at the very least, starting links which will take you to solutions, especially those which have been well-explored and are clearly presented, whether they are in books, journals, or websites. As you use them you learn which are trustworthy, and which require additional efforts to apply.

Of course as you proceed with building your collection, you will begin to notice

---

[56] Windle, *The Catholic Church and its Reactions with Science*, 52.

[57] Burnham, *Burnham's Celestial Handbook*, 5.

certain great themes – the methods or paradigms of dealing with problems. Try to be *catholic* [58] in your collection, as even dubious or extremely specialized approaches may have value in illuminating a difficult case. Also, begin to consider the solutions not only according to their classes, but by adjacency, which might be called the Principle of Cooperation: *Could these two (or more) techniques somehow be used together?*

* * *

The reader should bear in mind that our discipline is very young, even if one starts with Charles Babbage in the 1830s. There is plenty of work to be done, especially on those of its aspects which are philosophical, or self-descriptive: unfortunately these seem to be less immediately relevant to practical uses in industry, and less attractive to the hot topics of theory currently in vogue among academics. Think of how long it took until Linnaeus began (1735) the modern scheme of Taxonomy upon which Biology depends, or until Mendeleyev proposed (1869) the Periodic Table of the Chemical Elements – yet all workers in those fields know these systems and use them constantly. Hopefully we won't need to wait that long for a systematic approach to our discipline. [59]

---

[58] Note that the lower-case term means "universal."

[59] No, I am not ready to propose a systematic view of "Problems" writ large; the most I am doing is suggesting it as a topic for further study. But maybe this series will help a little: a depth of philosophy and a *catholic* viewpoint (ahem) will be essential.

Chapter 8
On Elementary Matters: the Hierarchy of Symbols

...there seems to be serious indication that the whole high human art of scripture or writing began with a joke. There are some who will learn with regret that it seems to have begun with a pun.

GKC *The Everlasting Man*, CW2:198

Chesterton made that comment about ancient Egyptian hieroglyphics, and while I am no scholar in that language, I have explored it slightly, and his insight seems to have hit on the "trick" of writing: that is, letting approximations of one sort "stand for" something else of another sort. But with that approximation there enters the possibility of alternatives, which means the possibility of puns. For example,

Q: What has four wheels and flies?

A: A garbage truck.

Which pivots on whether "flies" is a noun or a verb. There can't be puns when there is no opportunity for ambiguity: mathematics seems to present few opportunities for such low humor. (But see Appendix 8 for a counterexample.) In the end, of course, we manage to communicate, to get things done, even with exceedingly great accuracy, because we overload our language with redundancies in order to reduce ambiguities to their minimum. (Later we shall see a practical application of this technique, which might be called the "I tell you three times" trick.) There are other methods, some well-known academically (such as Grammar) and some which are common and well-used but hardly noticed, which we will mention shortly.

It would be very comforting to spend some time collecting puns and curious ambiguities of language, and there are books on such things by scholars of language. But my purpose in beginning with writing is to start with the fundamentals – not to examine them as subject matter, but to link them together with our discipline, and to farm these fields for often-overlooked fruits.

Yes, speaking strictly for myself, there is a real delight in considering printing: in the simple 26 characters of the English language. At a relatively early age (perhaps third or fourth grade) I encountered the Greek alphabet, and found further delights. It was some time later that I explored hieroglyphics... but this is not about me, even as an example of acquiring knowledge of human writing. Besides, our discipline is not about printing, or calligraphy, or the history of writing – and it comes as a shock to many when I tell them that computers do not have any internal arrangements for letters *at all*. They do not "know" an "A" from a "W" or from a "5"... because those things are *exterior* representations, occurring only in keyboards or display screens or printers. And this unexpected truth helps us understand this first and most fundamental of the elementary matters.

That is, our field requires a hierarchy of symbols: representations in one form which stand for realities in another form. (It may also be so for the field of human intelligence, but I am not ready to explore that topic here.) We see this readily enough in our own non-technical experience: the thing we call "speech" is a representation in sound, generated by lips and tongue and teeth and vocal cords, of something mental, some internal thought. That sound may be a merely biological expression of the body's feeling (like a sigh, or gasp, or groan), or it may be arranged according to some traditional rules, accepted without argument for the sake of utility, and likewise obeyed, since we speak with the expectation of being understood.[60] Hence, we should understand that "Speech is an audible representation of Thought."

Printing and writing, of course, follow from speech, as these things are likewise traditional representations. There are sometime frustrations, such as the prevalence of the "th" sound in English, which must now be written with two letters; the Greeks had their wonderfully shaped Θ, and the British of centuries past had the now-obsolete letters

Đ or ð called "eth"

Þ or þ called "thorn"

Worse is the case of the "sh" sound which has at least a dozen spellings:

sh	shoe	sch	schist
ch	chaperone	ti	function
si	tension	sci	conscience
se	nauseous	su	sugar
ss	issue	ce	ocean
ci	suspicion	psh	pshaw [61]

But even these are merely traditional. The point is not that English has punnish tendencies, but that there are symbolic representations in print of audible sounds – and while the spoken word came first in terms of that tradition, it is quite possible to produce plenty of printed matter directly from thought as I am doing right now.

Still, that is not what we are doing here: we are trying to get a sense of the possibilities of relations between things (say a fish) and their symbols (the word FISH as a sound, or *GHOTI* if you are Mr. Shaw), and even symbols of symbols (the printed thing "FISH" as four letters).

This may seem complex already, and a very long road to walk, but like the Witch told Dorothy, we have barely begun.

There is, after all, another bunch of these odd little symbols which are not letters, but are used in a similar manner. They too are traditional, but they have a strange property, that while the things they represent are ideas, they are among the most universal of ideas known to Man, so much so that almost anyone can understand them and deal with them from a relatively early age, even if he is not otherwise fluent in a spoken language. Those symbols are the *digits*: 0, 1, 2, 3, 4, 5, 6, 7, 8, 9. I use the term "digit" here to refer to those ten particular symbols, which we must thoroughly understand as *symbols*, not as "numbers" at least for the moment. While it is true the digits may be pronounced "zero," "one," "two," and so on, and therefore are related to the words "ZERO," "ONE," "TWO," etc., *and hence to the ideas those words convey*, we must preserve a very careful distinction from these *representations* and the ideas represented. We therefore have an additional layer – yes, our scheme of representations has a layered, or "hierarchical" quality.[62] We need this distinction when we try to understand what is meant by the symbols written "12" or "1.2" and so on, but also when we try to understand why "2" is not really a number at all inside a

---

[60] Sure, we can make babbling and nonsense noises all we want, of course, but we'll get funny looks if we do, or perhaps worse... For a fascinating insight into this topic see "The Noticeable Conduct of Professor Chadd" in GKC's *The Club of Queer Trades*.

[61] Speaking of Shaw, he concocted GHOTI, the famous spelling of "fish," with *gh* as in laugh, *o* as in women, *ti* as in action.

[62] It is always funny to hear people use this word, especially when they disdain the idea of a priesthood or of any sort of religion, especially in contact with topics in science. But it is well to recall that this concept of an ordered layering of classes of individuals comes from religion: from Greek 'ειρος (hieros) = "sacred, holy" and αρχη (*archê*) = "first, leader."

computer – and, in fact, what numbers really are.

We have to mention one other class of symbols, those little gnats like commas and periods, semicolons and colons, quotes, dashes, and so forth. Some of these are comparatively new, others date to classic times – but we have no time to explore that now. However, there is one other item to be mentioned which is very easy to overlook, since it is almost *impossible* to see it, or even think of it, until, by design, thatmarvellousitemisnolongerusedinthetextyouarereading, and then the idea of *white space* becomes incredibly obvious. Few people these days know that this "space" was devised comparatively late in the history of writing; both the ancient Greeks and Romans ran their words together. Even more than the much-discussed idea of "zero" as a number, the idea of an invisible character called "blank" or "space" is a triumph for those who read, even if it presents a challenge in other ways.

Are you getting tired? I hope not. We really do have a long way to go, but at least there's no one throwing fireballs at us.

There are important reasons for this tedious treatment of such simple things, and the first is that it is *extremely* easy to overlook such relationships as we are examining. We learn to associate our thoughts with sounds – both those we hear and those we produce – at a very early age, and until we take up an additional language in later years of education we don't ever think about what we are doing when we hear the spoken word, or speak them – and then, regardless of what language we study, we must struggle with an unexpected array of subtleties in pronunciation and auditory perception. Incidentally, such struggles go very far back in time: the very word *shibboleth* [63] iconifies this difficulty, as it served to distinguish one group of language speakers from another.

The array of subtleties begins with a strange paradox, the paradox of language – an incredibly binding collection of extremely arbitrary and traditional rules which are imposed upon us – yet these rules are such that we never notice them, and even in attempting to discuss them, revise them, or replace them, we are forced to obey them. No wonder Chesterton said "Free speech is a paradox."[64] This same sort of tradition extends to the character sets of computers... but let us talk about something simpler, and just as arbitrary: the Alphabet.

It is one of the first ordered things we learn, along with the first few counting numbers. But whereas the numbers exist in some fashion independently of the names given them by languages – so much so that even monkeys and dolphins and horses, nay, even chickens – can be trained to compare small integers. But the alphabet is a Grand Tradition, and one of the most arbitrary arrangements that exist.[65] In a future

---

[63] See Judges 12:6: "They asked him: Say then, Scibboleth, which is interpreted, An ear of corn [grain]. But he answered, Sibboleth, not being able to express an ear of corn by the same letter." To the best of my knowledge, the two sounds are what we hear as "sh" versus "s". In more recent times, the name of the letter "Z" is pronounced *zee* in the United States, *zed* in Canada, and even *izzard* in some places.

[64] GKC, *Robert Browning*, 174.

[65] Should you perhaps wonder what the alternative is, consult the appendix to Tolkien's *The Lord of the Rings* and see his discussion of the Elvish characters, the shapes of which are arranged according to philological and physiological principles. Also, every time you consult a dictionary or any sort of alphabetized index, you bear witness to the exceeding power and utility of this admittedly arbitrary arrangement; we will shortly hear about the comparable trick in computing. Indeed, a child ought to spend a lot of time playing with the alphabet so as to have a most intimate awareness of each letter and its neighbors: I recall doing such exercises (write the letter after S, the letter before Q) in first grade.

volume I will have more to say about these splendid characters, and you can find books about them; I may have to write one of my own eventually. What we here need to remember, and try to realize, even if we've never thought about it before, is that the alphabet was invented, almost in the way a story is invented: just for the simple delight of its originator. Yes it has undergone a number of alterations, from some likely Semitic origin, through Phoenicia, through Greece (which gave us the vowels), through Rome (which preserved the F which the Greeks had discarded, threw out the ones they didn't want like Θ and Ψ, gave us the odd conflicts of C (a variant form of Σ which was the Greek S) with G or K, and moved X, Y, and Z to the rear) – and which was tinkered with even in the Middle Ages (which took care of I and J, U and V and W). Then printing came in, and things began to settle down, except for the last gasp of the "thorn" which was used in spelling words like "the" (originally written "þe") but since the printers often ran out of that odd "þ" character they substituted a "y" which accounts for the fake old-fashioned "Ye Olde Inne" signs. (Which, it ought to be pointed out, is read *"the* old inn. *"*)

Now, leaving all this fascinating history for another time, let us remember what is going on. There are a bunch of sounds we can make with our mouths, and perceive with our ears, and It Has Been Decided By Our Past (meaning, by Tradition, as pugnacious a word as there is!) to associate those sounds with these odd little marks we call the Letters of the Alphabet. It may be observed that the Greeks or Russians or Arabs or other language-speakers have devised their own symbols for most of those sounds, and sometimes for others English doesn't use. But just as there is an arbitrary representation linking the idea *fish* to the spoken word "fish" there is also an arbitrary link from that spoken word to the four symbols F-I-S-H.

And therein lies a number of great principles we must recognize as we begin to approach our discipline.

First we have the idea of an alphabet: a collection of symbols which we call "letters." There are several secondary aspects to this idea which I should mention here, such as the distinction of "capital" and "small" letters, also called "upper" or "lower" case, and the variety of such symbols which might be called "fonts" by which the critical elements of the letter's shape are preserved while noncritical elements (such as size, slant, perspective, or lesser ornamentational aspects of those symbols) are altered.

Second, these letters are given a fixed order, taught and insisted upon at great length at an extremely early age, which serves as a master-rule for all sorts of things. No physical key opens so many doors as the master-key called the alphabet.

Third, these letters are associated with Something Else, typically a "sound" – and this association is a pairing, just as one might grab two things, one with each hand, and push them together so they are adjacent. This concept – association, pairing, mapping – is of extreme importance,[66] and so large it is even easier to overlook than the fact that the alphabet is a bunch of arbitrary symbols arranged in an arbitrary manner.

Finally, there is another sort of association which may occur with these letters – a

---

[66] Indeed; another topic for a chapter, or a book: this idea of abstracting the simultaneous grasp of two distinct things with one's two hands... pairs, mappings, functions, all the splendid complexities of set theory, relations, and analogies. But we expected this, since at the depths of Scholastic Philosophy we learn: "Everything that is in the intellect has been in the senses." See GKC, *St. Thomas Aquinas*; the quote may be found in CW2:525.

strange power which is so much tied to our physical body, and which deserves further analysis, which I shall supply in a future volume: that is, the marvellous *chirality* of the letters: the fact that each has a "left hand" and a "right hand" by which they may be chained together, thereby forming *words*. Such words may not be exactly like the spoken words, and not only because of the ambiguities of sound-representation.. but we *don't* have time to treat matters like contraction, elison or syncope here. The point we must attend to is another which is so easy to overlook, unless one has played with model trains, or perhaps stood by a railyard and watched the assembly of single cars into a train. Like a railcar, letters come with exactly two "couplers," one at each end, and can only be joined as links in a chain, or cars in a train: we give the term *concatenation* [67] to this formal action of linking characters together.

From such a complex list we learn something else, something metaphysical. It is essential to understand our materials and actions by both large and small views: treating things by their most large and generic senses to perceive their proper places, but also according to their most minute characters, even when such are perpetually overlooked. We need to think about forming words from individual letters as one does in playing "Scrabble" or as one did in the days when printing required true fonts made of type-metal, and these were stacked into a wooden backbone called a "composing stick" in preparation for printing.[68] It is, paradoxically, a limitation which provides the most intense and broad freedom.

But in all this we must not lose sight of why we bother with letters or digits, with concatenating them in computers, or on composing sticks, or with pen on paper. We are trying to do something very profound: to accomplish the transfer of thought from one mind to another. The amazing thing to contemplate is that this almost insanely impossible task has been accomplished in the utterly dim and distant past, and has been used with great success for over five millennia.

(At this very moment, as you read this, you are relying on those successes. It would be well for you to think of this, perhaps on the next Thanksgiving Day. It is a great victory of humanity. We ought to be grateful for our technology even in its simplest forms, and reach the point where we can say as Chesterton did over 100 years ago, "I have often thanked God for the telephone."[69])

Now that we have reached this idea of making words from letters, we must advance to a related topic, which will take us deeper into computing: that is *numbers*.

---

[67] From the Latin *catena* = chain.

[68] See Gaskell, *A New Introduction to Bibliography*, 43-5. All computer scientists ought to have some basic awareness of the old technology of printing.

[69] GKC, *What's Wrong With the World*, CW4:112.

Chapter 9
On Elementary Matters:
Numbers and Their Representations

Somehow, when it comes to the spelling of numbers, there is a far greater whine at hand than even the most controversial of issues in the spelling of words. Not that there are better or worse alternatives proposed, those taking history into account, or ease of remembering, or confusion of the simple, or simplification of the teacher's task; I don't mean anything like that. I mean something more controversial, since it is far less well understood: the idea that a number is something fundamentally *different* from its representation. This distinction, and the Scholastics of the Middle Ages were always careful about making distinctions, is a tricky one, and has confounded many who try to come at the realm of mathematics using the tools of another trade, or without trying to understand what that very remarkable field is trying to do.

You may recall the "Calvin and Hobbes" comic strip where the father tries to teach Calvin about addition. He gets out eight pennies and asks Calvin for four more, then says, "Now, you've added four pennies to my eight, so how many pennies do I have?" Calvin, wary of what he thinks is incipient petty theft, states: "Eight!"

Yes, indeed. That's the issue at hand. For grouping together, even of seemingly identical entities – the technical term is "fungible" – does not in itself constitute addition, even for mathematicians, and if you think otherwise, you have not yet ascended high enough in the field to begin contemplating Number. I mean no slighting; but then there are other ways one may "add" eight and four, which, depending on the "glue" one uses for "addition," might yield:

84 or 48	mere adjacency – positional notation
8.4	period – decimal point
8/4	slash – fraction
8^4	large and a small superscript – exponential
(8,4)	horizontal pair – vector of two dimensions
$\binom{8}{4}$	vertical pair – combinations of 8 things taken 4 at a time

and so on. The problem is not so much with those others, as exotic as they may be, since anyone can recognize that some other verb is active, not the elementary one which simply means addition. (One feels tempted to scream, "Calvin! ")

However, it is well that we consider these forms, as it will help us grasp not only the real mystery of addition in itself, but something which is far harder to notice: that first example of "addition" labelled "positional notation" which is properly called concatenation. Those two things, "84" or "48" are called "numbers" since those symbols are the agreed-upon convention for representation of the *ideas* which we also use the terms "eighty-four" and "forty-eight" in English, or "*octagina quattuor*" and "*quadragina octo*" in Latin, and so on in other tongues, being merely our spoken sounds for

eighty-four = •••••••••• •••••••••• •••••••••• •••••••••• •••••••••• •••••••••• •••••••••• •••••••••• ••••

forty-eight = •••••••••• •••••••••• •••••••••• •••••••••• ••••••••

that is, representations for the *ideas* of that many things.

Yeah... the idea of that many things. But we cannot go into the principles of Number now. We are only examining a far simpler matter, the *representation* of number, but *not* as a word (or compound of words).

The issue at hand is known as *positional notation*, and requires a handful of items which must also be decided upon:

1. The "base" b, a *number* (greater than one) upon which the enumerating system is based.

2. The "digits" or symbols to be used in the notation:

$$D = \{d_0, d_1, d_2, \ldots d_{b-1}\}$$

There must be b of these, all distinct from each other. It is agreed upon that each of these symbols are representations of the values of the *numbers* from 0 to $b-1$. That is, one can make a table listing all the distinct *digits* (representations) in the first column, and the *numbers* (ideas of quantities) from 0 up to $b-1$ in the second column. For example, we give the important representation called "hexadecimal" with $b = 16$:

Digit	Idea represented	Digit	Idea represented
0	zero	8	eight
1	one	9	nine
2	two	A	ten
3	three	B	eleven
4	four	C	twelve
5	five	D	thirteen
6	six	E	fourteen
7	seven	F	fifteen

3. A rule governing the meanings of the various positions. One common way is to let the positions represent a value which is a power of the base, and having the values decrease from left to right, with the rightmost position representing the "units" place, since $b^0 = 1$ for any non-zero integer b.

There are also various extensions, such as adding the idea of the "point" which signifies fractional values, the minus sign, and so forth. One other extension I use in this book, sometimes called the "e-format," derives from the old FORTRAN notation, and has become very common elsewhere; it is a shorthand for the scientific notation for the representation of very large or very small numbers, condensing them by using powers of ten. For example, to represent 46,000 one may write 4.6×10^4 in scientific notation which may also be represented as 4.6e4 in e-format notation. (Simply read the "e" as "times ten to the. ") Also see the table of metric prefixes later in the book.

Thus, in order to represent some number with the value n, we write a series of the appropriate symbols, arranged according to the rule governing positions, so that the arrangement represents, or stands for n. If the position values descend from left to right, placing the appropriate digits from D *next* to each other like this:

$$s_k\ s_{k-1}\ s_{k-2}\ \ldots\ s_3\ s_2\ s_1\ s_0$$

then the corresponding value of n is given by the following equation:

$$n = \sum_{i=0}^{k} s_i b^i$$

where the rightmost digit has subscript zero, and the index i increases as one goes left in the representation. For example, when $b = 10$, the common base ten system used by a very large proportion of humans on Earth, and the digits are $D = \{0, 1, 2, 3, 4, 5, 6, 7, 8, 9\}$ we have

$$n = \sum_{i=0}^{k} s_i 10^i$$

where the index i decreases from left to right, ending at zero, and the s_i are chosen from D so as to yield the above sum. Hence, the value symbolized by "348" can be computed as

$$n = 3 \cdot 10^2 + 4 \cdot 10^1 + 8 \cdot 10^0$$

or

$$n = 300 + 40 + 8$$

which is, as you expect, 348.

If this seems absurdly confusing, or even more absurdly trivial, that's because we are using numbers in two senses, which is my point. (The philosophers warn against this, calling it the Error of Equivocation. It's a *constant* threat in many fields.)

So, let's try it using something else, which may help by making the representation not look like a "number." We'll let $b = 2$, and for our digits, we'll use D = {◊, ♦} where ◊ represents zero, and ♦ represents one. This is just a variation of binary, or base two.

Now, let's consider the representation which is ♦◊◊♦◊♦, pronounced one, zero, zero, one, zero, one. What is that number?

There are six places, so we must descend from two-to-the-fifth to two-to-the-zero as we go from left to right:

one times 2^5, plus
zero times 2^4, plus
zero times 2^3, plus
one times 2^2, plus
zero times 2^1, plus
one times 2^0

or

$1 \cdot 32 +$
$0 \cdot 16 +$
$0 \cdot 8 +$
$1 \cdot 4 +$
$0 \cdot 2 +$
$1 \cdot 1$

which equals the number we call thirty-seven, represented as 37 in base ten.

If this is still not clear, you should get a book which discusses positional notation, both base ten and the three "special" bases used in computing: base two or binary, base eight or octal, and base sixteen or hexadecimal, also called "hex" for short – and then try a few exercises using these bases. They really are a lot easier than their first appearance. Binary is incredibly important, since it has only two digits; we may write them as zero and one, or in other ways as we just did in the example; in the typical electronic computer they are represented by two distinct voltage levels, usually +5 and −5 volts, or +5 volts and 0 volts. The other two, octal and hex, are merely binary grouped by threes or fours for compactness.

For example, here are the first few numbers in the four bases:

binary	octal	hex	decimal
0	0	0	0
1	1	1	1
10	2	2	2
11	3	3	3
100	4	4	4
101	5	5	5
110	6	6	6
111	7	7	7
1000	10	8	8
1001	11	9	9
1010	12	A	10
1011	13	B	11
1100	14	C	12
1101	15	D	13
1110	16	E	14
1111	17	F	15

binary	octal	hex	decimal
10000	20	10	16
10001	21	11	17
10010	22	12	18
10011	23	13	19
10100	24	14	20
10101	25	15	21
10110	26	16	22
10111	27	17	23
11000	30	18	24
11001	31	19	25
11010	32	1A	26
11011	33	1B	27
11100	34	1C	28
11101	35	1D	29
11110	36	1E	30
11111	37	1F	31
100000	40	20	32

(If you study the chart in Appendix 2 or, even better, write out for yourself the four representations for numbers from 0 to 255, you will readily see how the groupings for octal and hex are worked.)

Hexadecimal (or base 16) is a mixed blessing, because it requires the use of six additional symbols besides the usual ten common digits, as we gave earlier. Work with hex can sometimes be very annoying, but many computers arrange memory in groups of eight bits, which is conveniently represented as two hexadecimal "digits" ranging from 00_{16} through FF_{16}, which is 255 in base ten.

It is important to understand this idea of the representation of numbers for many reasons, but especially because it is necessary to understand how one might handle numbers in the general sense on a computer: that is, not as a human thinks, or as one has learned to perform manual computation, but within the very narrow constraints imposed by the electronic machinery at hand.

Just consider what sort of thing is going on in this eight-bit unit we call a byte, the values of which may take on any of the 256 possible patterns of zeros and ones from 00000000 to 11111111. Now that we know of binary, or base two, that is, the representation of a number using only two distinct digits, we readily grasp that this byte can be said to contain any integer (yes, a number) between 0 and 255.

We can also extend the idea to larger memory units; typical machines may be able to calculate using two, four, or even eight bytes considered together, which gives numerical ranges like this:

bits	bytes	total patterns
8	1	256
16	2	65536
32	4	4294967296
64	8	18446744073709551616

Typical computers are able to perform an operation which is called "addition" and which remains accurate as long as the limits imposed by the memory constraints are not violated. Otherwise it will do something else, and the expected "addition" will not take place. This ought to be clear enough: typical (non-military) clocks do not go past 12, yet we have no trouble in knowing what to do when it is 11AM and a friend tells us to meet in two hours – we gleefully add "two" to "eleven" and get "one" without committing math heresy. What a computer will do, however, in comparable cases, ought not be left to chance. (See the discussion on addition later in this book.)

But that is getting ahead of our topic. We need to understand the idea of the representation of a number using a base b and a set D of digits, which requires two particular operations: one which converts a given number into its representation in that base, and the other which takes a representation in a particular base and computes the corresponding number. We have already done the second, which is represented by the big-sigma equation a few pages back. Let us see how to turn a given number into its representation in a given base. I am not going to derive the method, or justify it, I will simply state it. To convert an integer n into its representation in base b with digits D = $\{d_0, d_1, \dots d_{b-1}\}$:

Start with an empty representation ρ.
Repeat the following steps
    1. Divide n by b, giving the quotient q and remainder r, with $0 \le r < b$.
    2. Augment ρ by placing the digit in D corresponding to r to the left of ρ.
    3. Replace n with the quotient q.
until n becomes equal to zero.

Let's try it for something juicy, like 2766 and convert this into hexadecimal, which means $b=16$ and the digits are $\{0, 1, 2, 3, 4, 5, 6, 7, 8, 9, A, B, C, D, E, F\}$.

Start with $n = 2766$ and ρ = [] (Yes, there's nothing between the brackets.)
First loop.
    Divide n (which is 2766) by 16, giving 172 and a remainder of 14.
    Augment ρ on the left with the base 16 digit for 14,
        which is "E", so now ρ = [E].
    Replace n with 172.
But n (which is 172) is not zero, so we must repeat.
Second loop.
    Divide n (which is 172) by 16, giving 10 and a remainder of 12.
    Augment ρ on the left with the base 16 digit for 12,
        which is "C", so now ρ = [CE].
    Replace n with 10.
But n (which is 10) is not zero, so we must repeat.
Third loop.
    Divide n (which is 10) by 16, giving 0 and a remainder of 10.
    Augment ρ on the left with the base 16 digit for 10,
        which is "A", so now ρ = [ACE].
    Replace n with 0.
But n is now zero, so we are done.

Hence, the representation for the number 2766 in base 16 is ACE_{16}.

Huh? Why are you trembling? Division? It feels like division? Are you scared by division? Oh, no, please don't be scared. Division isn't a hard thing – no, not at all – and with the right sort of friendly guidance you will soon be freed of such a silly phobia.

Yes, we need to talk some more about division, especially in light of that cunning little algorithm we just studied. Oh yes, that little thing was an algorithm. We'll talk about that also, a bit later. But first it's time to face your fear, and I assure you it will be dispelled. Wands out, people... er, I mean, pencils out – and let us proceed with the help of God.[70]

---

[70] In Juster's *The Phantom Tollbooth*, our hero Milo is given such a "magic staff" by the Mathemagician. You ought to have your own.

Chapter 10
On Elementary Matters: LONG DIVISION

Putatis quia pacem veni dare in terram? Non dico vobis sed separationem.
Think ye, that I am come to give peace on earth? I tell you, no; but separation.
– Luke 12:51

What a horrifying topic this is! But it's not. LONG DIVISION is truly a very important Problem-Solving Skill, in some ways one of the most important of all such skills. It is not merely important for simply finding a quotient; for some values one can use a calculator or computer, and get an answer, which might even be correct. But it may be the case that one has some sort of unique challenge, as I once did (though that concerned multiplication; see the Case Study later in this book). One may need to divide numbers with many places, or get a more accurate result than that supplied by the calculator or computer at hand, so one has to write a program which actually performs LONG DIVISION. But there are many problems which are very similar to that problem, and which no calculator or computer can solve directly, for example, to factor polynomials, to convert the representation of a number into an internal form, to integrate by partial fractions, and other more exotic purposes, such as in Galois Field Theory (a branch of mathematics which underlies error-correcting codes used in CDs, DVDs and elsewhere). But even considered at its elementary level, it is important, and not only for getting the answer. You ought to know by now that almost every elementary skill brings along a variety of secondary skills, and is taught for other purposes besides the primary and obvious one. It may come as a surprise for you to realize that LONG DIVISION will endow the student with additional skills – and we ought to understand more about it before we shrug it off as irrelevant.

In order to perform LONG DIVISION, a student needs to be able to multiply, compare, and subtract numbers; he must concern himself with important details like keeping the values correctly aligned with each other, performing all the simpler steps of arithmetic accurately, checking his work, and so on. But there are much more subtle reasons, which, like so many of the major subjects taught at the elementary levels, are fundamentally important – yet their importance is very hard to recognize, since the reasons are hard to notice.

LONG DIVISION is a means of teaching something much harder to describe than the very simple idea of getting the quotient. In fact, it exemplifies the First Problem Solving Skill one ought to have. It is simply stated, and something I would guess you've heard from your mother, especially if you've ever tried to make something in the kitchen. It is simply this:

Follow the Directions.

Furthermore, this idea of Getting Something Done By Following Instructions Correctly Even When They Are Boring is a very useful skill.

Another reason for studying LONG DIVISION is to teach the concept of Algorithm: that is, a formal series of instructions, like a recipe. The idea of Algorithm underlies many human actions, for example:

cooking – in the form of recipes
drama – in the form of playscripts
religion – in the form of ritual (liturgy or formal worship)
music – in the form of musical scores

and so on. It is a general idea, and one of the most powerful of "Problem-Solving Skills": one may be able to arrive at the answer to a problem by insight or intuition or some remarkable mental skill, but it is far more of a Solution to state a recipe-like or ritual formula by which the solution can be found for any problem similar to the one originally provided. In that case, one does not so much match the given problem to one already solved, one examines his toolbox of known solution-methods, looking for the one closest to the need, adapting it if necessary.

Such a skill – grasping the *concept* of Algorithm – is indeed powerful; it is also abstract. It may escape the notice of many otherwise intelligent individuals. However, there is another practical aspect to this study. LONG DIVISION also teaches the use of several simpler steps (all of which have already been learned) in order to perform a more complex task. This is another Problem-Solving Skill which we might call the Composition of Skills. Unlike other examples of this action, like the building of sentences from words, or the composition of a picture from various motions of a drawing implement, all parts of the operation are isolated and reduced to almost total simplicity; they succeed or fail almost instantly, and without any chance for debate or disagreement on points of style or aesthetics.

There are other aspects of LONG DIVISION which teach other, less obvious topics. The algorithm contains three interesting characteristics:

1. It uses a comparison: right in the middle it requires a decision to be made.

2. It uses a loop: the same sequence of steps are applied over and over.

3. It requires a terminating condition, which causes the stopping of the loop; and this is unlike the mere repetition of addition, subtraction, or multiplication which are based on the number of places in the values at hand. In the computation of decimals, even simple LONG DIVISION problems (like dividing 7 into 1) can proceed to arbitrarily many places, and one must know how to deal with such cases.

LONG DIVISION also happens to be the algorithm which is known to almost everyone, and so it provides a handy reference. It may not be something which one would want to perform manually; that is not the point. (If I had to use a pen to write, rather than a keyboard, I would not like it very much; my handwriting is horrible.) It is a simple skill which ought to be in one's toolbox; the fact that very few people have ever bothered to look at it, especially once they own a calculator, is beside the point. It's there, it's useful, especially as a point of reference for discussing certain abstract things – and one of the many advantages of Scholastic methods is to make use of analogy, working from something well-known to something less well-known, or even unknown.

An Assignment. If you think you're reasonably proficient at programming, and know all the basics of assignment, loops, conditionals, and are comfortable with the use of arrays, try writing a little program which performs "symbolic" LONG DIVISION of two numbers where their digits are given in two arrays. It requires a good bit more care than you may expect, but it is very satisfactory to get working, and may even be useful.

Chapter 11
On Knowing Your Tool

The precept "know thyself" did not fall from heaven; it fell upstairs from the other place. I decline to know myself; he is not in my set. He is an unknown benefactor of mine, who prefers to remain anonymous.

GKC "A Plea for Hasty Journalism" in *The Apostle and the Wild Ducks*

There is an ancient dictum ascribed to Plato and others, expressed in Greek Γνωθι σεαυτον (*Gnôthi seauton*) or Latin *Nosce teipsum* translated as: "Know thyself." This epigram was well-known to the Medievals:

> By reminding man of his origin, the divine Wisdom, Hugh says, keeps man from being like the other animals. The "tripod" of Apollo, with its superscription "Know thyself" is actually the threefold sense of Scripture, inspired by the divine Wisdom to teach man self-knowledge. ... [As Hugh says:] It is written on the tripod of Apollo: γνωθι σεαυτον, that is, "Know thyself," for surely, if man had not forgotten his origin, he would recognize that everything subject to change is nothing.[71]

A profound and suggestive start, which we have neither time nor space to explore further![72] But there is a far more modern variant, which is strikingly powerful, and is inarguably wise: **Know your tool**.

As we point out elsewhere, it is absurd to proceed into computing (even as a user) without knowing what is going on behind the screen, or inside that box. It's not magic. The machine is only performing some simple and elementary actions – a tiny handful of operations upon zeros and ones – with only one further strange and unbelievable power: that those operations proceed at a rate measured in *millions* or even *billions* per second!

But it is not sufficient for a diligent student or a serious worker to know only that. I don't mean you ought to order the logic diagrams of all the integrated circuits, or the source listings for the operating system – chances are they are not for sale anyway. Rather, I mean you ought to gain a working familiarity with the computer and its capabilities: with the machine itself, the operating system, and the language you are using.

What does "know your tool" mean? It means knowing both its capabilities and its limits, what it can do, what it cannot do. Flaunting such vast numbers one may readily think it may be *unlimited* – which would be very dangerous. No machine is unlimited; they are all finite, and will ever be finite. Sure, one of my professors once joked that "we approximate infinity by a terabyte" – one trillion characters – but that was in 1990. I was working on cable TV in 1999 when the company bought a video library capable of holding three terabytes and made of dozens of disk drives – it cost about a quarter of a million dollars. Now you can walk into a store and buy a disk

---

[71] Taylor, *The Didascalicon of Hugh of St. Victor*, 24 and 46. In a note on page 177 he states its ultimate source is Xenophon, *Memorabilia*, iv.ii.24-25.

[72] If you want it see Gilson *The Spirit of Medieval Philosophy*, chapter IX: "It was from the Delphic oracle that Socrates himself took the famous precept 'Know thyself'..." but adding the note "That, moreover, is why there can be no science of the individual as such." (note 1, p. 464) There is far more. Deep and thrilling but the matter deserves a different treatment than possible to the scope of this volume.

drive (at much less than a thousandth of that cost) which will hold a terabyte. Of course you can easily fill that up, and still want more space. As large as they are, these things are *not* infinite, not even close.

Let's pause briefly and review the metric prefixes.[73] Just in case you haven't gotten used to terms like gigabytes or nanoseconds, here are the ones you'll need:

kilo = thousand (1e3)	milli = thousandth (1e–3)
mega = million (1e6)	micro = millionth (1e–6)
giga = billion (1e9)	nano = billionth (1e–9)
tera = trillion (1e12)	pico = trillionth (1e–12)
peta = quadrillion (1e15)	femto = quadrillionth (1e–15)
exa = quintillion (1e18)	atto = quintillionth (1e–18)

At this point it would be well to insert a point which my good friend Jim reminded me of, one of the remarkable metric units which is not yet among those standardized by the ISO: the famous "millihelen," the unit of beauty which dates to Homer, defined to be the quantum of beauty necessary to launch *one* ship.[74] There are others which we shall defer for another time and place.

How big is a gigabyte? It's a billion bytes. A byte is a unit of computer memory which on most common machines is eight bits long – that is, a byte is capable of holding any of the 256 possible patterns of eight zeros or ones. A byte is often used to represent one printed character, since 256 is more than enough to handle both upper and lower case, digits, and punctuation.

So how big is a billion characters in terms of books? Here are three examples.

(1) The electronic form of the five-volume English translation of the *Summa Theologica* of St. Thomas Aquinas contains about 16 million characters, so a billion characters would be a stack of three hundred volumes (60 sets) of comparable size.

(2) Chesterton's collected *Illustrated London News* essays occupy about 13 million characters, which are 11 fat volumes (a good deal less dense in print than the Aquinas edition); printing a billion characters in such a form would give you a nice library of 846 books.

(3) A typical 200-page paperback with 10 words per line, 45 lines per page would have 90,000 words; assuming the usual 5-letter average plus a space would give 540,000 characters per book, so you'd need 1,852 such paperbacks to have a total of billion characters; they would take up about 80 feet of shelf space.

Human DNA contains about 3 billion bases which if stretched out would be almost a meter long – think of a molecule that huge! – though that merely demonstrates how small atoms are. It also goes to show what a huge library a typical human cell contains, comparable to the typical DVD of two to four gigabytes.[75]

---

[73] It may be fun for you to puzzle through these, especially when coupled with a review of that neglected skill called *dimensional analysis*: the accurate handling of equations which include "dimensions" or units of measure: time, length, and so on. For example, prove to your satisfaction that π seconds is very close to a nanocentury.

[74] Helen of Troy, said by Christopher Marlow to have had "the face that launched a thousand ships." See *Doctor Faustus*, Sc. 14.

[75] Since a DNA base may take on four possible values (A, C, G, T) it is comparable to two bits, or a quarter of a byte, so 3 billion bases is equivalent to 0.75 gigabytes. (It is a hilarious coincidence that "two bits" is also the slang for $0.25, a quarter dollar.)

Another way of showing a billion is to imagine laying a ring of quarters (about an inch across) around the Earth: since its circumference in round numbers is 24,000 miles, working through the dimensional analysis we have:

24,000 miles × 5,280 feet/mile × 12 inches/foot = 1,520,640,000 inches

The project requires 1.5 billion quarters, or $380,160,000.[76] So if you want to imagine a gigabyte, think of that ring of quarters around the Earth.

Now, rather than trying to save up that many quarters, perhaps you'd like a more practical project which will help demonstrate something about these numbers. This one, however, deals with the tiny nanosecond, a billionth of a second.

A Show-and-Tell Project: Making your own Hopper Nanosecond

Here is a nice little computer crafts project for you to do. It is a brief tribute to a major name in computer science: Captain (later Rear Admiral) Grace Hopper (1906-1992), who I am glad to have met in person. May she rest in peace.

Computers contain a master clock – an electronic device which governs its actions as a metronome or beat-keeper. In typical personal computers of the 2010s this clock runs at gigahertz speeds – that is, billions of ticks per second. And since time intervals are the inverse of speed, the work of the computer is measured in nanoseconds, or billionths of a second.

So *how long* is a nanosecond?

That was the question Grace Hopper once asked some engineers. And this is what they told her:

> The speed of light is almost exactly 300,000,000 meters per second. So in one nanosecond light travels 3e8 divided by a billion which is 0.3 meters, or 30 centimeters. That is 11.8 inches, just shy of 11 and 13/16 inches. So if you want to see "how long" a nanosecond is, get some wire and cut a length of 30 cm or 11.8 inches – and there you have it.

I have paraphrased, of course, but after she told us that,[77] she handed out pieces of wire which were 30cm long... yes, I own an authentic Hopper nanosecond. But you ought not be disappointed, since you can make your own which will be just as good. (I keep a handful of these for distribution at talks, etc.) They are useful since they suggest the limit to which any gigahertz-speed device may grow, and to demonstrate the astounding achievements in miniaturization which have made such speeds possible: the thousands of transistors which made up all the logic gates of the CPU in the 1960s required a huge 15x3x6 foot water-cooled box (these are my rough recollection of the dimensions of the CDC 6400) – now a comparably gigantic collection of electronics is reduced to a thin disk of silicon a few cm in diameter.

This business about the speed of light suggests a very interesting issue about knowing our tool. Clearly we are dealing with very large and very small numbers, and it can be hard to measure such things – like counting the number of quarters it would take to circle the Earth. It would be easy enough to write a simple program to fill up a disk drive in order to learn its capacity; there are tricks by which one might learn how

---

[76] I don't recommend doing this. Besides, due to the oceans it is not a practical project. Furthermore, as a young scholar once observed: "If the shoreline of Maine was straightened out it would reach to Mexico. But we must cut government spending somewhere." Quoted by Harold Dunn, *Science Digest* June 1972.

[77] She was a captain when I heard her speak in Philadelphia back in the early 1980s. She also mentioned that she had a microsecond, which is a huge hank of wire almost 1000 feet long.

much working memory one can use in a single program. But how might we go about knowing its effective speed, considered from the practical standpoint, that is, without consulting the relevant technical manual? Indeed, a fascinating question for the science of metrology: how can we measure something exceedingly out of range with relatively coarse measuring tools?

History reveals a very curious detail. In 1675 [78] Ole Rømer computed the speed of light by measuring the eclipses of Jupiter's moons. He noticed when Earth and Jupiter were on the same side of the Sun, the eclipses of the moons of Jupiter occurred a few minutes earlier than when Jupiter was further from Earth than the Sun. He estimated it took 16 minutes longer, which therefore enabled him to make an approximation of the speed of light: 240,000 kilometers/second or 150,000 miles/second. This is *an excellent approximation* considering the tools then available! The figure used today is 299,792,458 meters/second or 186,292.03 miles/second.

So, the trick is to somehow "enlarge" the experiment to such an extent that the value to be measured greatly exceeds the errors of the measuring tool at hand. The same sort of trick is used in the very important procedure called "PCR" – the Polymerase Chain Reaction – which is how molecular biologists acquire the sequence of bases in DNA. It would be utterly futile to attempt to learn this sequence from the DNA contained in a given cell, which is far too small to manipulate. The Polymerase Chain Reaction replicates ("amplifies") the DNA sequence, and by judicious use of both machinery and reagents, each run of the reaction doubles the number of DNA copies: as you will know by consulting the powers of two in Appendix 2, thirty repeats will amplify the original sequence a billion times.

An aside: In terms of the gross quantity as handled in the lab, this is still an incredibly tiny amount. For example, when I helped a molecular biologist friend with cancer research, one of his sequences had 194 bases with a molecular weight of over 62,400. After a billion repeats the weight would amount to just over 100 picograms – an absurdly small weight, but sufficient for performing the actual sequencing. For comparison, the paper I use to print with weighs 75 grams per square meter, so a piece of paper weighing 100 picograms would be a square 0.0011 millimeters on a side; on typical 600dpi printers, a single dot is 0.0423 millimeters square, so the speck of DNA would be about 38 times smaller. Amazing.

It may seem that we have veered away from our topic, but we need to have a sense of the right tools to proceed. Since we are not dealing with a natural thing (a star, or rock, or living creature) we may proceed with some assurance about what it is we are studying – and yet, at the same time, as scientists we ought to keep all our senses alert as we investigate what this thing we call a computer actually does. And the first thing we need to do is dispel the mythology which the Media and popular talk has built up about these devices.

Case Study: Computers Can't Add.

A few years ago I shocked a young friend when I told him how easily computers can make mistakes, even in doing the simplest sort of arithmetic. Yes, people actually think that computers are especially good at mathematics, until one actually begins to

---

[78] See *The Timetables of Science*, 160. For reference, at that date pendulum clocks could beat time in half-seconds, though they were not yet precise. It was not until the 1700s that intervals of 0.1 second could be measured accurately. See Usher, *A History of Mechanical Inventions*, 304-331.

study them. It is one of the first errors to be dispelled: computers do *not* do mathematics. (This book is not the place to give a complete exposition of what it is they really do, but I will provide enough to justify our immediate purpose, of knowing our tool.)

I am sure this comes as a surprise to many, but it is true: the computer cannot even perform addition. It really doesn't do arithmetic in the way in which human beings "do" such things: that is, intellectually, with a grasp of the nature of the thing being done: being a machine, there is nothing "grasping" about it.[79] The fact that its work is being carried on by ultra-miniaturized fragments of doped (chemically treated) silicon, switching circuits on and off at a rate measured in millionths or even *billionths* of a second is irrelevant; it could just as easily be steel gears turning, or even little chunks of wood shifting back and forth, though a good deal slower.[80]

This, however, is not a discussion of the nature of addition, as fascinating as that would be; I am not going to argue this truth here and now. Not when it is far easier to give a tidy little program which demonstrates by counterexample that the computer cannot add.

But first it would be best for you to assure yourself that *you* can indeed add.

So I ask you to turn to a blank page in your notebook and spend a few minutes doing a little chore. You might do it tidily, maybe on a page at the back, as the result will be handy to have for future reference.

A Little Chore: the Powers of Two

At the top of the page in the center write "Powers of Two." Then, you are going to form two columns of numbers, and the first of them will grow fairly large – so go down a line or two, and maybe an inch in from the *right* side of the page put down the digit 1, and after it, almost at the right edge, put the digit 0.

Now, you'll do the following step over and over. Take the *last* number in the left column you've written, add it to itself, and write the answer on the *next* line just underneath the previous value, keeping them aligned in a neat column. Then take the number in the right column and add one to it – and write that result below the previous value. While you do the adding, you might sing the "Inchworm" song,[81] if you know it... Ahem! Soon you will have something like this:

```
        Powers of Two
                        1   0
                        2   1
                        4   2
```

---

[79] This is why the two epigrams of Scholastic Philosophy quoted earlier (beginning *Nemo* and *Quidquid*) are relevant for our discipline.

[80] Most believers in Artificial Intelligence would hesitate to impute "intelligence" to either of these machines, which seems a bit unfair. (Hee hee.) Though this raises an interesting topic: what sort of computational speeds could one get if the machine was *mechanical* (as opposed to electronic). As we shall hear later, Babbage claimed that his Analytical Engine could perform 10 steps in a minute, which is 0.166 Hz, but then it was cranked by hand. At present there are dentists' drills which rotate at 800,000 rpm which (if driving a computational machine) could give a clock rate of 7.5 μsec/cycle, or 0.13 Mhz. This is some 10,000 times slower than typical machines of 2013 which clock at gigahertz speeds. (The one I am presently using, though a little old, does about 1 instruction per nanosecond, which is 1 Ghz.) Even more curious was the technical barrier which existed against Babbage's machines, a barrier which has since been lifted. We shall consider that also at the right time.

[81] It is from the 1952 movie "Hans Christian Andersen" with Danny Kaye.

```
        8    3
       16    4
       32    5
       64    6
      128    7
      256    8
```

Huh, stop? When *are* you supposed to stop?[82] Well, probably when you get to the bottom of the page, at which point hopefully you will have at least 33 lines of numbers. If your notebook is small, then turn over a page and keep going until you have gotten to these:

```
1073741824   30
2147483648   31
4294967296   32
```

All right, very nice. You now have a reference chart for the powers of two. (There is a longer one in Appendix 2, so you can check your work.)

The Mistake of the Machine

Yeah, that's the title of one of Chesterton's "Father Brown" detective stories in which he observes that machines can neither lie nor tell the truth. (It is wise for us to keep such things in mind.) Now, let's have the computer do the *same* job, and see what happens. I suggest you try it for yourself – write the program in any language you like, but here is my version in the language called "C":

```c
#include <stdio.h>
void main()
{
  int i,s;
  i=0;
  s=1;
  printf("%12d %3d\n",s,i);
  while(s>0)
      {
      s=s+s;
      i=i+1;
      printf("%12d %3d\n",s,i);
      }
}
```

Code for intlimit.c

Huh? You are wondering about that odd-looking `while` statement? You don't see how doubling a *positive* number can *ever* become *smaller than* zero? Ah well, it's a good thing you're about to learn. After all, this is one of the most basic ideas about a computer: they do *not* really perform addition, and when they try to do it, they sometimes get the wrong answer.

So... now. (A drum roll, please.) Let us see what we get as an answer to this simple problem:

```
   1    0
   2    1
   4    2
   8    3
  16    4
```

---

[82] This is called the "Terminating Condition" and it is a very important concept, as we shall see when we consider recursion later.

59

32	5
64	6
128	7
256	8
512	9
1024	10
2048	11
4096	12
8192	13
16384	14
32768	15
65536	16
131072	17
262144	18
524288	19
1048576	20
2097152	21
4194304	22
8388608	23
16777216	24
33554432	25
67108864	26
134217728	27
268435456	28
536870912	29
1073741824	30
-2147483648	31

Yes... you see, when it tried to add 1073741824 to 1073741824, it got the wrong answer – a *negative* number! How curious.

Of course, perhaps you already have learned about how data is represented inside a computer. You know that on typical machines (the consumer-style PCs known and used in most of the world these days) the values called *integers* are stored in 32 bit-sized chunks.[83] Also, what we humans call "addition" is performed in two different ways within a computer: *integer* addition, wherein two values stored in 32 bits (or another size) and representing whole numbers are added, or *floating-point* addition, wherein binary representations of numbers with decimal points and exponents are added.[84] In neither case are *actual* numbers being added, since the idea of a number (to us humans) carries along with it the idea of being of arbitrary size.

Yes, the word "carries" is a pun with respect to addition. It's like the kid riding along in an old car: "Watch the odometer, Johnny: it's gonna go back to zero, and all of a sudden we'll have a *new car*!" The odometer overflows, and there is no provision for a carry. But since the computer uses bits which represent the powers of *two*, the overflow occurs at the appropriate power of *two*, not of ten as in the car odometer.[85]

---

[83] The growing availability of 64-bit machines only changes the point of failure. You can work the same problem using a 64-bit value, and will get this:

1152921504606846976 60

2305843009213693952 61

4611686018427387904 62

−9223372036854775808 63

[84] Typically there may be at least two others, called unsigned integer addition and double-precision floating point addition. More sophisticated machines may provide other arrangements, such as the CDC 6000 series which had an indexing addition of smaller range than the usual integer addition (18 bits versus 60 bits); this was used in computing array subscripts and so forth.

[85] Overflow occurs at 31, not 32, since one bit is used to indicate whether the number is positive or negative. You can do the work using "unsigned" arithmetic and see for yourself.

If not accuracy, how about speed?

Now, let us try something quite different, which will perhaps clarify the real nature of the computer and remind us of why we bother with them.

Sit back, close your eyes, and count to a billion. Well... no, don't do that. Even if you could say one number every second, you will be counting for almost 32 years! Yeah... boring. Probably you have better things to do.

Say... Even though we know the computer can't *always* add correctly, it seems to handle small values without difficulty... so, do you think maybe if we ask the right sort of question, it might do this accurately? Well, as a good friend of mine likes to say, "Computing is an experimental science." Since our previous experiment indicates that the computer can handle up to 2^{30} accurately, let's stop at a billion. So, here is a little program to try:

```
void main()
{
  int i;

  printf("Let's count to a billion... ready? Go!\n");
  i=0;
  while(i<1000000000)
      {
      i=i+1;
      }//end while
  printf("Done\n");
}
```

Code for intspeed.c

It will do no good to show you the "output" from this program, since the point is to *watch* it run – and maybe use your watch to time the pause between the two lines of output. (It is a very good example of how computing is an *experimental* science.)

As you will see, this experiment is just like Ole Rømer's use of 17th-century clocks to measure the speed of light, or like the Polymerase Chain Reaction of the molecular biologists, since we have "amplified" the thing we are trying to measure to a level where even relatively simple, imprecise measuring tools can be useful. In fact, on my machine this program took about four seconds, and there are four actual machine instructions (I checked the actual assembly from the compiler) which are repeated a billion times. Hence each instruction takes about a nanosecond (a billionth of a second) and that sounds about right for a gigahertz-rated machine.

What does this experiment tell us? Something much more important than the internal clock speed of the machinery.

It tells us that the computer can do certain things much, *much* faster than a human. That's no surprise: our cars can go faster than we can walk or run, and there are other machines which can do other kinds of jobs with facilities which transcend our human abilities. But we don't use our car to take us upstairs, or to cook dinner; nor are stoves, toasters, or microwaves street legal.

We need to remember this *constantly* as we work with the computer: it is just a machine, and has no innate "intelligence"; it will, however, execute our instructions in a most literal manner, and perform them with almost unthinkable rapidity. That can be very useful for us: for our enlightenment, our entertainment, and especially to aid in the performance of the various needs of business and industry in our world.

Getting to Know Our Tool – an Outline

Here is a brief overview of some major points in knowing our tool. To give you the rule in an epigram: **Have *some* sense of what's under your hood!** Always try to gain some awareness of even the simple limits of the thing.

1. Limits of the machine
   a. limits of its various numerical forms: integer, floating-point
   b. machine operators (versus those performed by library routines)
   c. memory addressability (indexing, indirection, etc)
   d. ability to check for overflows of integers, floating-point
   e. ability to check for out-of-bounds memory access
2. Limits of its Operating System
   a. file names and directories
   b. method of handling program execution
   c. concurrency and related issues
   d. input/output limitations, whether constrained by real devices, security, or by options permitted for programmatic use
3. Limits of the programming language(s)
   (It is hardly worth trying to enumerate details here.)
4. Basic awareness of timing
   a. instruction speeds
   b. central memory access speeds
   c. speed of disk access
   d. network speeds and limits

But you should also have an awareness that such details may be misleading in both directions. Compilers can produce unexpectedly odd translations, even from comparatively simple source code, and some machines have very peculiar rules of execution; there are some in which instructions may actually overlap in execution, or be wilfully deranged from the Fundamental Law of Linear Flow of Control, also called the Great Law of Sequential Execution, which we shall hear about shortly.

Even the problem itself may be misleading. For example, everyone knows that in Euclidean space, the *shortest* distance between two points is a straight line. However, it is not always the *fastest*. I saw a demonstration of this at the Franklin Institute long ago: two balls were released simultaneously down two tracks, one straight and the other curved, obviously longer than the straight path – and the ball on the curved track won every time. That curve is called the *cycloid*, the solution of the *brachystochrone* problem [86] (from the Greek for "short time"). Hence, be sure the problem is stated clearly, and investigate it thoroughly.

Also, do not expect the compiler's optimization feature to tidy up your messy code. Finally, you must recognize that solutions for the real world will not always be a "Big O" question, as we shall discuss in a future volume.

I will add just two further points:

(1) About getting used to a new language/system: My suggestion on a good way to start such a task is by writing a tool to deal with that language: a re-formatter, a symbol cross-reference generator, or something of that type.

(2) About instrumentation: Always be ready to build your own tool, as *ad hoc* as it might be, just to learn more about the machine. This is an important skill – er, tool

---

[86] See e.g. *VNR Concise Encyclopedia of Mathematics*, 699.

for our toolbox: be ready to build test-beds (or test rigs, or experimental setups) to explore the machine and also to test your work. This is especially recommended for deep library/utility routines destined for use in many places, or for anything tricky, even if the solution is being taken from published literature.

Chapter 12
On Algorithms and Design

...you cannot make a statue unless you have an idea...
GKC ILN June 15 1907 CW27:487

In so far as religion is gone, reason is going. For they are both of the same primary and authoritative kind. They are both methods of proof which cannot themselves be proved. And in the act of destroying the idea of Divine authority we have largely destroyed the idea of that human authority by which we do a long-division sum. With a long and sustained tug we have attempted to pull the mitre off pontifical man; and his head has come off with it.

GKC *Orthodoxy*, CW1:236-7

...Suppose some friend of mine (say, the Vicar) says to me on some stormy and dangerous occasion (say, the Church Congress), "Keep your hair on." This use of the imperative may be considered illogical at either extreme of interpretation. If it be held to mean, "Do not, at this moment, forcibly remove the whole of your hair from your head," the advice is superfluous. No such proceeding has formed any part of my plans. If, on the other hand, it be held to mean that I have entered into a positive agreement between Paul Pentecost Potter (hereinafter called the Vicar), of the one part, and Gilbert Keith Chesterton (hereinafter called the Hair-Restorer), of the other part, that no hair of the said Gilbert Keith Chesterton shall fall out till he is ninety-two – then the advice is again superfluous, for it would be practically impossible to enforce the fulfilment of the contract. And it is difficult to see what "Keep your hair on" (considered as an exact or legal phrase) could mean, except one of these two extremes.

GKC, ILN Sept 6 1913 CW29:548

Algorithm. With that prefix *al* the word sounds Arabic, and it is, but the idea goes back to the ancient Greeks; one of the famous algorithms still in use today is Euclid's algorithm to find the Greatest Common Factor of two numbers, a and b:

1. If b is larger than a, swap the two values.
2. Perform the following three steps
    2.a. Divide a by b, giving the quotient q and remainder r.
    2.b. Replace a by the present value of b.
    2.c. Replace b by the present value of r.
until r becomes zero.
3. Then the desired value is a.

So, what is an algorithm? There are niceties which may be required when handling these things in formal study, but for now we only need to state that an algorithm is a *series of clear unambiguous instructions*. These instructions may be considered a series of "commands": indeed, if we are in the kitchen we would call such a thing a *recipe*, which is simply the Latin command meaning "Take..." (Abbreviated as the initial calligraphic "Rx" symbol of medical prescriptions.) If we are musicians, we would call it a musical score; if actors we would call it a playscript, or perhaps a libretto; if clergy we would call it a rite, or perhaps a Ceremony. The idea of having a planned formula for doing something is quite ancient,[87] and such things are worth

---

[87] For example, see the book of Exodus about the rites of Passover, the plays of ancient Greece and Rome, or the curious cookbook of Apicius from the days of the Roman Empire.

exploring. Plans for any organized activity, especially those involving many people, are very important if one wants that activity to succeed.

But we are speaking as computer scientists, and we have in mind a plan for instructing a computer to perform a series of mathematical or symbolic manipulations – so we need to consider the various characteristics of such things. (You can find a thorough treatment of this topic in algorithms texts; this is just a brief introduction and review, with some comments.)

As algorithms are usually treated, there are three great classes of instructions... I am tempted to draw analogies to those other Arts I have just mentioned, but I ought not risk wandering off topic. Perhaps I might merely hint at the matter by noting how a typical Play might have (1) Dialog, (2) Stage-directions, and (3) Larger Structure like act and scene, along with details about structure, background, properties, lighting directions, etc. There are also things important to the performance not included in the script: like availability of actors, what plays will be put on this season, how big is the stage at the theater, how many seats are there for the audience, and so on.

So we will arrange our study under these titles:

1. Data motion (the ubiquitous "assignment statement")
2. Flow-of-control (what to do next, and upon what conditions)
3. The Hierarchy of Routines (libraries and making your own tools)
4. Concurrency and Larger Issues (threads, processes, and so on)
5. System Issues and Other Things

Some of these topics are not what one usually thinks of under the heading of "Algorithms"; they seem to be more related to "Design," that is to *implementation*. But when the design of software proceeds in the abstract, there is a blurring of boundaries between sketching the details of a formal algorithm and the corresponding details of a "dry" implementation (where one is not actually at the keyboard, or even ready to commit to a particular language and system).

Part a. Data Motion

Motion of data is the most fundamental operation of algorithms, since there is always some data which must be manipulated; it is invariably stored in a designated place using a convenient name or *identifier*; such things are often called "variables" but they are emphatically *not* like the variables of mathematics.[88] They are more like addresses than like names, more like Proper Nouns than like pronouns... but you ought to consult a manual for further discussion of things like "types" – that is, what sort of data can be stored in a variable, and so on. In formal algorithms, there is often a great degree of informality, which requires the one writing such things to clarify the intention in advance; be warned, whether you are using an algorithm, or writing one.

And then there's symbolic ways of stating this operation, the commonest form of which is generally known as an "assignment statement." There are some languages which use curious verbs to reveal this operation:

---

[88] Such abstractions are not necessarily the "variables" of common programming languages, but could be hardware registers or files or database elements or other forms of data storage.

```
A ← 0                          APL [89]
MOVE ZEROS TO A.               COBOL
(SETQ A (QUOTE 0))             LISP
a:=0;                          PASCAL (and some derivatives)
```
But others simply write
```
A=0                            FORTRAN and implied-LET dialects of BASIC
a=0;                           "C" (and some derivatives)
```
You should note that despite the appearance, these assignment statements are *not* equations, but commands to evaluate the expression on the right side of the "assignment operator" and store the result in the place indicated by the thing on the left side. There are all sorts of fascinating details to these things, as fascinating as the varieties of dialog in plays, which may include their own stage directions...

Among other things to note here are pestilences like the ++ and += operators in "C"; these are inane ways of trying to pretend to help the compiler, and for the most part optimizers have improved since the days when those things were invented, but the linguistic guidance provided by an explicit assignment operator is *LACKING*. There are whines which sometimes come from the opposite side of the realm relating to what are known as "side effects" – when an expression contains a call to a function which alters something elsewhere. These whines come from people who like to prove a theorem, but never have to finish a programming project for a customer *by tomorrow*. My point in mentioning these is not to whine, criticize, or compliment, but only to call attention to issues which concern this most fundamental operation.

It's funny that the whines in both the academic journals and the coding shops relate to such trivia, since there are other matters which don't get explored, matters which I would find helpful. For example, a way of handling dimensional units, of solving algebraic equations, or at least of performing substitutions: it seems a bit arcane to think that there isn't yet a standard library for doing that. Ah, another project for another day. Then there's the development environment itself... I don't think we are still using punch cards, this *is* the 1980s now! Ah well. There is also relatively little concern paid to the inherent limits of the data representations, and this is not healthy. Also neglected are safety tricks for things like solving the quadratic equation and taking cube roots, or guides to the wise use of trig functions. You can find the second topic in a later Case Study; I will supply the others now.

Case Study: On Computing the Cube Root

I once had a bitter argument with a friend about this. It was rather disheartening, since he was an engineering student at Lehigh University, and older than me, but it demonstrates the serious dangers of trusting too much in machinery instead of knowing the principles of mathematics. We were discussing the cube root of negative one, and he claimed that it was complex, because when he tried to compute it on his powerful calculator, it gave him an ERROR. But I told him:

Since
$$(-1)\cdot(-1)\cdot(-1) = -1$$
that means the cube root of -1 is -1.

---

[89] I am not an APL expert, but this assignment notation happens to be my own preference. The only problem is that few of the "modern" keyboards have such a character; indeed, they seem to have fewer and fewer keys, not more and more. Quite frustrating.

Now, there *are* complex cube roots of negative one. They are easy enough to work out, being simply the conjugate pair of the three roots of the equation

$$x^3 + 1 = 0$$

which are (-1) and $(1 \pm i\sqrt{3})/2$. I leave the algebra for you as an exercise.

The reason for the calculator rejecting the computation is related to the series expansion used for computing such things; the same thing is done by most run-time libraries. The particular issue is due to the fact that the cube root of x must be expressed by raising x to the 1/3 power, and 1/3 is an infinite repeating decimal, which can't be represented accurately in the usual floating point representations. However, it is easy to show that when $x<0$,

$$\sqrt[3]{x} = -\sqrt[3]{|x|}$$

so we may merely define our own "cube root" function to handle negative values, something like this, with the precision of the constant depending on your machine:

```
float CubeRoot(float x)
{
    if(x<0)
        return -pow(-x,(1.0/3.0));
    else
        return pow(x,(1.0/3.0));

}
```

A comment about the constant. Some compilers will reduce explicit constant expressions, and generate the equivalent value in the object code; you should investigate this for yourself, and manage the case as necessary. Of course repeating decimals are a difficulty in any case; in most encodings for floating-point, only fractions with a power of two in the denominator will be accurate. For example, on my computer, the two closest single-precision floating-point values to "one third" are:

```
aa,aa,aa,3e = 0.33333313465118408203125   (error 1.9868e–8)
 one third  = 0.333333333333333333333333...
ab,aa,aa,3e = 0.3333333432674407958984375 (error 9.934e–9)
```

However you wish to handle it, a routine for managing the sign of cube roots is useful when one wishes to solve cubic equations. These may require the solution of a quadratic equation, and that technique deserves investigation also. But first we will digress briefly to consider a tool to handle floating-point representations.

Case Study: the "Real" Value of a Floating-Point Number

In many situations the nature of the problem will make it fairly obvious whether you can "get by" with a single-precision floating-point number, or if you ought to use double-precision. (And then, of course, there may be times when you'll have to consider alternatives.) But it is handy to have a way of looking into the internal representation of floating-point numbers. This is usually supplied somewhere, in a manual about your computer, or perhaps in the help-files for the compiler or development tools you are using. Just in case you cannot locate these, or if you wish to explore the machine for yourself – which I most heartily recommend – I will give you two tools to take along.

The first tool finds the number of bits used in the mantissa of the floating-point representation. It uses a standard technique in physiological measurements (such as hearing acuity) called the Just Noticeable Difference. It simply loops around a doubling, watching to see when the computer can *no longer* distinguish the doubled number from the value which is (arithmetically speaking) one greater than it. Note that the final value should be *one greater* than the actual number of bits used in the mantissa; for my computer the correct values are 23 and 52. Also note that I have explicitly computed the increment, since some compilers (like mine) compute expressions using higher precision than the actual storage. When I used a conditional comparing f with f+1 in single-precision, I obtained the result for double-precision.

```
void Doubler()
{
  float f,ff;
  double d,dd;
  int i;

  i=0;
  f=1.0;
  do
      {
      printf("%d %f\n",i,f);
      i=i+1;
      f=f*2.0;
      ff=f+1.0;
      }
  while(f!=ff);
  printf("float (%d) stops at %d\n",sizeof(float),i);
  i=0;
  d=1.0;
  do
      {
      printf("%d %f\n",i,d);
      i=i+1;
      d=d*2.0;
      dd=d+1.0;
      }
  while(d!=dd);
  printf("double (%d) stops at %d\n",sizeof(double),i);
}
```

Code for doubler.c

The other tool uses a symbolic arithmetic to print the *actual* value for a given floating-point number. This is handy since the run-time library might not manage this correctly, especially out near the frontier. It is funny to think that our base ten decimals happen to provide a particular challenge, since the value one-tenth, which is 0.1 in base ten is an *infinite repeating* value in base two: 0.0001100110011... Such difficulties often result in accounting programs maintaining their values in pennies, or using another mechanism for accuracy. Let's see what our tool shows us is going on here in single-precision. The first item is the "nominal" value as represented by the compiler. The second is the hexadecimal for the four-byte internal representation; the repeated hex "c" can be seen in the repeated "1100" of the binary. The third is the actual decimal corresponding to that representation, as computed symbolically.

```
0.10000000149011612000 = [cd,cc,cc,3d] 0.100000001490116119384765625
```

By manipulation of the internal representations, we can see what values correspond to its two "adjacent" values:

```
0.09999999403953552200 = [cc,cc,cc,3d] 0.09999999940395355224609375
0.10000000149011612000 = [cd,cc,cc,3d] 0.10000000149011619384765625
0.10000000894069672000 = [ce,cc,cc,3d] 0.10000000894069671630859375
```

(Yes, this machine is "little-endian" and a single-precision number has four bytes.) You should explore both single and double precision on your own machine.

Case Study: On Solving Quadratic Equations

This problem is a bit more subtle than the cube root problem, as the danger of error is not as likely, but it provides a good example of the niceties of numerical computation. The solution most of us learn in Algebra is certainly straightforward, and like me you no doubt know it by heart. Given the quadratic equation

$$ax^2 + bx + c = 0$$

its roots are:

$$x = \frac{(-b) \pm \sqrt{b^2 - 4ac}}{2a}$$

Applying some algebra, you can revise that equation to this form:

$$x = \frac{2c}{(-b) \mp \sqrt{b^2 - 4ac}}$$

However, though the first formula is well-known, it is not safe to use it in programming: when a or c (or both) are very small, the value of the square root will be very close to b, and one of the two roots (in the case where the signs of the two parts of the addition/subtraction are different) will be inaccurate. (For extra credit, work out an example of where this goes wrong on *your* computer.)

There is a way [90] of avoiding this danger, which merely alters the order of computation slightly. First, compute q:

$$q = \frac{b + sign(b)\sqrt{b^2 - 4ac}}{-2}$$

Then the two roots are given by

$x_1 = q/a$

and

$x_2 = c/q$

Of course you should first check whether the discriminant (b^2-4ac) is negative, which indicates that the roots of your equation are a complex conjugate; depending on what you are doing, you may need to handle that case separately.

Case Study: Comparison of Heterogeneous Data Structures

There is another sort of subtlety involved in the handling of heterogeneous data structures – which sounds like a mouthful and probably of exquisite complexity, yet is really a very simple idea, almost obvious – something most people can do by mere common sense without special training. It's because it *is* so simple and obvious that it

---

[90] See (e.g.) Press et al, *Numerical Recipes*, 145.

can readily be overlooked that the *computer* cannot do such things, and has *no* common sense which might correct your sloppiness.

So what is this thing anyway? The easiest way of telling you is to give an example: like comparing two dates in order to decide which comes first in history. The dates, you see, are given in three parts: a month, a day-of-month, and a year. A "date" data structure, then, is *heterogeneous*: it is *not* a composition of three integers of like qualities as in a vector in three-space, but three integers each having very different meanings and ranges, interlinked according to a very special arrangement. Granted there are difficulties with some details, as anyone who tries to play with calendars soon discovers: 1 B.C. is followed by 1 A.D. (there is no year "zero"), and in 1582, Pope Gregory XIII ordered that the day immediately after "October 4" be designated "October 15," along with the adjustment of the leap-year computation.

However, almost anyone would have no difficulties comparing something like the date of Columbus' discovery of the Western Hemisphere (October 12, 1492) with the birthdate of Galileo (February 15, 1564) – and could determine that the Columbus date comes *before* that for Galileo, even though the month for Galileo comes *before* the month for Columbus, and the day-of-month for Galileo comes *after* the day-of-month for Columbus.

Why? Because we know that in order to determine which date comes earlier, we must *first* compare the *years*. If the years are different, the month (and day-of-month) is irrelevant to the comparison. But if the years are equal, we must compare the months; only when years *and* months are equal must we compare the day-of-months.

Now, it is always permitted to check *equality* in any order we like: If two heterogeneous values are equal, *all* their parts are equal, but if they are *not* equal, one or more of their parts will not be equal. To compare equality of heterogeneous data structures *a* and *b*, we must check if part 1 of *a* equals part 1 of *b*, AND if part 2 of *a* equals part 2 of *b*, AND if part 3 of *a* equals part 3 of *b*, ... and so on, for all the parts of *a* and *b*. Clearly, there is an implicit iterated AND at work here:

$$a = b \quad \text{if-and-only-if} \quad \bigcap_i a_i = b_i$$

By commutativity of the AND operation, we may perform these tests in any order we like, making sure we only declare equality once *all* parts have been found equal; inequality in any part means inequality of the whole.

However, when we are performing the ranking form of comparison in which we wish to know *which* of the two values is lesser or greater, we must proceed according to the specific meaning of the data itself. We may sometimes want to control this dynamically based on the situation at hand, in which case we specify a series of sorting "keys" by which we declare the priority of the values to be ordered. But in some cases (like dates) the comparison is fixed, and may be coded directly.

In either case, however, there is a very simple arrangement which is used: we consider the corresponding parts of the two data items in *descending* order of their priority. When the two corresponding parts are *different*, we know the result of the comparison, but if they are equal, we must proceed to compare the next highest corresponding parts in descending priority. For example, to compare dates:

```
int DateCompare(int Ayear, int Amonth, int Aday,
                int Byear, int Bmonth, int Bday)
{
  int k;
  k=Ayear-Byear;
  if(k!=0)return k;
```

```
    k=Amonth-Bmonth;
    if(k!=0)return k;
    k=Aday-Bday;
    return k;
}
```

Such an example may seem too trivial to spend time on, and yet it is all too easy for someone to try coding such trivialities *incorrectly*. These things ought to be set up and tested carefully, especially when they are being used in many places.

At the opposite extreme, there are some apparently simple expressions which can be very mysterious, and yet are remarkable in their practicality: we will see a stunning instance of this in the last Case Study of Part III.

Case Study: Making a Perfect Hash of Things

I have rather slighted more complex data structures, since they would probably deserve a book unto themselves, and also because there are good texts available for them. Also, rather to my surprise, I also seem to have neglected the very important topic of food in this study, though I have mentioned "the supreme art" of cooking. This case, however, is not a recipe for food; I recall the difficulties Nero Wolfe encountered [91] in the challenge of preparing perfect *corned beef* hash, but this is the hash used in a certain efficient form of data storage. This is no doubt very amusing; there are a variety of hashing techniques, and you can find them discussed in just about any algorithms or data structures book. I like to tell students that hashing provides the computational analogy to the teenager's room: it looks utterly random, but everything is very easy to get to. It's called hashing because one "hashes" the data value into a reduced form called a "key" which is then used to locate that data.

The classic form which I have often used is the "open" form with bucket lists, where all keys hashing to the same value go into that "bucket" from which depends a linked list of the distinct values hashing there. Another is the "closed" form, which is limited because it does not use lists, and for which one must decide on a collision strategy to handle the case when two data items hash to the same value.

The "nice" kind of hash, however, is called the "perfect" hash, in which the data value is itself the key: this is only possible when those values are all "small integers." One classic example is in treating standard DNA: since there are only four nucleotide bases – usually represented as their initials A, C, G, T, which we may readily transform into 0, 1, 2, 3 – we can also map *DNA strings* of length k into values ranging from 0 to 4^k-1, using the same sort of positional arrangement by which numbers are represented in base 4. (Here "base" has the mathematical, not the biological sense.) Thus, for strings of length $k = 4$, "AAAA" maps to 0, "CCCC" maps to 85, "GGGG" maps to 170, and "TTTT" maps to 255. The underlying reason which enables this is the *finite* number of possible keys, together with a simple and direct (inexpensive to compute) mapping which makes each datum itself a useful key.

So... what if we had some other finite collection of data, a set S of strings

$$S= \{\sigma_1, \sigma_2, ... \sigma_n\}$$

to which we wanted to apply the efficiencies of hashing? One answer is to mix the strategies, and attempt to propose a simple hashing function which provides the same effect. For example, let's say we are given a string σ, and we'll compute its hash by the following pseudocode where p and q are some constants:

---

[91] See "Cordially Invited to Meet Death" in *Black Orchids*.

```
function hash(τ, p, q)
argument
    in string τ
    in integer p, q
returns integer
local
    integer i, h
begin
    h←0
    for i ← 1 to |τ|
        h ←((h*p)+τ[i]) mod q
    endfor
    return h
endproc
```

Now, since we know the set S, we want to find the value for p and q such that *no two* of the σ_i in S will yield the same value from our hash function.

Some time ago I needed such a thing, and built an experiment to try finding the appropriate values. It simply proposes values for p and q, and checks to see whether every member of the given set hashes to its own location; I did put limits to the possibilities for p and q, but it worked fine for several different sets.

You still need to verify that the thing you've hashed to matches the thing you have, but you only need to do such a comparison at most *once*, not multiple times, which saves time when those strings are long. It would be a nice little piece of research to determine where (with respect to the number of strings and their lengths) this method becomes effective – but then it is handy to know that such an approach is possible: that one should be able to make a "perfect hash" from any given fixed set of distinct strings.

For a simple example, imagine that we have some huge data collection which needs verification, and one of the items in it is the name of a month. My experiment provided a perfect hashing when p=13 and q=28, thus the hash table would be:

0	APRIL	8		16	FEBRUARY	24	JULY
1		9		17		25	
2	JUNE	10		18	JANUARY	26	OCTOBER
3	MAY	11	SEPTEMBER	19	DECEMBER	27	
4		12		20			
5		13		21	AUGUST		
6		14	NOVEMBER	22			
7		15	MARCH	23			

Another example was the two-letter abbreviations for the 50 United States; for these, the values are p=69 and q=157; here are the hash values:

8	AL	154	CT	89	IL	44	ME	54	MO	121	NM	38	OR	75	TX	110	WI
7	AK	51	DE	91	IN	43	MD	59	MT	133	NY	90	PA	140	UT	126	WY
22	AZ	39	FL	78	IA	40	MA	113	NE	111	NC	79	RI	52	VT		
14	AR	97	GA	77	KS	48	MI	130	NV	112	ND	142	SC	33	VA		
135	CA	17	HI	83	KY	53	MN	116	NH	28	OH	143	SD	102	WA		
149	CO	81	ID	128	LA	58	MS	118	NJ	31	OK	65	TN	123	WV		

In such a case, since there are only 26·26=676 pairs of letters, one could manage this another way, which I will leave for you to implement.

Part b. Flow-of-Control

I must have really confused my students when I told them I was going to introduce that day's topic by reading to them from a famous classical children's fantasy. But, as I pointed out, the author was a professor of mathematics, and spread remarkable *truths* throughout his tale, though few know his real occupation, and even fewer know that the name of his heroine [92] means "truth" in Greek... But I would like to give you the same delight (or confusion) I gave my students, so I will simply quote the same lines:

> The White Rabbit put on his spectacles. "Where shall I begin, please your Majesty?" he asked.
> "Begin at the beginning," the King said gravely, "and go on till you come to the end: then stop."[93]

This, of course, is the Fundamental Law of Linear Flow of Control, also called the Great Law of Sequential Execution: unless otherwise directed by some conditional, branch, loop, or routine-invocation (or other such things) control begins at the Beginning, and goes on linearly until the End is reached.

In the huge majority of cases, a program is not an exercise in musical harmony or counterpoint: a work for keyboard, xylophone, or any string instrument is not an appropriate analogy. It is a composition for a solo monophonic instrument (or for the human voice) producing exactly one tone at a time.

It is splendid to call upon music as an analogy at this time; it is an exceedingly rich source of material. Typical music certainly has symbols [94] for indicating the repetition of a portion of a work; these often have branching notations showing what to perform at the first or second repeats. The composer may also include various options, such as to include (or omit) a cadenza; a musician might even decide to save time when a performance is running long by "taking the second ending" instead of repeating the indicated portions according to the score. Another trick known to pit musicians is the "vamp until ready" in which a certain musical phrase is repeated until (for example) the actor has reached a certain position on stage. All these sorts of flow-of-control arrangements, and many others, exist for use in algorithms and also most common programming languages.

This brings up one of the most hotly debated things in all of computing: the scorn heaped upon the "GOTO" statement. It always comes from people who do not program; people who have struggled with "spaghetti code" of archaic FORTRAN or BASIC make other sorts of protests. (I know I did. But this is not the place for recounting such things; I won't even take up arms about object-oriented or other "modern" styles.) The reason for the existence of the GOTO is obvious: it is an elementary control command which has no other substitutes; when one has both the GOTO and any sort of conditional (an "IF" statement) one can accomplish any other form of control. Moreover, as we shall see in our discussion of recursion, there are algorithms [95] in which there is no clean way of describing the necessary control

---

[92] Alice, from the Greek Αληθεια (*Alêtheia*) = "Truth," was the daughter of Henry George Liddell (rhymes with "fiddle") a professor of Greek, famous for the great *Greek Lexicon*.

[93] Carroll, *Alice's Adventures in Wonderland*, Chapter 12.

[94] Sorry, that is *not* a percussion pun, though it *sounds* like one.

[95] One of my favorite examples of this is the Dinic Maximum Flow Algorithm found in Tarjan's *Data Structures and Network Algorithms*, 102-104.

without a very confusing collection of conditionals and flag-variables – in which case one is not programming a solution, but conforming to an inappropriate style. I don't have a style reason, much less a philosophical reason, to avoid the GOTO; I am in the business of getting things done. (Besides, block-structured control forms compile into GOTOs, just as ethanol is produced by anaerobic glycolysis even in teetotallers. But (ahem) this is the sort of thing we can discuss over a beer, not at the keyboard.)

Case Study: Sorting out IFs

I mentioned conditional forms of flow-of-control, which are almost always referred to as "IF-statements." Yeah, they can appear boring to the experienced programmer, but like anything else they can surprise you. Not very long ago, as I was researching another curious matter, part of which may appear in a future volume, I bumped into the question of efficient modes of sorting. I had been looking through my collection of notes, and spotted one of those old brain-teasers: you are given 12 coins, one of which is counterfeit and hence does not weigh the same as the others. You need to find which one it is using *only three weighings*. No doubt you can solve this for yourself... but the riddle happened to bear on my question about efficient sorting. I wanted to know what sort of sort would perform the *minimum* number of conditional tests. It's easy enough to realize that *two* things can be sorted with just one comparison: that's how one finds the lesser of two things:

```
if a<b then
     the order is a,b
else
     the order is b,a
endif
```

To sort *three* things requires a total of five IFs, though at most three will be executed:

```
if A<B then
   if A<C then
      if B<C then
         the order is ABC
            else
         the order is ACB
      endif
   else
      the order is CAB
   endif
else
   if A<C then
      the order is BAC
   else
      if B<C then
         the order is BCA
      else
         the order is CBA
      endif
   endif
endif
```

Such an approach is very interesting, and indeed demonstrates a very tricky sort of efficiency, but one soon needs a program to produce the appropriate nestings of IFs since the number grows as the factorial: in fact, to sort n items requires a total of $n!-1$ IFs, though only at most $log_2(n!)$ of them are executed. To my surprise, when I generated the solution for $n=9$, I found I had written the *single largest program I have ever written!* In fact it had over 4.3 million lines of code in one routine, including

74

362,879 IFs, and probably exceeded the entire sum of all the code I have ever written in my life. It was so large the compiler refused to handle it. It was loads of fun to work on, and so was the one to check that every permutation would sort correctly.

Yes, I know, with that factorial in the picture it smells like recursion. We shall cover recursion separately though it also is a form of "flow-of-control"; it also requires larger structures which we shall see shortly. Let us, rather, look into one of the more exotic control structures which has a very important practical use.

Case Study: the Case of the Adventure of the Finite State Machine

One interesting control mechanism might be given the generic name "branch on integer" which behaves like a rotary switch, or a roundhouse in a rail yard, choosing one from among several alternative pathways. In old FORTRAN these are called "computed GOTO" statements, in PASCAL they are "CASE" statements, and in "C" they are "switch" statements. Internally, they are extremely efficient on most computers, being performed by indexing a transfer of control into an array of pointers to locations within the code-space of the running program, provided that the collection of case values are all "small integers"; otherwise the thing degenerates into a bunch of hidden IFs, and there is no efficiency gain. They have their popular uses: the standard message-processing "window procedure" for a WINDOWS application uses a "switch" statement to handle the various messages. But there is one famous use for "switch" statements which you will encounter when you reach the study of Finite State Automata (FSAs for short; also called Finite State Machines) and the related Regular Expressions and Grammars.

FSAs are fundamental mathematical objects lying at the heart of computing, and they are eminently practical for many sorts of simple parsing or syntax handling. It is often easier to use a development tool (like LEX for example) or write one as I did, in order to use Regular Expressions directly, but sometimes it is faster to build the automaton by hand. In either case, however, the main component of the automaton is a "switch" statement, which is governed by an integer variable called the "state" – yes, that's why they are called *state* machines. It would unduly lengthen this book to present all this here; I strongly urge you to explore the topic, and you will readily see how the "switch" statement applies.

But there is a related topic which provides a marvellous, attractive and practical analogy to the more abstract (and seemingly more complex) FSA. That is the topic of computer games, and the first of all such games, if not in formal chronology, in precedence, is the one called "ADVENTURE." If you have never seen it, you ought to hunt for it, as it is in many ways the prototype of all subsequent video adventure games, no matter how gory the enemies, how nasty the armaments, or how slick the graphics. Here is a miniature statement of how it works:

1. The game tells you where you are, giving its description.

2. You type in a "motion verb" which takes you somewhere else, then the game returns to step 1, describing that new place. Sometimes these verbs are magic words like "XYZZY" or "PLUGH."

There's stuff to pick up, and stuff to do, and enemies to deal with, but actually the weapons, enemies, booty, and scoring are almost incidental to the enticing geography of the game.

The nice thing about ADVENTURE is that it teaches about FSAs. Except in an FSA you are "in a state" and you execute a "transition" to a new state based on something, like the next character in the string you are trying to parse. If you get to a "winning state" the input string is valid, and it has been parsed; otherwise the input has a syntax error and **YOU LOSE**. (Insert an appropriate sound effect here.)

The wonderful thing about knowing automata theory is that you likewise know the fundamental design of *all* such adventure games, since they are all based upon such a scheme; you may add all the rest – the treasures and the bad guys and the weaponry – and the slick graphics – to make the result more exciting, but deep inside you are still using an FSA. It's hard to beat that score.

Part c. The Hierarchy of Routines

Very early in one's studies of programming one hears about "routines" which are also called "procedures," "subroutines," "functions" or other terms depending on the language. These things provide another sort of control option, one which has a very curious and interesting property. They allow one to construct what we might call a "black box": a curious little device which does whatever we want it to do. However, we also give it a *name*, and thereupon we may treat that device in just the same way we treat other components of programming: almost as if *it came with the language, or system, or development kit*. It becomes in some sense an *atomic* action, which performs a given task, or computes a given value, based on given parameters.

These routines of course might be provided by the Operating System itself, or by a run-time library for the given language, or by your company – or you may have composed them yourself many years ago, or earlier today. It doesn't matter very much, except in the case of those from "others" where you don't get to see the source code, or alter it. (There are times when this limitation becomes irrelevant, but we won't go into that here.) You may consider this little device either as that atomic (here meaning "having just a single purpose") black box, or you may make it transparent and see all the elegant internal gearwork, like those awesome grandfather clocks with glass sides, where you may watch things happening, or tracker organs, which use purely mechanical means to cause the pipes to play. In many cases you may have to *imagine* seeing it, as few computers provide any sort of visible indication that they are working, or what they are doing, alas – but like a serious student of music, you can look at the source code (I mean the score) and "watch" the orchestra as you listen to the music playing. (Unless it's a player organ or such.)

Now, this is all very nice and appealing, and perhaps enticing to serious study. But I have another reason for talking about these routines. Simply that they are the elementary (and in some ways the only) means by which one organizes the work of a program. We may group them into a rough hierarchy (though this "calling tree" may be made precise by a suitable symbolic analysis and cross-reference tool) such as the major working routines of the program, their lesser supporting routines, and a variety of utility functions much like those of the Operating System or run-time libraries. Some languages provide other organizational schemes, permitting a division of these routines among several files, depending on the style and complexity one prefers, or demanded by the project in hand. (Yeah, some of this sounds a bit dated, but almost all of our field remains stuck in the punch-card world of the 1960s. Punch-cards were sometimes easier to deal with than files, though it is far less likely that you will ever drop a "file" in the snow, as I once dropped one of my decks of punch-cards.)

Another reason for mentioning routines is that they are essential for enabling the very important tool known as *recursion*: that is, the use of a given routine *from within its very self*. We shall explore that more shortly.

Routines are, in some ways, analogous to the cells of multicellular organisms which are each assigned its very special physiological duty within the living creature. Hence they enable a kind of programmatic "histology": Histology is the branch of Biology which studies the "tissues" of the living creature: groups of cells woven together to form a functional unit. Routines play a very similar role in the structural study of programming.

Part d. Concurrency and Larger Issues

Having mentioned routines, we may now ascend to the larger organization of programs into complete processes, or collections of processes (sometimes referred to as "packages") or even into Systems. These of course are themselves applications, and hence subject to the Operating System, but the Operating System is itself a system in this sense, a collection of programs.

The formalisms are not as strict here; the terms depend on the system within which these things reside, or even on the character of the purpose. We need not concern ourselves with any formulations, but merely note that any given project requires serious study of what individual programming entities will be required; some may be available, some may need to be written, and suitable "plumbing" may be needed to interlink the various components. All this must be considered at an early stage, if only to plan for sufficient resources in development personnel.

There is also the matter of concurrency, that is, of programs (or portions of programs called "processes" or "threads" or other names) which are in execution simultaneously. That last word demands a qualification: the simultaneity may be authentic, either because the computer contains multiple CPUs, or because there is more than one computer in the picture. Or, the simultaneity may be only apparent, being handled by an appropriate multi-tasking Operating System, or even by a suitable run-time environment. (See our discussion on Concurrency elsewhere in this book for more on this.)

This concurrency must arise from specific requirements of the project; there is little point in attempting to drag it in for simple, *ad hoc* applications. But as one advances in treating more and more complex problems, it becomes a very important tool to wield.

One important aspect of design for such things is answer the question "Who does what?" where "who" refers to a program or software unit. Another is the idea of "systems flow": that is, the pathways by which the various kinds of data – think of them as "raw materials," "intermediates," or "finished products" – are flowing between the various processing components. Such things may become very intricate, but all developers require knowledge of the master plan. One of the best examples I can suggest is the wonderful "Chart of the Metabolic Pathways": you can find it on the "net" but you ought to acquire a poster-size copy for future reference.

Part e. System Issues and Other Things

This is rather a catch-all subdivision which I mainly meant to deal with any relations between a given project and the Operating System within which it resides, but it also includes some other matters which don't readily fit elsewhere.

We must consider how a given project fits within an actual Operating System: is it a simple application, *ad hoc* perhaps, and run at need, or maybe a unique tool having an intimate connection to a specialized external device, or is it a complete package handling a variety of projects, or a multi-user scheme for handling larger matters (like order-processing, inventory, shipping, and so on) or perhaps a multi-computer system handling the work of a business? Each sort of thing will make special demands on its host system in order to accommodate its use; also, each will require its own special sort of supporting functions – so the interrelations in both directions must be carefully considered.

One must also remember where one is working: any industrial application (and even certain ones used in academic settings) require a distinctly different sort of discipline than those developed for the sake of coursework, or indeed for research. There are several points which ought to be mentioned in this regard:

1) Usage ought to be tracked, including performance statistics.

2) Internal logs, primarily for debugging, but also for tracking activity, ought to be generated.

3) Any aborts, whether arising due to hardware, software, or application-specific problems, should be tracked, and when appropriate, *let someone know that something has gone wrong*.

4) Keep the Teleology of the *user* in mind, not of the project. The program is not an attempt at proving a theorem, or a means of justifying a hypothesis; it is supposed to be satisfying some particular need of a User. The User's satisfaction must be met, as far as that is possible, even if it means abolishing any hope of a formally efficient implementation. Very few users know or care about "big-O" – and though they will complain if your program runs what they think of as "slow," they will complain far more bitterly if it does not satisfy them with its answers. (We shall hear more on this in a future volume: trust me, it is fascinating.)

Another important case to be considered is when the project becomes a miniature Operating System in itself (or, in the extremely unique case where *you* are working on an actual Operating System!) Then there are several points to note:

1) Keep "TRON" in mind, and remember that the purpose of the System is to serve the Programs, and the purpose of the Programs is to serve the Users.

2) A System has its Teleology inverted from that of a user-based application: its End is *not* to end (that is, to come to the completion of its computation). Thus a certain sort of self-defence and protection should be considered in its design.

3) There are unique issues of maintenance which arise in perpetually running programs; you must arrange for such things, and design and implement any necessary utilities.

4) Status monitoring, run-time statistics, logging, and other such matters become even more important than in common applications, as well as planning for fail-safes, backups, and other remedies in case of disasters.

Chapter 13
On Errors

It is easy to be a madman: it is easy to be a heretic. It is always easy to let the age have its head; the difficult thing is to keep one's own. It is always easy to be a modernist; as it is easy to be a snob. To have fallen into any of those open traps of error and exaggeration which fashion after fashion and sect after sect set along the historic path of Christendom – that would indeed have been simple. It is always simple to fall; there are an infinity of angles at which one falls, only one at which one stands.

GKC, *Orthodoxy* CW1:305-6

"No machine can lie," said Father Brown, "nor can it tell the truth."
GKC, "The Mistake of the Machine" in *The Wisdom of Father Brown*

What is an error? In the general sense, as it applies to computer science, an error is any malformation in design or implementation which defeats the Purpose of the item (algorithm, routine, program, tool, system) under consideration. I have often contemplated making a collection of such things, just for the intellectual fun of the thing: it would probably be useful, and maybe I will do it in a future volume. But such things do exist:

Medicine has subdivisions known as Pathology (the science of treating diseases), Etiology (the science of the causes of disease), Teratology (the science of developmental malformations), and so on. Medical students spend a significant amount of time studying the many things which can go wrong with the human body – so much so that there is a famous disease they supposedly catch when they take the course on diseases and find themselves experiencing the symptoms then being considered.[96]

Theologians can list about two millennia of heresies, beginning with those spoken of by St. Peter.[97] Broadly speaking, a heresy is a form of error in which one truth is chosen to be exalted, and hence it usually displaces other truths. It is curiously relevant to computer science, since the very famous ancient heresy called Arianism (4th century A.D.) claimed that the Son was merely *similar* to the Father, not *consubstantial* as St. Athanasius argued that the Church taught. Consider the critical terms as they appear in Greek:

ʻομοιουσιον (*homoiousion* = like in being, similar)
ʻομοουσιον (*homoousion* = same in being, consubstantial)

Do you see the difference?

Note that the Greek words differ by only *a single iota*, which passed into an epigrammatic phrase, "not a single iota of difference." Not only verbal battles were fought over this single letter of difference. In the same way as a theologian, or indeed a specialist in any field of Wisdom, a computer scientist must constantly be on guard against error. One single letter or character can make a huge difference, as anyone

---

[96] Variously called third-year syndrome, medical-school-itis, or hypocondriasis.
[97] See 2 Peter 2:1. I have looked around for a taxonomic treatment of heresies; so far the only text which helps is the commentary by Aquinas on the Apostles' Creed in his *The Three Greatest Prayers*.

who has mistyped a logon password will know. Such instances are not limited to theology or computer science: the gene for the beta-chain of hemoglobin A which carries sickle-cell anemia [98] differs from the normal ("wild" type) by one single DNA character: the change from A to T alters a single amino acid from Glutamic acid to Valine. Later in this book we'll see a Case Study where a single letter difference gives rise to another kind of illness.

The term "error" does not only mean such simple "typographical errors": in programming these are usually caught by the compiler. Far more insidious are those semantic errors where the program does not perform as specified (or expected) – we shall mention some later. Such errors are often called "bugs" and are hopefully eliminated by the debugging and testing stages of development.

There are some other errors, even more hazardous – as hazardous as heresies. Perhaps we might call them *classification* errors: I mean the cases of choosing [99] the wrong tool. I am not here dealing with the dull dispute about "artificial intelligence," a pointless and futile waste I may comment on another time. I am talking about the very simple problem of not really grasping what a computer is, what it does, and what it is capable of doing.

Another issue, particularly encountered by recent graduates, is understanding why industry is not like academics. When I went back for my M.S., I had already worked in industry for seven years tackling a strange and varied array of puzzles, and as a result I often found the class assignments trivial. The reason is simple: the professors almost always know the answer, and have gauged the problem to be accomplished in the chosen time-frame – but this never happens in industry. The customer walks in with a riddle, and probably wants it *tomorrow*, or even while he waits... he has no idea whether there even *is* an answer, but he expects you to find it, and get it arranged for him to use, while your boss is anxious about your using up time for *that* project when there's another four or six he's got waiting for you to handle! But this might simply be the challenges of management, and the chasm between a customer problem and a class assignment. Actually there really is an important difference, and it needs to be stated, as bitter a pill as it will be to the theoreticians.

The explanation is that the customer wants AN answer, which will probably not be THE answer. In fact, sometimes, he will be perfectly satisfied with a WRONG answer, according to the views of our discipline! I know this is startling, and maybe disconcerting to the academic mind, but it happens to be true, and getting used to it is an important part of dealing with life in industry. (We shall see a stunning example of this in a future volume, well worth waiting for.) However you will recall how I insisted on making meticulous inquiries as to what the user truly wants and needs, as well as careful planning and continuing contact during both design and implementation.

Another very important aspect of industrial programming (as opposed to academic) is the need to deal with failures: to capture them, acknowledge them, track them, and eventually to deal with them.

Case Study: the MCP, Reformed

In a later Case Study I will tell you about September 19, 1977, my first day of regular employment, at the small consulting company known as Frankel Engineering

---

[98] See (e.g.) Rawn, *Biochemistry*, 143.
[99] The word "heresy" derives from a Greek word meaning "to choose."

Labs, or FEL. At that time they had two HP 2116 timeshare machines running a timeshare BASIC operating system. The computers were large things physically, over six feet tall, maybe five wide and two deep; each had two large hard drives attached, around 2x3x4 feet, with a clear plastic cover over the platters: they looked a bit like washing machines, and sounded like them too... ah, in the rinse cycle. Customers with Teletypes dialled in and used FEL's numerical control or business software. Unfortunately, the disk drives failed rather often, and when that happened, this message on all presently connected terminals:

```
DISK ERROR - WAIT 30 SECONDS.
```

Granted, this was a very misleading message: the immediate aftermath almost always was that the system crashed, and we all tramped back to the computer room to watch Charlie reboot the failed machine. The humor of the message arose from the fact that one day a very annoyed customer called us and said, "I got this message: 'disk error, wait 30 seconds'. I waited *thirty minutes* and nothing happened!"

Those crashes *were* annoying, and I wrote a song about system crashes, which I have used countless times at many companies. But in 1978 we got our new HP 3000, and the crashes became far more rare.

The challenge of errors and users arose in the early 1990s at another company, when one of the data-processing programmers realized that someone had made erroneous multiple entries in one of the databases. She tracked down the source of the data and called the user who had done it. "What did you do?" she asked.

"Program X aborted, so I just tried the same thing again," was the reply.

"You tried *five* times?" she asked, delicately refraining from asking why the user hadn't called our department for assistance.

So we discussed the matter. The users won't always tell us (the programming department) when there's a problem. Hence, we ought to be told *by the machinery* whenever an application aborts.

That was a good idea, of course, and perhaps some sort of steps should have been taken during development: hindsight is always far more clear than foresight. But there were lots of programs, and the language (compiled BASIC) did not have the mechanisms for error-trapping provided in some more recent systems. That meant deep system stuff, so they looked at me.

After some study, I told them: "If you want this done, we can patch the run-time library to handle all fatal errors by means of a new error-recording routine, and generate a report. That way, if *anything* aborts, we'll know about it."

This project became a part of another which handled the "menu" program (a sort of primitive desktop/"Start" button thing) by which the users could select what they wanted to do – which we gave the haughty title "Menu Control Program" or "MCP" for short. The system library was patched so as to send any of the various machine or library errors to a single common routine, which would generate an "error log" output. (Yes, a reformed MCP, which now served the Users, as is right and just for all Programs, no matter how exalted.)

Soon the users were amazed to learn that when something went wrong and a program aborted, they would get a phone call from our department: "Were you having a problem with Program X?" And so, things improved.

Case Study: the Complaint System

This same issue arose during my work in cable television, but there the situation was far different in one important sense: while again nearly all the software was being written in-house, unlike the previous example most of it was stand-alone, indeed having some essential character of the Operating System itself, since these programs were to run perpetually, and *never* end.[100] We arranged a common routine to handle any sort of software abort; it would generate a special file which we called a "complaint" detailing the computer name, date and time, program and many other details. These files were delivered by our file transport machinery to a common processing site, which had an arrangement for e-mailing a complaint to any designated group of users; it also archived the files for later study.

This "complaint" arrangement proved to be so useful we used it for other purposes besides error-reporting. Several informative reports, including the very critical "Daily Summary" of headend performance statistics, were generated and dropped onto the Complaint System's conveyor belt for processing.

Here are two samples. The first shows a fatal error which was the famous out-of-range exception I called the "C-thousand-and-five" error.

```
Computer 2WODB
DateTime 2003-09-06 04:00:00.067
Command zbaloeis
Compiled Nov 26 2001 12:04:47
Process 204
Thread 150 Monitor_Chores
Routine Monitor_Chores
Source mtr_chor.c line 901
Severity FATAL
Problem X_FatalError was called!

Fatal Error
Caught exception c0000005 at 41d080

Thread 150 Monitor_Chores
File mtr_chor.c line 901 routine Monitor_Chores
```

The second complaint isn't about a programmatic error or failure; rather it was intended to inform the Traffic Department of an anomaly in the files being processed. By comparing it with the previous one, you will observe the standard header which appeared in all complaints: the computer, the date and time, the program, thread, routine, and the nature of this complaint. Among other interesting things to be noted in this example is the timestamp we used for files, which has the format *yyyymmddhhmmss*. It also provides a statement of the corrective action taken (the duplicate logs are moved to a holding directory called "latelogs").

---

[100] That is the philosophical pun about an Operating System: its End is to *not* end.

```
Computer STARGATE
User nustar
DateTime 2005-01-14 16:00:00.007
Command snns
Compiled Dec  3 2004 11:00:56
Process 280
Thread 149 Monitor_Chores
Routine SendDenverStaleLogs
Source chores.c line 104
Severity Information
Problem Denver Stale Logs

15:07:49 Region ALBU    Zone 006 DEM    Net 01 CNN    (Y)
Log ALBU_10601006_20050114234705.dtv This log is stale
Denver log ALBU_10601006_20050114234705.dtv
matches existing log, new (duplicate) is put in latelogs
15:07:49 Region ALBU    Zone 007 SLI    Net 01 CNN    (Y)
Log ALBU_10601007_20050114234705.dtv This log is stale
Denver log ALBU_10601007_20050114234705.dtv
matches existing log, new (duplicate) is put in latelogs
```

There were, of course, some difficulties: since most of our programs were to run perpetually, there were tricky arrangements for making them restart when they aborted – but when something went wrong (like, say, a playback device failed) an infinite loop of retrys and almost immediate failures resulted in a cascade of complaints. That was readily fixed by adding a reasonable delay to the retry machinery; fortunately these cases were rare, but at least we knew right away when things went wrong.

Another matter was the case where the user who needed to know about the situation had shunted complaints away from his e-mail's inbox. This, however, leads to a very important and interesting discussion about monitoring, enshrined in the ancient epigram from Juvenal's Sixth Satire: *Quis Custodiet Ipsos Custodes?* = "Who Will Watch the Watchers themselves?" We shall consider this topic at length in the volume on ad insertion.

Case Study: Memory Leaks

When one thinks of "errors" on computers, most people think of major catastrophes: system crashes such as the BMR (Bad Monitor Request) of SCOPE or the "Blue Screen of Death" of WINDOWS. Or, if you are closer to the field of programming, you may think of syntax errors, design errors and oversights, coding errors, timing errors, or program aborts. Some of these have become famous in their own right: SCOPE's "ERROR MODE 4," the curious WINDOWS run-time out-of-bounds error I called the "C-thousand and five" error, the "stack dumps" and "File System Error tombstones" from HP's MPE system, IBM's "abend" (which is also the German word for "evening"), and so on. There are errors which are detected by the machine itself (the so-called "traps" such as overflow, out-of-range, illegal address, etc.), those detected by library routines, and those which are detected by the program itself, some of which go under the term "ASSERT." There are others, countless others, most of which do not announce themselves, but lurk, an ever-present hidden threat, within all software. (Alas: it is a truism that every non-trivial program has at least one undetected bug – but that is, after all, only another sad result of something that happened long ago: "I call it what it is – the Fall."[101])

---

[101] GKC, *Orthodoxy*, CW1:321

There is one error in particular which may arise in any program or run-time environment which provides the programmatic memory-management structure called a "heap," chunks of which may be requested, allocated, and used as required, and abandoned or returned when no longer needed. Not that there is an *inherent* problem with such a thing; the device is extremely handy and generally of reasonable efficiency. This heap may be native to the language as in the new() of PASCAL, supplied as a library routine as in the malloc() of "C", or it may be an essential element of the run-time environment for languages such as LISP.

Once a program becomes very large or complex, it may happen that the programmer's tracking of these allocations and abandonments are no longer under control. The disposal mechanism will usually try to detect invalid abandonments, that is the attempt to get rid of a memory chunk which has *already* been disposed of, but the opposite case, the allocation of chunks which are never disposed of, but no longer in active use, is the problem. For then, as the program continues to run, more and more of the heap is allocated, used, and slowly "forgotten" and never returned... sort of like a computational hardening of the arteries. Sooner or later there won't be any more memory to allocate. (The "garbage collection" used by LISP isn't an option.)

As you will hear in the Case Study about Qs, the famous finger-pointing blame game once accused WINDOWS of having such "memory leaks," resulting in the eventual unexpected termination of an important program. It won't spoil the story to tell you now that the problem was elsewhere – but oddly enough, the development environment did not provide any tools for managing the use of the heap, and it required someone who designed with a system-tools viewpoint to tackle the larger matter.

It's reasonably clear how to proceed: one merely replaces all the explicit allocations and disposals with newly written "wrapper" routines which track the details. There are three distinct alterations to be made:

1. Every allocated memory structure must be marked with its own unique type identifier and index. I chose to use a four-byte label for the first, and an unsigned 32-bit integer for the second.

2. Every request for allocation must store the appropriate type and the incremented index in the newly allocated memory chunk – *and then log the fact*.

3. Every request for disposal must *log the fact* of the type and index being disposed.

A very straightforward plan. This marking with an appropriate type id provides an additional gain: one can now install additional ASSERT tests to verify that a given memory chunk has the expected type.

```
// An example declaration:
typedef struct TreeType_
    {
    unsigned int memcode;
    unsigned int memindex;
    // (all the other fields for this struct)
    } TreeType;

// An example allocation:
p=malloc(sizeof(TreeType));
p->memcode='tree';
allocated_TreeType=allocated_TreeType+1;
p->memindex=allocated_TreeType;
LogAllocate(p);
```

```
// An example disposal:
LogDispose(p);
free(p);

// An example ASSERT:
if(thisnode->memcode!='tree')
    ASSERT("expected pointer of type 'tree'");
```

Then, in order to discern proper behavior of a program instrumented with such alterations, one runs a test of that program, producing a log of the allocations and disposals. The log is then analyzed, discarding every match of an allocation and disposal, and the resulting mismatches are investigated. Some, no doubt, will be required, due to the relative permanence of the data structures. But if there are others which ought *not* be permanent, or for which no enduring use is expected, the code must be studied, and the pathways of allocation and disposal checked. In this way, memory leaks may be abolished, and a program made effectively "water-tight."

Case Study: One Way of Watching the Watchers

The famous epigram from Juvenal's Sixth Satire: *Quis custodiet ipsos custodes?* = "Who will watch the watchers themselves?" seems to be aimed at computer science and especially at its division which concerns the *watching* or monitoring of the machinery. We shall explore this topic at length in the volume on ad insertion. But since I mentioned the old SCOPE operating system of the CDC 6400 and its famous "BMR" form of system crash, it seems very appropriate to describe one very simple and interesting way of performing this classic duty.

The CDC 6400 was really eleven computers united in one machine: the Central Processor (CP) which clocked at 10 MHz but had absolutely *no* ability to do any sort of input or output; and ten Peripheral Processors (PPs) which ran ten times slower than the CP and handled all the I/O for it. The first of these, PP0, continually ran a PP program called "MTR" (for "monitor"). It continually cycled around its main loop performing tasks which included governing the master clock, checking the activities of the CP, and assigning tasks to the other nine PPs. If it encountered an invalid request, it would "crash" the system, displaying the infamous message
BAD MONITOR REQUEST – XYZ
in large letters on the operating console.

That, of course, makes sense. If MTR could not recognize a request, it had to "give up." But there was another kind of system failure which could occur, announced by the message:
CM0 IS NOT ZERO
One of the strategies for efficiency used by SCOPE relied on having the zero word, the lowest word of central memory, continually set to zero. (This was no doubt an echo from of the machine hardware, in which the B0 register of the central processor was hard-wired to zero.) That value could thus be copied by any PP in order to clear memory – but all sorts of very difficult bugs could arise if that memory location ever became non-zero: terrors like corruption of disk drives, and so on.

So one of the very trivial tasks performed by the MTR program running in PP0 was to verify that CP0 was still zero, and if it wasn't zero, to "crash" the system before the mess had spread too far.

What does this tell us? Simply that it makes sense to have your program pay attention to its own activities and those programs associated with it. Such things are often quite inexpensive, and while it may seem odd to make a program report a failure in such a strange way, it is just another example of the ASSERT idea: that the current state of affairs within the machine ought to be maintained as expected, and as soon as this is no longer the case, to STOP THINGS COLD, and cry for help. Hopefully, someone will be watching who can deal with the situation and get it fixed... but that topic of monitoring is beyond the scope of this book.

A Motley Collection of Errors
    Herewith are a handful of interesting or annoying issues which I felt worthwhile to jot down, for your amusement or edification.

1. Typos in coding (sometimes called "fat-fingering"). Not all typos will be detected as syntax errors. One notably annoying case (which I was often guilty of) was mistyping the confounded backslash in the oddly formed string literals of "C"; such things cannot be detected at compile time, but only at run-time, and then only when one attempts to use the erroneously spelled file name!

2. Oversights. It's easy enough to miss something, overlook something, forget something. It just hurts more when one is trying to be meticulous and detail-oriented. It is best to correct the issue and proceed to the next task at hand, since it will likely happen again.

3. Pay attention to symmetry, and to the dangers of interchanging similar names or terms in equations. Such things as parallel names (e.g. "lft" and "rgt" when dealing with binary trees) have their pros and cons, but one ought to be aware of the symmetric situation regardless of one's naming preferences.

4. The Error of Plus or Minus One, also called the Fencepost Error. This is a major nastiness which occurs in many forms. Its classic appearance is in situations involving the arrangements for the "first" member of a list or array: is it numbered "zero" or "one"? But it also occurs in various kinds of counting problems, whence its other name: when arranging a fence, do we count the railings between the posts, or the posts? There is usually one more post than rail.

5. Speed and timing issues. Some of these have to do with large and complex matters of concurrency; one ought to be very careful with such things, lest the program deadlock waiting for something which can never occur. But there are others, involving performance.

Case Study: Why Does This Program Run So Slow?

One instance I had to handle started when my boss came to me and said:
    "Peter, all the users of program X are complaining about it, and we saw that it's consuming a lot of CPU time. Look into it and find out why it's running so slow."
    Unfortunately X was in COBOL and it was doing some abstruse business thing which I did not understand. I used some deep tech tricks (a performance utility) to find out where (in terms of the object program) the CPU was spending all its time. Then I dis-assembled the object program and tracked down the corresponding "paragraph."
    To my surprise, I found something (yeah, I can *read* COBOL; most people can) but I won't try to give you the code. Rather, I will give it as a mathematical equation:

$$z = \sum_{i=1}^{y} x$$

Of course you might not know what that means, though I figure you'd have a better shot at math than at COBOL. But it has a very standard reduction, and one which humans can perform. One can simply write

$$z = x \cdot y$$

instead, since *multiplication is simply repeated addition*. I reported my findings, the program was soon revised, and performance improved radically. (Alas, this reduction is not readily recognized by typical optimizers.)

6. Tests of underlying routines. If you didn't write it, maybe you ought to check it out, since **you ought to test-drive things** anyway. You will hear more about this in a later Case Study.

7. Omission of status checks, use of "ASSERT." Be sure to check status-returns from system library routines, especially critical things like file manipulation, external I/O, and process-control routines. Augment your code with ASSERT statements whenever possible, indicating both what you expected to have, and what you actually are experiencing at that moment.

8. Over-design *and* Under-design. It is possible to do both, maybe even at once. If you over-design, you may never get the project sufficiently established for use – and the same can happen if you under-design. Keep in mind the classic epigram, *Medio tutissimus ibis* = "You will go most safely in the middle."[102] Also keep in mind that academics and industry are two different worlds, and remain squarely on the fence, reverting to methods of the 13th century in order to get things done.

9. Odd or exotic cases of exterior devices. It seems to be one of the real frustrations of our discipline that those who should be our closest allies (in hardware design and manufacture) are often our most terrible foes, thwarting us in countless unforeseeable ways. It was a sad thing for me to try to explain such things, when my boss would credit me with technical prowess (accurate or not) but such knowledge is irrelevant when it comes to making a guess at the inner workings of *this* particular device. We saw so many hilariously frustrating cases – for example:
   – Three different HP 3000s each using a completely different parity for I/O. Yes, three kinds: "even" parity, which was then correct for ASCII; "odd" parity, which is an anomaly, and "zero" parity, which has now become the common form. And yes, there are times when such things matter.
   – Plotters ordered by major companies for which *no* documentation was available anywhere in this country.
   – A complex networking system for VSAT communications via satellite to remote locations which was IP-based, but was definitely *not* IP since it could not perform a broadcast.
   – Dozens and dozens of other oddities of special hardware which *had* to be brought online as soon as possible. There were more subtle instances, like the spot

---

[102] Ovid, *Metamorphoses*, 2, 137.

playback devices which had to track framecounts independently for two spots being played back-to-back.

There are no answers to problems like these, except to constantly resort to the Experimental Method (and to prayer!), to keep good notes, to cultivate patience, and finally to keep asking politely for assistance from the hardware guys.

10. Files requiring a date-stamp in their names should always follow the method of heterogeneous data comparisons so they sort lexicographically: hence, the correct form is always *yyyymmdd*. Alas, yes: there are places which continue to use only a month and day for their thousands of daily files, and hence they are often plagued with difficulties in, ah, let us call it the *freshness* of their files.

11. Any program which deals with "real" time (that is, where the current *time* as normally seen on a clock or watch plays a role in its function) *must* handle the infamous "Clock Day" alterations of Spring and Fall as mandated by Congress (typically known as "Daylight Savings"). If your work is sensitive to such an alteration occurring in the System behind your back, so to speak, you should add code to handle the change as necessary, or take other precautions.[103]

12. Dangers of *obscure* or stenographic code. While you will sometimes need to pay strict attention to performance, when one is dealing with hardware or with certain time-sensitive situations, you must always (especially in those cases) strive to be *utterly clear* in your coding style, documenting at length to explain any subtle matters whenever necessary.

a. Our first warning is against obscure coding techniques, often resulting from an inappropriate conformance to a pompous and impractical style:

> **Your code, as in the style of the Latin poets, with subject as remote, with modifier piled upon modifier, of word-order most careless, injecting clauses and curious yet classic allusions to Zeus whose thunder is awesome, or garlic, the Senate, wine, and other matters for grand effect, from the rest of the operations as possible, leaving for the very end the verb, you ought not write.**

You see what I mean? Yeah, I've seen code like that. Sometimes it comes from an infection I call *cool feature-ism.* (Also called "μ-softening. ") You may have heard a programmer exclaim: "Hey, look at this new trick! Cool! Let's find a way of using it." (And soon it's been jammed into production.) Maybe it *is* cool, but be on guard against such things, and don't go revising code just for the sake of "Change."

There was a famous stupid example in a word-processing tool I heard about: the command to show a line of text was "P" for "print"; the command to remove a line was "D" for "delete." Then a new version was released, but *now* the command to show a line was "D" for "display" and to remove a line was "P" for "purge." (Oh yes, it really happened.)

---

[103] Incidentally, in cable TV time was critical, and we had another kind of confrontation about time, which I will not elaborate upon here. However, it raised the question about Time Travel, and so I looked into the matter. To reduce it to a simple and practical question: "Can the Past be Changed?" I think it is worth telling you what I found. The answer is that *not even God* can change the Past, since "there does not fall under the scope of God's omnipotence anything that implies a contradiction." See Aquinas, *Summa Theologica* I, Q25 A4.

Remember what Chesterton said: "There must in every machine be a part that moves and a part that stands still; there must be in everything that changes a part that is unchangeable."[104] – and control your urge for novelty. *Dic cur hic* – know why you're doing it. Know your purpose, know your users.

b. Be reasonable about where you try to go for savings, and consistent in your concerns. Don't try to jam all sorts of data into a tiny memory unit with bit fields and convoluted mappings, *and then* overlook gross abuses of time and memory space:

Don't be *bit*-wise and *byte*-foolish.

c. Don't write production code with a pretentious "APL" accent, trying to take up as little space as possible. (This is a sort of inverse sesquipedalianism, more akin to the old tachygraphy of telegrams.) Or maybe an example is more effective:

Don'tcodelikethis;whitespacematters.

A related topic is "why we do not usually code in machine language" – but that is misleading, so we shall let it go for the present.

11. Problem Mis-statements, or Incomplete Characterization of Solutions. This is all too common, and can be prevented by more careful interaction with the requesting user – who, incidentally ought to remain involved in the stages of development insofar as that is possible. Sometimes, of course, there is no way around this; the user is aiming for something all but inexpressible, and the best we can do is produce a reasonable approximation. Humility, Patience, Clarity of Expression, a Willingness to Learn – and a Willingness to Teach without condescension – all these will be helpful in such cases.

Case Study: Faulty Pseudo-code

In a rather sad conclusion to this discussion I wish to mention two errors I have observed in books. (A professor once referred to a "famous wrong proof" but I have lost the reference.) More precisely, the first is a caution against unfortunate oversights, all too easily made when one presents "pseudo-code" which is neither implemented nor tested. Here is an example for finding the root of an equation, taken from a textbook [105] on numerical methods:

*CAUTION – FOLLOWING IS **ERRONEOUS** – DO NOT USE*

To find the root x where $f(x)=0$, rearrange to the form $g(x)=x$.
DO WHILE $|x2-x1| >$ tolerance
    Set $x2=g(x1)$
    Set $x1=x2$
ENDDO

---

[104] GKC, *What's Wrong With the World*, 116-7.
[105] Gerald, *Applied Numerical Analysis*, 23 and 56. Similarly 50 versus 44-5 and 56 versus 16.

The above will always stop after one cycle, since at that point x1 will equal x2. Obviously, this is not what was intended. (Possibly the pair of assignments are intended to occur in parallel, which would give a valid algorithm.) Fortunately, that text includes actual source code which shows the correct way of doing the work.

Case Study: Turn That Crank, Chas!

The other error occurs in the famous *Ninth Bridgewater Treatise* of Charles Babbage, which was first printed in 1837. It is a very fascinating book, the first to explore the frontier between computing and philosophy, indeed, theology itself, and includes some of his reflections on Miracles and other such topics. He actually speaks about his Calculating Engine in his discussion of Free Will, providing the following example:

> When calculating a table of squares, it [the Engine] may be made to change into a table of cubes, the first time the square number ends in the figures 269696; an event which only occurs at the 99736th calculation; and whether that fact is known to the person who adjusts the machine or not, is immaterial to the result.[106]

Now, his argument does not depend upon the accuracy of that statement – that the square of 99736 ends in 269696, and it is the first such integer to do so. But we defer an investigation of the metaphysics in favor of examining the mathematics.

It is certainly easy to show that 99736 squared is 9947269696, which ends in 269696 as stated.

However, 99736 is *not* the first such number.

The square of 25264 is 638269696, which also ends in the desired six digits.

Chas! Er, I mean, excuse me, Mister Babbage! What happened? Did you get some kind of *bug* jammed in your Engine? (Yes, it's hard to believe I am debugging a program written almost two centuries ago, written by the First Computer Scientist.)

Don't we have *any* clue about this riddle? Maybe. Earlier in that book he gives us a clue about how fast his machine works:

> It has been supposed that ten turns of the calculating engine might be made in a minute, or about five hundred and twenty-six millions in a century.[107]

That comes out to one turn in six seconds, a very slow CPU, but remember it's completely mechanical! Thus, to use his machine for the computing of the squares of integers and checking for those last six digits, assuming one case was checked by a single turn of the crank, it would take 9973.6 minutes, which is 166 hours, 13 minutes, and 36 seconds: just shy of *one solid week* of cranking. Somehow I don't think he did that. (Crank-turning, 24/7, in the 1830s?) I might make a guess about what happened –

---

[106] Babbage, *The Ninth Bridgewater Treatise*, 168. I wonder if Babbage had in mind that most awesome description of the Master Designer found in the Psalms: "The designs of the Lord shall stand for ever, the plans of His heart for all generations." (see Ps 32/33:11)
[107] Ibid., 42, note.

maybe *he* made a guess at where to start hunting for the solution – but there is no further data available to me at present.

Writing is a risky business, I know: it's so easy to make a mistake. Putting things down in print (be it software or literature) is *always* a risk, but then "The only way to avoid becoming a metaphysician is to say nothing."[108] But this matter of 269696 is a curious riddle about a fascinating project of an amazing man.

I cannot conclude this chapter without a brief digression in order to mention a few of the classic absurdities that have occurred in other Sciences.[109] I will not belabor them, but we ought to be aware of such things, as they have admonitory value for anyone who thinks he has it all figured out.

Case 1. Phlogiston. It's the "element" which makes fire. (Try not to laugh when you look it up.) Bear in mind that "It was the precision of Lavoisier's balance that led to the abandonment of the concept of phlogiston and made possible the reorganization of the study of matter on a basis that was designed to emulate the clarity of the Newtonian system."

Case 2. The Ether. I do not mean organic compounds like $(C_2H_5)_2O$, but the "stuff" that fills outer space, which light and radio makes "vibrate." It was no less a physicist than the great Maxwell who wrote the article on it in the Ninth Edition of the *Encyclopedia Britannica*. "There can be no doubt," he asserted categorically, that the ether "is certainly the largest body of which we have any knowledge."

Case 3. Another great physicist, Lord Kelvin, "felt that ether vortices, about which he kept writing highly mathematical papers, were the last word in physics. He saw the physics of his day as a clear sky with only two small clouds, soon to be dispelled." Those clouds were (1) the specific heat of gases and solids as a function of their temperature; (2) the null result of the Michelson-Morley experiment. As Jaki observed, "Both clouds turned out to be huge storms for physics." Just in case you are wondering about this, the answers are (1) quantum mechanics and (2) "relativity" – but to go further would be even more of a digression.

---

[108] E. A. Burtt, *The Metaphysical Foundations of Modern Physical Science*, quoted in Jaki, *The Relevance of Physics*, 344.
[109] See Jaki, *The Relevance of Physics*, 249, 81; "The Last Word in Physics" in *Patterns or Principles and Other Essays*, 215; "The Relevance of Materials Science" in *Numbers Decide and Other Essays*, 183.

Chapter 14
On Being Wrong About Errors

There is no better test of a man's ultimate chivalry and integrity than how he behaves when he is wrong...

GKC, "The Real Dr. Johnson" in *The Common Man* 120-1

When first the giraffe was described by travellers it was treated as a lie. Now it is in the Zoological Gardens; but it still looks like a lie.

GKC ILN Oct 21, 1911 CW29:176

Having been so severe with errors, it will be a pleasant change to see another sort of error: the kind where the data are so remarkable there *must* be something wrong – but there isn't. It's the gentle nudge which tells us we are near a discovery.

At first it would appear that such things cannot happen in the rigorous and logical world of Science, let alone in computing: but they do. I am making a collection of examples of the weird things which didn't make sense when they were first encountered, and how they led to the unexpected and remarkable. Things like argon, or nebulium, or helium, or gravimetry, or Uranus, or the parallax and proper motion of nearby stars, or Cepheid variables in the Magellanic Clouds. Most of these discoveries revolved around the precision of observation, and could have easily been dismissed as sloppiness or carelessness – or errors. It takes a special sort of professional to admit he is wrong, but it takes an even more special sort to *humbly* admit the possibility that everyone else is wrong too.

Case Study: a Different Sort of Floating Point

This example occurs in the study of gravimetry, a valuable tool of geophysics, by which the character of deep geological structures is learned. The change in the period of a swinging pendulum due to change in altitude was known to Newton in the 1600s, and as the precision of time-keeping improved, more subtle variations began to become apparent. One of the most curious of these occurred in the mid-1800s during a topological survey of India. The skill of surveying had already been brought to an excellent level of precision, so when the field data began to go awry and the data were checked by other means, the engineers began to look for an explanation in physics. Two locations, Kaliana (at about 30°N, near the Himalayas) and Kalianpur (at about 25°N, some 350 miles south) were studied. Since the surveying depended on the use of a plumb-bob to fix the vertical position of a given measurement, it was guessed that the gravity of the Himalayas themselves was pulling the plumb-bob off vertical. That was true, and the differences in latitude were

> 5° 23' 42.29" measured by triangulation
> 5° 23' 37.06" measured astronomically

giving a discrepancy of 5.23". But this would mean an error of some 160 meters, far too large to attribute to errors of surveying. After further investigation of the expected deflection, the effect of the mountains was found to be *too small*. Something else was going on – and this led to Pratt's Hypothesis of Isostasy: the Himalaya mountains are higher because they are *less dense* than the surrounding material of the Earth, and hence are "floating" on the underlying layer.[110]

Case Study: an Inert Error in the Thousandths Place

This example arose from the study of the density of gases in the mid-1890s.

> Lord Rayleigh had for some time been engaged in determinations of the exact densities of a number of gases. Among these was nitrogen. In his experiments Rayleigh found that the density of nitrogen obtained from the air was slightly but consistently higher than that obtained from artificial sources. [That is, nitrogen generated by chemical reactions, such as the decomposition of ammonia.] Writing to *Nature* in 1892 he says "I am much puzzled by some results as to the density of nitrogen and shall be obliged if any of your chemical readers can offer suggestions as to the cause. According to two methods of preparation I obtain quite distinct values. the relative difference, amounting to 1/1000 part, is small in itself, but it lies entirely outside the errors of experiment." The difference in the weights of one liter of the gas obtained in the one case from atmospheric air and in the other from ammonia varied by about 6 in 1200, or about 0.5 percent, but the accuracy of the method did not involve an error of more than 0.02 percent.[111]

An intrepid chemist named William Ramsay took up the challenge; after removing oxygen from the air, he absorbed the nitrogen using heated magnesium – and so found there remained another gas, an *inert* gas, to which he gave the name *argon* (from the Greek for "inert"). Here is a little more about the background of this discovery:

> The establishment of well-equipped physical laboratories, first in German and French and later in British universities, clearly evidenced the general recognition of the extraordinary importance precision has in physics. The rewards were at times spectacular, particularly when unknown entities, such as new elements, were discovered. The case of argon was perhaps the most characteristic, resting as it did on the worries of Ramsay and Rayleigh as to why some samples of nitrogen had a weight of 1.257 grams per liter instead of only 1.256. [112]

Such subtleties are enough to shake up anyone who has to deal with numerical methods, and even the less sophisticated forms of mathematics used in business applications – but then it was not a mathematician or a data analyst who pointed out this important truth:

> A woman cooking may not always cook artistically; still she can cook artistically. She can introduce a personal and imperceptible alteration into the composition of a soup. The clerk is not encouraged to introduce a personal and imperceptible alteration into the figures in a ledger.[113]

(Neither are such things permitted to those who write business applications.)

Case Study: Missing a Discovery of Planetary Proportions

This example goes beyond any other sort of warning I might propose; it is the sort of thing which really makes you think about the way you work. Indeed, the story of the discovery of Uranus ought to be required reading for all scientists, especially in the "cautionary tale" form Sidgwick gives in one single critical chapter:

---

[110] See (e.g.) Gilluly et al., *Principles of Geology*, 13-15.
[111] Harrow, *Eminent Chemists of Our Time*, 48.
[112] Jaki, *The Relevance of Physics*, 254-5.
[113] GKC, ILN Apr 7 1906 CW27:161

It is generally true to say that an unrecorded observation is an observation wasted. Communication of results is an essential condition of the progress of science.

When planning the form that the observational record is to take, and subsequently while making the actual notes at the telescope, the characteristics to keep constantly in mind are: clarity and unambiguity, conciseness, objectivity and comparability, orderliness, legibility. The record should be immediately intelligible to anyone familiar with the subject, without any supplementary explanation.

... **In the history of astronomy can be found numerous cautionary tales which illustrate the fatal consequences of messy and muddled observational records, as well as of preconceived ideas regarding what is likely or possible, and of emotional bias – expectation, disappointment, surprise, hope.** No fewer than 19 pre-discovery observations of Uranus have been identified, from 1690 (by Flamsteed) onward.[114]

(Oh yes; I know I've been messy and muddled...)

Very well, my dear friends: let us consider ourselves warned.

Now, let us see something rather remarkable in our field which, ahem, involved a preconceived idea regarding what is likely or possible. Oh yeah.

Case Study: the Maybe Gate

The FORTRAN I used on the HP 3000 at FEL in July 1983 provided an extension to extract a given number of bits starting at a given bit from a variable X:

```
X[startbit:numbits]
```

I happened to use this expression in a relatively large piece of software, and *sometimes* found some strange behaviors. Sometimes? Yes. I could not quite tell what was going on. It would have been easy enough to just abandon that hunk of code and try another way, or to claim it was because of some "user error," the old "finger-pointing" excuse which comes up all too often in industry.

But that is not for us. Somebody has to do the hard jobs.

So I put in code to trace the activity of the program. Sometimes everything looked fine... but then, when I removed it, I got wrong results. Whatever it was, it was subtle...(Maybe as subtle as the actual density of nitrogen?) Slowly but surely I worked as Ramsay did, removing all the other code which might be interfering, until I had reduced the entire thing down to the following. (The array and its values are required in order to, ah, set the stage properly.)

```
PROGRAM MAYBEGATE
LOGICAL K
INTEGER ARRAY(5)
LOGICAL MYFUNCTION
MYFUNCTION(K)=K[0:1]
C
C Initialization...
C
K=%177777L
ARRAY(1)=0
ARRAY(2)=1
ARRAY(3)=0
```

---

[114] Sidgwick, "Observational Records," *Amateur Astronomer's Handbook*, ch. 32, emphasis added.

```
      ARRAY(4)=0
      ARRAY(5)=-1
C
C      What is K? TRUE or FALSE?
C
      IF(MYFUNCTION(K))DISPLAY "TRUE"
      IF(.NOT.MYFUNCTION(K))DISPLAY "FALSE"
      STOP
      END
```

Oh man! I thought I understood FORTRAN... Well, maybe you think you understand FORTRAN... and maybe you do. What do *you* think was the output?

Care to make a guess? (*Maybe* you can tell already?)

Nothing in my experience prepared me for the shock of seeing those *two* lines of output:

```
:RUN MYPROG
    TRUE
    FALSE
END OF PROGRAM
:
```

Ah. Immediately I dumped the assembly language, and found that the compiler had inserted a *spurious* instruction, such that the actual value upon which the IF statement depended was whatever happened to be on the stack *below* the value which should have been tested! Hence, the subsequent action of the program was not according to the given instructions. (That's the reason for that strange array in the above code.)

What was learned, then? What was my amazing discovery? Simply that production compilers from well-known companies could have errors.

That was well worth the debugging exercise. Maybe it was just a rude awakening, but it is better to be aware that such things can happen than to proceed in a naive sort of trust.

Another remarkable experience occurred when I attempted to apply the classical Knuth-Morris-Pratt string-searching algorithm to strings over the so-called "wildcard" alphabet of DNA and RNA. I will present a study of this in great detail in a future volume of this series. Similar to this was the complexities I encountered at FEL in working on two very difficult problems for a customer with an NC punch press; those also shall be dealt with in a future volume.

The moral of this chapter, then, is to be cautious and meticulous, and not to overlook minor errors. There may be some more subtle truth waiting for you to discover.

Chapter 15
On Recursion

Part a. Recursion and Its Rules

Since I brought up recursion, I thought it best to talk about it a little, and state the rules about the use of this very powerful technique.

When I introduced the topic in class, I used a wonderful "visual aid." This is one of the famous Russian nesting dolls, also called *Matryoshka*. [115]

Recursion is simply the use of a given function from within itself. It is based on the very powerful theoretical tool known as **mathematical induction**:

Given a function or other property suspected to be true for an entire series possessing a "successor" property such as integers, graphs, trees, or so forth, one establishes its validity by the following:

1. Demonstrate that this property applies to a starting element which we call the *basis*.

2. Assume that the property holds for some arbitrary value n.

3. Using that assumption, prove that the property holds for the successor of n.

---

[115] I told the students that it's one of the cases in which computer scientists are allowed to play with dolls.

Whereas mathematical induction works forwards from a basis value by successors, recursion works by reduction backwards (each doll splits open to reveal a smaller doll), moving towards the starting point (the basis of induction) which thus becomes what we call the "terminating condition." Sooner or later, the reduction can go no further: there is a smallest doll which itself does not open.

Recursion is a case of problem-solving by "Divide and Conquer": chop the problem up into ever-smaller pieces, and eventually the sub-problem can be solved trivially.[116]

Recursion is relatively easy to implement, being simply a fancy use of a *stack* – a data structure having the first-in, last-out property like those plate dispensers at a cafeteria or buffet. There are two forms of recursion in software:

1. Explicit, in which the routine actually contains (either directly or indirectly through other routines) a call to itself. The existence of an unseen stack is assumed.

2. Implicit, or what I call pseudo-recursion, in which a routine does not actually contain an explicit call to itself, but uses flow-of-control to accomplish the effect of recursive execution. This typically requires an explicit stack to store the intermediate parameters and local variables, and a flag to indicate where to send control after a nested "call." Note that the following warnings also apply to such implementations, but there is a good deal less danger since there is nothing hidden: all memory and additional supporting code is visible.

We should note that for certain recursive functions, there exist *closed* forms: that is, formulas which do *not* invoke the function itself, but rely on some algebraic or other transformation to give the same result. This idea relies on the fact that a single recursive call can have the identical effect of a simple "while" or other repeat-loop. We shall see an example of this shortly.

Explicit recursion is possible only when the language and its underlying run-time environment provide a stack for the storage of its return-address and local variables. Note that this stack may exist in hardware, or may be implemented by the compiler. As strange as it may sound, on the HP 3000, routines in both BASIC and FORTRAN could be recursive since the primary "registers" for that machine are stack-based.

---

[116] A tongue-in-cheek article on "Simplicity Theory" in *SIGACT News* many years ago called this method "multiply and surrender": you *multiply* the problem into more and more parts until you have to *surrender* and solve them. See Appendix 8 for the reference.

Implicit or pseudo-recursion must sometimes be resorted to when the nature of the work to be done in the routine exceeds the capabilities of the supporting language or machine, or where some inherent complexity in the algorithm precludes a tidy implementation, perhaps because the algorithm is still being designed. In general such code gets very confusing to read; there is a real gain in quick understanding from a clean and simple recursive routine; the classic example of this is the tree-walking routine, which we'll see in just a moment. Hence, to use this powerful tool safely and wisely, we should remember the following rules:

Recursive Rule 1: a recursive routine must have a *terminating condition*.

A recursive function *must* have a conditional character: that is, there must be a situation wherein that function *is not called*. This is known as the **terminating condition**: it is the case in which the routine does not call itself. It corresponds to the *basis*, the starting point of mathematical induction.

A common recursive example is to walk a binary tree. This is a classic piece of code which ought to be in your personal memory, as it is very short. My version returns the maximum depth of the tree it traverses. You may implement or remove any of the three "visit" routines as you may require.

```
int Walk(TreeType * p)
{
    int depthleft,depthright;

    if(p==NULL)
        return 0;
    else
        {
        VisitPrefix(p)
        depthleft=Walk(p->left);
        VisitInfix(p);
        depthright=Walk(p->right);
        VisitPostfix(p);
        return 1+max(depthleft,depthright);
        }
}
```

In this routine the terminating condition is a "leaf" with no descendants (both its left and right pointers are NULL).

Just for reference, consider this simple tree:

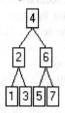

Then, assuming three runs, in of which just one the "Visit" routines simply prints the value of each node, we get the following results:

```
VisitPrefix:   4 2 1 3 6 5 7    depth 3
VisitInfix:    1 2 3 4 5 6 7    depth 3
VisitPostfix:  1 3 2 5 7 6 4    depth 3
```
(See the web site for the code.)

Recursive Rule 2: a recursive routine should have a bounded depth.

This can be hard to enforce, especially in cases where the routine is dealing with complex data structures such as a graph or tree. (Generally this will be bounded by the number of nodes, but it depends on the algorithm. That is why it is wise to add statistics/performance code to tracks entries in a data structure and depth of recursion.)

You ought to arrange things so that you can track the depth, just in case you do overflow the stack – and if you cannot determine any bounds for your problem, you should pay strict attention to the next rule.

Recursive Rule 3: a recursive routine should use as few arguments and locals as possible.

The reason for this rule is that all parameters and locals must be allocated on the stack, and even on today's large-memory computers it is possible to overflow the stack. There are various tricks for this. For example, in the above tree-walking routine, don't process the node being visited within the recursive routine, but call another routine to do that job. Another trick (if you know that the heap is larger than the stack) is to build a "parameter block" on the heap, and pass a pointer to it as the argument. If you are desperate, you may need to revise the routine to make it pseudo-recursive: that is, arrange an explicit stack and manage it yourself, using appropriate flow-of-control code to perform the effective recursive call. Here is the code for testing your machine's stack size:

```
#include <stdio.h>
void Try(int level)
{
  int waste[1024];
  // note there is NO terminating condition!
  printf("at level %d\n",level);
  Try(level+1);
}
void main()
{
  Try(1);
}
```

On my machine this stops with stack overflow after printing "at level 251" implying a stack of about a megabyte, which is the default value. (Real-world programming may require you to learn how to alter this allocation.)

Recursive Rule 4: write good documentation for such routines.

Of course you should always write good documentation for all your code. (What a grand thought that is, and so rarely accomplished. Ahem.) But it is very good style to annotate any routine which relies on recursion, mentioning its terminating condition and its bounds if you have any idea about them.

Unwinding Recursive Code

There are some cases where the problem in question does *not* require recursion. The factorial is often used as an introduction to recursion since 1!=1 and for $n>1$,

$$n! = n \cdot (n-1)!$$

but later we will see the standard definition using the big-pi notation [117] which can be performed by a loop. Many times there are simpler iterative solutions, but in some cases there are simple *closed* forms which give the result without recursion or loops. However, often complexity or tidiness will preclude such unwinding (as in tree-traversal) and sometimes there is no closed form to be had.

A very simple example is found in the famous story of the "Gauss Seatwork Problem," which I like to tell students about. Here is the version as I recall it being told to me. You can find the original in Bell's article on Gauss in *The World of Mathematics*, I, 298.

> Scene: a certain elementary school in Germany, during the late 1700s.
>
> The students were being noisy that day, and the professor had some paperwork from the headmaster he had to get finished by the end of the day. He checked the clock; he was supposed to do mathematics now. Hmm, maybe there was a way...
>
> He sighed and stood up, and the class settled down, apprehensive about the stern look on his face. "Take your notebooks. Write this: *A review of addition. Add the whole numbers starting at one, and continuing to one hundred.* Begin."
>
> There were some brief groans, but he ignored them and sat down. He would have a good fifteen, perhaps twenty minutes of relative silence, and that should suffice.
>
> But he had barely started when he heard a student stand. He looked up: "Yes, Mr. Gauss?"
>
> "Professor, I have the answer."
>
> He gasped. "*What?*" The class murmured in astonishment.
>
> "Yes sir. It's five thousand and fifty. I have the equation which computes the result for any starting and ending number, as well as the proof of its correctness..."

A nice little story. (The real one is even better, as the problem was harder and he was only ten years old!) Now, let us see the equation for the sum of the first n integers. Let $S(n) = 1 + 2 + 3 + ... + n$, or, to write this iteration compactly using big-sigma:

$$S(n) = \sum_{i=1}^{n} i$$

This also has a recursive form:

$$S(n) = \begin{cases} 0 & n < 1 \\ n + S(n-1) & \text{otherwise} \end{cases}$$

But there is a simple closed form which avoids both iteration and recursion, and you can try to work it out for yourself as you admire ten-year-old Gauss – it's not hard to do. Just in case you have some paperwork to get done, here's the closed form of the answer:

$$S(n) = \sum_{i=1}^{n} i = \frac{n(n+1)}{2}$$

---

[117] Big-pi of course is easy to implement, being simply a loop around a multiply starting with one, just as big-sigma is merely a loop around an add starting with zero.

So now you can check: yes, 100·101/2 is 5,050. I like to call this the "beer can formula" since it gives the number of beer cans stacked in a complete triangle with n cans in the lowest row. (If you want a pyramid that big, you'll need 211 cases. Let me know and I'll come and help.)

I want to make one little addition to this observation. Not long ago I wanted to know how the size of the base for such a triangle, given the total number – which is simply the inverse of S. It is readily solved by the quadratic equation, and is:

$$S^{-1}(z) = \left\lfloor \frac{\sqrt{8z+1}-1}{2} \right\rfloor$$

For example, if you want to know what size triangle you could build with 168 beer cans, the answer is a base and height of 17, with 15 cans left over.

Non-recursive tree-walking

One of the more unusual problems I worked on was to convert the above classic tree-walking routine to a non-recursive form. Yes, it can be done, assuming the tree has "parent" pointers; no, it is nowhere near as tidy and simple as the recursive form, but with it one can do all three forms of traversal (prefix, infix, postfix). I don't recommend doing such a thing – indeed, I would advise against it, unless you find yourself stuck (as I did) with a very simple language or computer, or some other severe limitation. Nevertheless it is instructive to see how it may be accomplished.

As part of the testing of this iterative routine I set up a "test jig" which generated all possible binary trees of a given depth. This was also a very interesting problem, as was the question of counting such trees. That number grows *very* rapidly:

Depth	Total trees
1	1
2	3
3	21
4	651
5	457653
6	210065930571

Here is the recurrence: let $T(d,k)$ be the number of trees of depth d having k leaves on level d. Then:

$T(1,1) = 1$

and for $d, k > 1$,

$$T(d,k) = \sum_{j=\left\lfloor \frac{k-1}{2} \right\rfloor+1}^{2^{d-2}} T(d-1,j) \cdot \binom{2j}{k}$$

The proof of the equation is left to the reader. (Ahem. I always wanted to say that.) Here are the first few values of $T(d,k)$:

Trees of depth d with k leaves in the lowest row

d \ k	1	2	3	4	5	6	7	8
1	1							
2	2	1						
3	8	8	4	1				
4	80	144	168	138	80	32	8	1

Note that the sum of each row

$$T(d) = \sum_{i=1}^{2^{d-1}} T(d,i)$$

yields the number of trees of that depth as given in the previous table. Yeah well. Turns out that OEIS [118] has it, and provides a much simpler generating equation:

$$T(d) = (T(d-1))^2 + 2T(d-1)\sum_{i=1}^{d-1} T(i)$$

Which sure grows fast! By the time we get to d=9, the number of trees is 3.79e90.

Searching non-recursively

Let's see a practical non-recursive routine which applies to trees. It searches a given tree for a given value, and requires no additional pointers, flags, or memory.

```
/* FindInTree  returns NULL if the value is not present,
                else a pointer to that node.
   It requires a comparison routine KeyCompare(a,b) returning an
integer indicating whether a is less, equal or greater than b. */
TreeType * FindInTree(ValueType sought,TreeType * root)
   {
   TreeType * p;
   int k;

   p=root;
   while(p!=NULL)
      {
      k=KeyCompare(sought,p);
      if(k<0)
          p=p->lft;
      else if(k>0)
          p=p->rgt;
      else //k is zero
          return p;
      }//end while
   return NULL;
   }
```

This is a good example of why one ought to think carefully about a problem before resorting to recursion, since the recursive approach requires somewhat more intricacy to get the same result. Hence, it makes as much sense to search by means of a loop as it does to do the infix traversal by means of recursion.

Furthermore, this technique may be used to perform insertion of a new key into an *unbalanced* binary tree, requiring only the addition of another variable pointing to the previous node visited, and a flag indicating whether the last branch went left or right. It also is worth some study.

---

[118] See the On-line Encyclopedia of Integer Sequences: http://oeis.org/A001699

I would like to call your attention to two things about the above code for searching the tree. First, there is a studied symmetry in handling the left and right cases, which is why I traditionally use the field-names `lft` and `rgt` for such trees. Such things appear very often in code for binary trees; it is a personal style, and others may find more appeal in less-symmetric names – yet the final effect ought to possess chiral symmetry, that is, the symmetry of the left and right hands; this occurs in important tree algorithms such as those for AVL-balanced trees.[119]

Second, the use of the comparison routine (which you will observe is called only once within the loop); it enables the three-clause conditional (less, greater, and equal). We shall examine another role for this three-way trick later.

Part b. The Famous "Towers of Brahma" (or Hanoi)

As we know, it is very helpful to learning and understanding an abstract idea to give examples, and visible ones are often the best. One of the classic examples used to explain recursion is an old solitaire game [120] sometimes called the "Towers of Brahma" (or "Towers of Hanoi"). A friend of mine who had to do this as a programming project called it the "Towers of *Annoy*" and it *is* a bit annoying, but then it is handy to use as an example. You can actually buy one of these toys, or if you like woodworking, make one for yourself.

The idea is simple enough: there are three posts, and seven [121] disks of different sizes, each with a central hole, are piled on one of them, stacked from the largest at the bottom to the smallest on the top. The object of the game is to move all the disks from one post to another, while never placing a larger disk on top of a smaller one.

Of course there is a simple recursive solution, which goes something like this:

To *move a stack of disks*:
    If there's just one disk to move, move it to a spare post.
    Otherwise, *move the stack of disks* (all but the largest) to a spare post,
        then move the bottom disk to the third post,
        finally *move the stack of disks* (all but the largest) on top of it.

As you see, I put the two recursive calls in italics; the terminating condition is to move just the smallest disk, which may always be performed.

From this algorithm it is easy to determine an equation for M(d), the number of moves needed to shift d disks:

$$M(d) = M(d-1) + 1 + M(d-1) = 2 \cdot M(d-1) + 1$$

---

[119] "Chiral" (pronounced "KEER-ul") is a term from the stereochemistry of organic compounds; it comes from the Greek χειρ (*cheir*) = hand. AVL-balancing is useful since such trees will never exceed 1.5 times the depth of the minimal-depth tree, and the implementation is relatively easy as well as efficient. See any algorithms text for details.

[120] It was invented by Edouard Lucas. See *Creative Puzzles of the World*, 175.

[121] There is a legend often told as stage-patter to explain the toy. One version says there is a secret temple in which sixty-four disks of alternating gold and silver are being transferred on posts of diamond, and when the tower is completely transferred, the world will end. Yeah. (In just a moment you will learn just how many moves that would require, and can make your own estimate.)

Since we compute M recursively twice at each successive level, one suspects a power-of-two lurking, and indeed, this recurrence equation has a simple closed form:

$$M(d) = 2^d - 1$$

which you can prove readily by mathematical induction.

This simple form suggests other patterns may be found once one charts out the positions of the various disks, providing one is careful not to overlook what is going on. For example, one "boundary condition" to be specified is *which* of the other two posts is to be the final destination of the stack of disks. We arrange the three posts in a circle (at 12:00, 4:00, and 8:00 on a clock face) and number them zero, one, and two starting at the top and going clockwise. Then, if the starting post is zero, and we wish to end up with the disks on post *one*, the number of disks to be moved will tell us which post we ought to move the first disk:

If there are an *odd* number of disks, move the first disk to post *one*.

but if there are an *even* number of disks, move the first disk to post *two*.

If, on the other hand you want them to end up on post *two*, just interchange the terms "odd" and "even."

The closed form for the problem

It is not hard to derive a closed form of an equation $p = P(n,f,m,d)$ for n disks which all start on pole 0, and the final pole f where all the disks will end up is either 1 or 2, such that disk d (where $1 \le d \le n$) at move m is on post $P(n,f,m,d)$:

$$P(n,f,m,d) = \left(3 + (-1)^{n+f}\left((2-(d \bmod 2))\left\lfloor \frac{m}{2^d} + \frac{1}{2}\right\rfloor \bmod 3\right)\right) \bmod 3$$

Here is an example result:

Towers of Hanoi 4 disks 16 moves to get to pole 2

m	Post0	Post1	Post2
0	1 2 3 4		
1	2 3 4	1	
2	3 4	1	2
3	3 4		1 2
4	4	3	1 2
5	1 4	3	2
6	1 4	2 3	
7	4	1 2 3	
8		1 2 3	4
9		2 3	1 4
10	2	3	1 4
11	1 2	3	4
12	1 2		3 4
13	2	1	3 4
14		1	2 3 4
15			1 2 3 4

Part c. Other Graphical Examples

There are three other elegant examples which demonstrate recursion by graphics, and are very easy to implement in software. (I omit the code since you ought to have the fun of doing them for yourself.)

1. "Mondrian" art.

This is based on the artwork of Dutch artist Piet Mondrian (1872-1944). We are given a rectangle. To generate its "mondrian" we perform the following:

If the given rectangle is "too small" color it in. Otherwise, randomly choose a direction (horizontal or vertical) and divide the rectangle into two smaller rectangles at some random interval, and generate the "mondrian" for each one.

The result is stunning on a color-graphics screen, but even in black-and-white it's interesting:

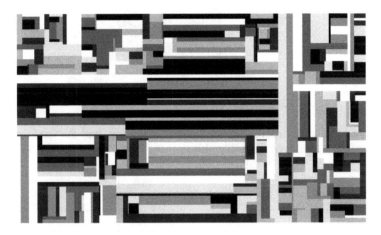

2. The n-bugs problem.

We are given a circle, on which we place a fixed number n of bugs (ants are usually chosen for some reason). These have been trained to walk towards the nearest of their fellow insects. Our objective is to show their positions at regular intervals... however there is a more artistic way of presenting the problem, which I also omit so you will have the fun of trying to work it out for yourself. (I had only seen the final result, and had to do the same; I've already given you a hint.)

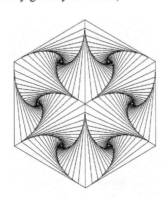

3. Islands.

One day when I was at grad school I was sitting outside the CS building talking with some fellow students when another one came up and asked, "Anyone have a program that can draw islands?" We laughed, and he explained. In order to enhance his presentation, he wanted any sort of programmatic way of producing irregular shapes that might be islands in some imaginary sea. The current buzzword at that time was "fractals," which are recursive [122] abstractions, but which when truncated can sometimes give a "realistic" character to computer-generated shapes. We discussed the matter, and the general idea was something like this:

Given a "random" polygon, apply the "island" function to each edge. The "island" function said: if the edge is "too short" draw it. Otherwise, randomly distort the edge into a "few" sub-edges, and apply the "island" function to each of them.

I went back to my room, did some experimentation, and the next day showed him my result which looked rather like this:

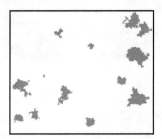

(It looked so realistic I naturally put an X on one of them and wrote "Secret Treasure buried here! ")

Again, you'll have a lot more fun trying this for yourself.

---

[122] Fractals, however, do *not* have a terminating condition. That is what makes them a fractal, a sort of limit to an infinite series, like an asymptote. See the literature for details.

Chapter 16
On Concurrency

It used to be the idiom for doing simultaneous things, and a kind of challenge about competency: "Can you walk and chew gum at the same time?" The human being is competent to do several things at once, depending on their complexity, but in most cases works best when attention is focussed on a single project. Computers, however, cannot do more than one thing at a time unless they are of the class of machines called *parallel processors*, in which a number of standard CPUs are united to form a single machine. A cunning arrangement called *time-slicing* built into operating systems since the 1960s enables a feature usually called *multi-tasking*: by this means a single-CPU machine can perform a number of different tasks, apparently "at once" but in reality shifting its attention among them, and actually doing *only one* at a time. To the annoyance of computer scientists, this term has been distorted by popular usage, and it needs correction.

Lebrecht's collection of anecdotes about musicians contains an interesting detail about Karl Czerny (1791-1857), whose study contained four desks, each holding an unfinished score. As Czerny explained to a visitor, he worked at one desk until he had finished a page, then he got up and went to the next desk and worked on that score for a page – and so on. That visitor said, "Such was the mechanical labor of this musician's life."[123]

In computer science we have another word for this: *multi-tasking*. Contrary to the popular use of the term, it emphatically does *not* mean doing several things at once. It means doing a lot of different things, but *one at a time*, by working on each task in *slices* or relatively small chunks of time. A multi-tasking version of the "walk-and-chew-gum" idiom would be for a person to repeatedly do two actions:

1. Stand still and chew gum once.
2. With mouth motionless, advance one step.

The difficulty with considering human behavior is *attention*. We can walk and chew gum at once (two actions truly performed in parallel) since both are to a large degree habitual, relying on motor circuits in less-conscious parts of our nervous system. Like Czerny we do not typically perform more than one significant intellectual task at a time – though there are famous exceptions like the astounding creative counterpoint of Bach, or multi-writers such as Caesar, Aquinas, and Chesterton.[124]

---

[123] Lebrecht, *The Book of Musical Anecdotes*. No. 235, p. 103.

[124] **Caesar:** I have not yet been able to find a citation for his having this remarkable gift. In my explorations I encountered something worth our consideration as relevant to my purpose: "The great contributions of Rome to military science were organization, discipline, attention to details, far-sighted preparation, the realization that battles could be won before they were fought." [E. S. McCartney in *Warfare by Land and Sea*, 101 and 137-8, quoted in *Latin for Americans*, Second Book, 235.] A stunning insight! Programs also can be "won" before they are run, providing those contributions of Rome are kept in mind, and carried out. Relevant to this are the comments about Authority and Obedience in the episode of the Centurion [Matthew 8:5-13], and GKC's related comments [in *The Everlasting Man* CW2:323].
Aquinas: "Still stronger is the testimony of Reginald his *socius* and of his pupils and of those who wrote to his dictation, who all declare that he used to dictate in his cell to three secretaries, and even occasionally to four, on different subjects." [*The Life of St. Thomas Aquinas*, 51.]
Chesterton: Maisie Ward reports: "The most startling thing told me by Mrs. Meredith was that Gilbert often wrote two articles at the same time on totally different subjects, steadily dictating

Mechanically, such remarkable skills are achieved by multiple CPUs, each of which performs a single task; other arrangements handle allocation of project portions and any necessary inter-machine communications. These machines are called "parallel processors" and there are a variety of such things actually available: some with relatively few CPUs are intended for high-performance interactive games; there are others with more CPUs targeted at difficult technical problems such as simulation. The matter of managing such complex machines is interesting, but we are here concerned with the common single-CPU machine running an operating system which provides for a number of effectively (but not actually) simultaneous multiple and independent processes – that is, which performs multi-tasking by allocating slices of time to any process presently wanting to execute.

It is important to note that this multi-tasking feature is necessarily *inefficient*, since the system must take time to arrange the transfers between the various running processes – but in the very large majority of cases this tradeoff is well worth the cost, since the common activities of an Operating System, typical simple user-oriented applications, and even software for the solution of some fairly complex problems (like, say, just about everything which needed to be done for the local ad insertion system we shall examine in a future volume) can be handled by a number of independently running but cooperating processes – which, moreover, rarely need to be running in an utterly simultaneous fashion. Only very complex problems of the kind we call "CPU-intensive" can benefit from the concurrent efforts of multiple CPUs.[125] In such cases the pretence of concurrency by multi-tasking on a single CPU defeats the intention: splitting up such problems for handling by multiple processes on a single CPU gives far worse performance than the straightforward single-process implementation. Observe carefully the distinction: a *parallel* (multiple-CPU) machine can make significant gains in run time by suitably dividing the problem among several concurrently running processes, but those same processes on a *single-CPU* machine will take longer due to the cost of performing multi-tasking than if the entire problem were solved by a single process. (E.g. Czerny's work took longer since he wasn't composing while he was walking between desks, moving lamps, checking where he left off, etc.)

Furthermore, once the arrangement to provide multi-tasking is made – be it for the sake of simplifying the System itself, to enable multiple users, or for handling the

---

one to her while writing the other by hand. The dictation came slowly, but this was always so even when he was only dictating. Rhoda Bastable too had often watched him writing something else while she took his dictation; after his bad illness this seems to have ceased." [*Return to Chesterton*, 157] However GKC's secretary Dorothy Collins reported it continued afterwards, and so informed Aidan Mackey, who informed me.

[125] It is extremely unlikely that any user-oriented program will take advantage of the *full* power of a given CPU: most of the time such programs must sit idly, waiting for the disk drive to read (or write) the next sector of a file, waiting for the next packet over the network, or waiting for the user to decide what to do next. ("The net, the disk, and the user" seems to echo "the world, the flesh, and the devil." Hmm...) No matter how fast you type, the typical CPU has time to execute *millions* of instructions between any two characters. The classic examples given for CPU-intensive purposes are (1) simulation/modelling of things like weather or chemical and nuclear reactions and (2) exploration of recalcitrant mathematical problems, such as the pursuit of huge primes. Even in such cases input and output of intermediates, etc., are required, and issues like the memory-bus timing also get in the way. It's very hard to keep the CPU of a common commercial machine busy at productive work, which is really rather a disappointment. This needs some further contemplation.

complex tasks of a single user – that arrangement begins to reveal the strength of thinking of a project in terms of its concurrency. A given system may be simultaneously handling any number of projects (up to its designed and configured level of efficiency) – and in the same way, a single project may be divided into several programs, each of which are running simultaneously – these we may call independent processes. By the application of the hierarchical paradigm, a single program may be divided into various simultaneously running entities (which may or may not be "independent" as its needs may require) – such entities are often called *threads*, which are part of a single program, but are just like processes in their simultaneity (be it real or apparent), and may share certain resources such as memory. Consult the relevant manuals for the internal run-time library for your System, which should provide the technical details.

Case Study: What Runs on HOME?

Here is an example from my system for local ad insertion. The computer called HOME had six different programs running perpetually:
1. PUMP – performs all file transport to and from the Field.
2. DUP – repeats the Field's monitoring information for use at our headquarters.
3. CUELOG – records the cue signals being repeated by the cue-machines.
4. TIMESYNC – keeping HOME in sync with STARGATE.
5. TIMESYNC – keeping the Field in sync with HOME by the satellite network.
6. TIMESYNC – keeping machines on the video subnet in sync with HOME.

All these programs arose at different points in the life-history of the system, and were dramatically dissimilar, so there was little point in forcing such disparate functions together into one somewhat monstrous factotum. Note that the TIMESYNC program was specialized for our use: it could synchronize the machine on which it ran (as in #4), or (when run differently, as in #5 and #6) it would provide synchronization to other machines on a given network. It might have been unified, but it was simpler to arrange as it was.

To go one level deeper, the PUMP program contained six threads besides its main thread, which handled user requests for its status. Those six were:
1. Monitor_Receive – handles new files arriving from the Field.
2. Monitor_SendNonMPEG – sends non-MPEG files to the Field.
3. Monitor_SendMPEG – sends MPEGs (spots) to the Field.
4. Monitor_ProcessNonSchedules – handles spot triggers from encoders.
5. Monitor_ReceiveJobs – checks status of underlying file transport software.
6. Monitor_Chores – handles regular and scheduled chores.

All six were remarkably independent, but shared certain code making it reasonable to keep them united in a single program. (Further information may appear in a later volume of this series which will examine that local ad insertion system in detail.)

Case Study: The Mutex

This term for a certain tech device sounds a little like a third-declension Latin noun with its final *x* (like *index*)[126] – or perhaps like a name from the taxonomy of biology. (*Murex* is a genus of marine gastropods whence came the ancient Tyrian

---

[126] Latin *index* comes from *in+dico* = "I inform or disclose"; its sense was transferred to the primary finger of the hand, which led to the meaning of "pointer" as used in computing.

Purple dye.) But the term is actually formed from the first fragments of the words MUTual EXclusion, and that is what the device does: governs a scarce resource by enforcing a policy by which two or more independent competing processes are *mutually excluded* from using that resource simultaneously – or indeed from performing the same thing at the same time.

Such things are quite common in the non-tech day-to-day world. We all know the famous common-sense rule "Two bodies cannot occupy the same space at the same time" resulting from the strength of the various forces which hold matter together. Perhaps a human-contrived example might serve better: at most street intersections some sort of mutex (traffic signals or signs) is erected to try to regulate drivers according to that rule: as Chesterton described so vividly, it is "a place where men, in an agony of vigilance, light blood-red and sea-green fires to keep other men from death."[127]

In the computer, the mutex is provided by the operating system,[128] whose privileged character guarantees exclusivity. A mutex is reasonably easy to use, requiring only a small handful of routines besides creation and destruction: one to request access, one to relinquish access, and one to check whether access is permitted.

Now, I have a nice little story to tell about the "Abominable Snow Monster of the North" from the famous old Christmas special on Rudolph the red-nosed reindeer.

This happened at the cable TV company, and was related to a lesser project, not local ad insertion, known as "National Marketing." This required processing and delivery of some 17,000 schedules per day, along with the same number of logs (the results from the previous day) – this huge number represents some 50 cable networks being handled at over 350 headends nationwide. Initially there was just one group of these files, being handled by the Traffic-and-Billing group called "NMI." Our customer was satisfied with the performance and expanded the project to an additional group known as "Bigfoot." This extension would require a nearly identical replication of all machinery, except that at the destination there was to be only *one* schedule, formed by a kind of "merge" of the corresponding NMI and Bigfoot schedules, and each log file had to be "split up" in the same way.

Now, these two groups each used their own unique spot-ids, so splitting up the logs was very easy. The "merge" required for producing the schedules, however, was very intricate: not algorithmically speaking, but because the customer had some particular requirements regarding the arrangements of alternation and priority – the details of which do not concern us here.

The interesting situation came about relatively early in the project, just after Bigfoot had been added. We were still using the file transport machinery of the local ad insertion system, which had a special gate-keeper program called GATE to handle submission of schedules: when our customer had prepared some schedules for delivery to the Field, one of their Traffic department called our Control Room to request transport, which was performed by our operator using GATE.

At that time, NMI was already using this same arrangement for delivery of schedules, with the exception that they could go into the Control Room and request this themselves. (Local ad insertion required Traffic to interact with Operations constantly, and generally these departments were on very good terms with each other.)

---

[127] GKC, *Heretics*, CW1:55.
[128] It may also be implemented in the hardware, or rely on special machine instructions designed to aid in the demands of concurrency.

One might expect that the addition of Bigfoot would be straightforward. But as I said, there were issues about performance of the schedule merge, and the final step in the processing was proving to be difficult to make stable, due to the challenge of specifying the process to the customer's satisfaction. At the same time, however, there were several special cases to be handled, such as when an NMI schedule existed, but not the corresponding one for Bigfoot, or vice-versa. Even more interesting was the fact that the processing and transport of such a huge number of files did not happen "instantly," and there had to be some sort of arrangement to deal with the possibility of one of the two groups wanting to perform transport very soon after the other.

Given the demands upon the development department (ahem) there wasn't any time to handle this situation as proper design would permit. Surely, I said to myself, it needs a mutex to govern the outbound pathway, to be shared between NMI and Bigfoot... but there was no easy way of altering the programs at that time.

My boss and I were over in the Traffic Department discussing this; we had just decided that for the short term, it had to be handled by the Traffic personnel being extra careful. Then I spotted a stuffed toy of the "Abominable Snow Monster of the North" from the old "Rudolph" Christmas show. I grabbed a piece of paper and scribbled "MUTEX" on it and pinned it to the Abominable, then told the Traffic people: "From now on, you have to carry this with you when you go to trigger the schedule transport. If you don't have it, you can't trigger it. When you're done, put it back here, in case the other guy needs it."

And so, for a while, until I finished altering GATE and the related programs, there was a visible – indeed, *tangible* – mutex at our company, relying upon the underlying mutex-like privilege of matter that only one thing can be in the same place at the same time – and providing authentic governance of a scarce resource for competing processes.

(Postscript: After the software had been appropriately modified, the poor old Abominable sat lonely on a shelf, still grinning his toothless grin and proudly wearing his MUTEX label.)

Chapter 17
On Reinventing the Wheel

...none of these makers of imaginary scenes have tried to imagine what it must really have been like to see those things as fresh which we see as familiar. They have not seen a man discovering fire like a child discovering fireworks. They have not seen a man playing with the wonderful invention called the wheel, like a boy playing at putting up a wireless station.

GKC *The Everlasting Man* CW2:198

The above title refers, in a paradoxical manner, to one of those epithets usually heard in the following sarcastic form, usually from a clueless superior:

"Don't reinvent the wheel."

Of course that's of dubious value, if not plain silly. One would never say it at Goodyear or Dunlop or Firestone, etc. There are *whole industries* where engineers are busy all day doing just that: reinventing the wheel.

There is nothing wrong with reinventing the wheel – or discovering America, or the Sun, or water. Most of us need to discover these things for ourselves, maybe more than once. I myself have invented several things which are recorded in the literature as having been invented by others: disk caching, a standard plot library, succinct status-reporting (or "twitting") and I forget what else. There is nothing wrong with that, as long as I do not put on airs about such things: I do not claim to have been chronologically "first"; I invented them before hearing of them.

It is very hard to read all the vast amount of literature there is, even in one special field. Besides, so many algorithms are mere mental exercises, and the literature will record the first person to reduce the solution to a formal paper as "discoverer" but even in the pure sciences there are instances of simultaneous workers achieving duplicate results: calculus (Newton and Leibniz) or oxygen (Priestly, Scheele, Lavoisier) and so on.

Moreover, there have been infamous slip-ups where good scientists didn't follow up the possibilities: "No fewer than 19 pre-discovery observations of Uranus have been identified, from 1690 (by Flamsteed) onward."[129] And the great Messier, who made a catalog of those annoyingly fuzzy objects which distracted him from finding comets, seems to have included one or two comets among the galaxies and nebulae. The brilliant Father Mersenne, who served scientific Europe as a kind of one-man INTERNET in the 1600s, made some guesses about prime numbers which have since been proven wrong: as F. N. Cole showed [130] in 1903: the "Mersenne prime" $2^{67}-1$ is 193707721 times 761838257287.

The point is to be diligent in looking for things, both in the literature and by one's own cleverness – but also to follow up on the work once it's been done. It may not be the case that your tricky little algorithm will end up in a future textbook, but if it's sufficiently novel it may be helpful somewhere. There are an awful lot of different sorts of wheels, and what's useful on a wheelbarrow or a jumbo jet has no place in an automobile trunk. Wisdom is what matters, not precedence, nor prescience.

---

[129] Sidgwick, *Amateur Astronomer's Handbook*, section 32.
[130] Bell, "The Queen of Mathematics" in *The World of Mathematics*, 503.

Part III
Random Access Memories

"It is a waste of energy to do the same thing twice..."

Yes, that ought to be the motto of computer scientists, shouldn't it? It was written almost a hundred years ago by a chemist named E. E. "Doc" Smith, in his famous "Skylark" science-fiction series. It's worth hearing just a little of the context, since he seems to have so perfectly envisioned a most elegant form of organ-console-style environment for program development. Our hero Richard Seaton (also a chemist) is on the planet Norlamin working with an alien genius of physics named Rovol...

> Rovol seated himself beside the younger man, like one organist joining another at the console of a tremendous organ. Seaton's nimble fingers would flash here and there, depressing keys and manipulating controls until he had exactly the required combination of forces ...
>
> He would then press a tiny switch and upon a panel full of red-topped, numbered plungers the one next in series would drive home, transferring to itself the assembled beam and releasing the keys for the assembly of other forces. Rovol's fingers were also flying, but the forces he directed were seizing and shaping materials, as well as other forces. The Norlaminian physicist set up one integral, stepped upon a pedal and a new red-topped stop precisely like the others, and numbered in order, appeared as though by magic upon the panel at Seaton's left hand. Rovol then leaned back in his seat – but the red-topped stops continued to appear, at the rate of exactly seventy per minute, upon the panel, which increased in width sufficiently to accommodate another row as soon as a row was completed.
>
> Rovol bent a quizzical glance upon the younger scientist, who blushed a firey red, rapidly set up another integral, then also leaned back in his place, while his face burned deeper than before.
>
> "That is better, son. Never forget that it is a waste of energy to do the same thing twice, and that if you know precisely what is to be done, you need not do it personally at all. Forces are faster than human hands, they are tireless, and they neither slip nor make mistakes."
>
> E. E. "Doc" Smith, *Skylark Three*

Herewith I present a variety of problems – some intricate, some trivial; some arising in the formal, mathematical, or academic realm, others from the practical, implementational, or professional (industrial) realm; some solved, some barely resolved. They are not presented to demonstrate any sort of technical acumen, but as an example of the challenges which arise in the discipline, and to give a hint about handling them. As I stated elsewhere, these presentations are unavoidably autobiographical, but perhaps that aspect will provide some comic relief, as well as a glimpse into an odd branch of archaeology: technology in years gone by.

And, perhaps, they will aid you from having to do the same thing twice.

Case Study: Music on the CDC

My undergraduate work began in 1973 at Lehigh University. I have considered commenting on it in a professionally polite but critical manner, but I prefer to avoid getting bitter about it, especially since good things happened despite the huge disappointment.

Indeed, many good things did occur there. For example, I was given the greatest advice I have ever experienced, or have ever heard of anyone being given: when the Dean of Students told me: "Did you ever hear of a book called *The Idea of a University* by Newman? Read it." [131] I heartily recommend it to you also.

Also I joined a fraternity, which has also become a signal disappointment even greater than that of that University, but in which I have met many good friends.

Furthermore, I met a wise and brilliant teacher, Samuel L. Gulden, who became my advisor for my M.S., and this significantly offset some of the more dull and difficult earlier encounters with others among the faculty and staff.

But most importantly was not what that school did, or the faculty, or the administration – but simply one of the resources they had. For down on the dismal first floor of the mechanical and electrical engineering building, past a machine shop and through a warm and noisy room smelling of machine oil, was a glorious piece of equipment from the 1960s: a machine costing some two million dollars, using a special 400 Hz power supply, built of nothing smaller than transistors and containing miles of wire: a computer made by Control Data Corporation, the CDC 6400.

I am not going to give you all the technical details of this machine, its 60-bit words and its Central Processor (CP) and ten Peripheral Processors (PPs) – they would deserve a book in itself. Even now I can recite most of them without going hunting; I can list most of the machine instruction set, both mnemonics and opcodes, from memory, and talk at length about its amazing architecture designed by Seymour Cray, its famous SCOPE operating system, or its Operating Console with those two awesome animated screens. Even now it dominates everything I've seen since, if not in clock speed [132] in overall power and majesty. (It deserves a poem, or maybe another volume in this series, but we have other things to do today.) It was a high point in my technical career, and thank God a great first experience, as was my first real-world employment, which you shall hear about shortly.

Yes, there is a lot I could say about the CDC and my years of hunting to know more and more about it and its system. But this case study is actually going to focus on one of its peripheral units, and hopefully teach you an interesting little fact.

I don't recall the date; it was surely very early in my undergraduate time, possibly late August of 1973, or early September. As a freshman in the Engineering School, we had tours of the various departments: I recall seeing two massive Analog Computers, chock full of everything I expected from a computer: lights, meters, switches, knobs, and bundles of wires and electronic components, and an oscilloscope. (My only reference at that time was television; except for brief encounter with a "programmable" desktop calculator, I knew nothing about real computers.) Oddly enough I never saw those analog machines after that first encounter.

---

[131] I also heartily recommend it for anyone, teachers or students. God willing there will be another book on this topic, though not in *this* series. And if you are curious, explore my Saga *De Bellis Stellarum*, paying close attention to a school called the Ambrosian University, which is a fictional implementation of Newman's ideas.

[132] The "minor cycle" of the CP clock was 0.1 microseconds, so it ran at roughly 10 MHz (ten million cycles per second). Slow by the machines of 2013, but remember it was built of transistors in the late 1960s, and think of how much more it was doing in each cycle!

But I did also tour the main Computer Center, which as I said was on the first floor of the same building. A junior who was employed by the Computer Center was the tour guide; he took us past a window labelled "118" and we looked in. There was a massive piece of machinery (maybe six feet long by two wide and nearly four feet high) chattering away as a student fed it stacks of punch cards; beyond it were two units spewing paper (these were the line printers as I later learned).

Then we walked down the hall to another window: there I saw for the first time the famous Operating Console: an operator was sitting there, peering intently at the green animated twin displays showing the current system activity.[133] In the distance were four tall magnetic tape units on which tapes were rotating. But the truly memorable item was none of these.

On the right, just inside the window, on a narrow table were a pair of drum plotters. Perhaps you have never seen such a thing: maybe you have seen a seismograph, the device often depicted in movies when there is an earthquake? It is a cylinder on which a paper is scrolled by a clock-mechanism, and against which moves a pen on a sort of movable arm, responding to the motions of the Earth.

In this case, the computer caused the motions of the drum and pen, not the Earth. But it was earth-shaking for me, since I had already seen the printouts produced by the line printers, which seemed to only be able to handle letters and numbers and symbols, and no drawings of any sort. But with such a plotter – Oh! With motion possible in both X and Y (from the action of the drum and the perpendicular motion of the pen against it) it was obvious that this device could be used to produce almost *any* sort of diagram one might desire... and to me at that moment, the most desirable of all diagrams was MUSIC.

I immediately mentioned this to our guide, and rather to my surprise, he said, "Oh, no, I don't think so. The treble clef isn't a function, so you couldn't draw it."

I didn't pay any attention. Before I had finished my freshman year I had implemented a relatively simple program which could handle single-part music. It always caused a stir when I ran it, and people went by that window and saw the plotter's pen coursing across the drum as it drew the lines of the musical staff, or wriggling like a wet dog as it filled in a quarter-note...

Plot made April 9, 1974 at 19:28.

---

[133] Again nothing I have seen has ever approached this marvel, though my WATCHER had it in mind. See the volume on local ad insertion or my *Subsidiarity* for further details, and the Case Study on Simulation later in this volume.

That music program was an amazing little introduction to non-academic programming for me, and my first non-trivial experiment [134] in stating a problem to be solved, then solving it. However, as I advanced into the field, other puzzles began to attract me, and I didn't continue to extend that program. But I did not neglect the plotter: three years later I wrote another, less intricate but more mathematical tool which converted the CDC into a two-million-dollar SPIROGRAPH. More on that later.

What was the problem which our tour guide had voiced? It is interesting to recount, though I did not work it out until some time later. Most of the plotting which was done at that time was accomplished by a library routine called QIKPLT, which took a pair of arrays and some additional information and produced a rendering of a "plot" – that is, a plot in the mathematical or Cartesian sense: a chart with X and Y axes and a curve representing the function implied by the given arrays.[135] As I imagine it, the tour guide must have assumed that I would somehow fill in two arrays with the "function" to represent the five-line staff, clefs, and so on.

But I had not done that. I had gone to the documentation and learned that QIKPLT used a lower-level library routine called PLOT which took three parameters: an X coordinate, a Y coordinate, and a third value which indicated motion with the "pen-up" (3) or "pen-down" (2). With this single fundamental tool I was able to draw any of the various musical symbols.

(Later on I learned how PLOT worked: it generated a series of 4-bit units which indicated one of ten primitive instructions to the plotter: two stood for pen up or pen down, and eight stood for – ah – let us call it the motions possible for a king in chess, either straight or diagonal, along a grid with sides of 0.01 inch.)

And that is the lesson, which is indeed a fundamental one for computing. One must always seek the fundamental abilities of one's tool, for that will provide its effective range of achieving results. I do not have the time or space to spell out those details for computers, but they exist, both in theory (we call it the "Pumping Lemma" in automata theory) or in practice (the actually existing machines, systems, and languages of the real commercial and industrial world.) Don't be a misleading leader: know the limitations and abilities of your tools.

Case Study: Debugging a Plot Program (Part 1)

Having left Lehigh in May of 1977, my first job was at Frankel Engineering Labs in Reading, PA. This place, affectionately known to us as FEL, was a small consulting house which had two departments: the NC department did engineering projects (especially those requiring Numerical Control of machine tools), the DP department handled traditional accounting, inventory, payroll, and other Data Processing for businesses. I was there over six years with many ups and downs, and though some memories have faded after 36 years, other images are still quite vivid.

My first day was Monday, September 19, 1977. I got to FEL and struggled up

---

[134] I had already done a plot of $y=2^{-x}$, which measures the length of organ pipes, a verification of the 256 "functions" of Boolean Algebra for three variables (which I had hand-computed in high school), the Lorentz-Fitzgerald time contraction, and other things I cannot recall.

[135] In our day this is readily accomplished by the "Insert Chart" command in typical spreadsheets.

the stairs, my foot in a cast.[136] I met Sam Frankel, the president, and he introduced me to Charlie, the head of the NC department.

Sam and Charlie knew I did not then know BASIC but was very good at FORTRAN, so they gave me the listing of a FORTRAN program to debug. It was something called "a plot program for a Bridgeport NC milling machine" – whatever that is. (I did understand plotters – see the previous case for more.)

It took Charlie some time to explain what was going on: the whole "Numerical Control" idea of how machine tools such as milling machines, lathes, flame cutters, and punch presses were mechanically controlled by instructions punched into an inch-wide strip of paper-tape. I won't give an overview here; it's not necessary, besides which there are dozens of formats. But the general idea is very simple, akin to that used in a player-piano: a paper-tape is punched with holes representing a "part-program" which is simply a sequence of "motion instructions": a series of locations (given by their x and y and z coordinates) which the tool must visit, cutting as it moves.[137] Other instructions tell the machine to move in an arc, change the cutting tool presently being used, alter its speed, stop, or other utility functions. The purpose of such part-programs was to produce actual metal parts using that machine tool in an accurate and reliably repeatable manner.

Generally an engineer started with a blueprint for the desired part, and after doing some preparatory work using geometry and the technical knowledge of the raw metal, the machine tool, and its programming methods, produce that part-program. The engineer could do this by hand, working out all the geometric calculations and engineering steps, writing out the correctly formatted instructions on paper, then transcribing them on a special typewriter [138] which produced the paper-tape. Or he might use software, into which he would input a series of generalized geometric and machining instructions; that program would then generate the corresponding part-program in the proper format for his machine tool.

At that time, there were many shops which had NC machine tools, ranging from small specialty production houses to very large truck or aircraft construction industries. I should here mention that FEL provided a whole range of facilities: we could do the NC programming from blueprints (either by hand or using our own software), or a company could arrange to use our software and do things themselves.

The program I was given was simple enough: it would scan an input tape and produce a "plot" – a graphical representation on paper – of the motions represented by the instructions on that tape. The purpose was to verify that the part-program was correct, comparing the "plot" of the part-program to the original blueprint. Like any other "program" be it a musical score, a recipe, or a piece of software, these part-programs have a strict syntax which must be obeyed, or the machine tool will fail to produce the desired part, or even (in extreme cases) break itself. So such plot-generating programs were an important item in our software.

As I said it took a good while for Charlie to explain that particular part-programming language, and once I had a sufficient understanding of the idea, I began

---

[136] How I hurt myself has to do with a tree, though not a binary one, but that story is not recounted here. It is, however, a sign that God the Master Designer always has a plan. And yes, there was an elevator, but I had no idea where it was; I found out later that day.

[137] Yes, this is almost exactly the same as the fundamentals of a plotter, as we have seen.

[138] At FEL we had Teletypes for punching tapes using the ASCII character set, and Flexowriters for punching those in the EIA character set.

going over the listing of the program. After lunch I told him I felt I had the corrections ready to apply, and asked which terminal I could use to edit the program.

And he said those very curious words, words that I didn't understand, having come from Lehigh where I used the CDC 6400, not only by punch cards, but also by interactive terminal: "What do you mean, 'edit'? Besides, it's *after lunch*, so we can't do FORTRAN now."

There were two mysteries here, both of which are extremely interesting for us to consider in this PC-literate INTERNET age, not even forty years later, and I will explore them separately.

O Radiant Editor!

At FEL in those days, when you wanted to produce a new (altered, or revised) version of a paper-tape from an older one, you had to use a Teletype or Flexowriter. You fed the original tape in and started the machine copying until it reached the place where you wanted to change. Then you typed your alteration, which was simultaneously punched into the growing tape – after which you had to advance the original tape past the altered point, and let the copying proceed. Yes, that sounds old-fashioned, but then what was the alternative? The two workhorse computers [139] at FEL only ran a time-share BASIC system, and there was *no* arrangement for storing a simple file of "text" and altering it: a common, extremely useful tool which some like to label a "word processor" but I still call an "editor."[140]

And no, Charlie was not being stupid; indeed he was a very experienced engineer and knew a wide range of machining practices and blueprint reading, besides being competent in math and programming. My experience at Lehigh did not make me "superior" at all: it merely meant I had seen a sophisticated interactive text editor, and expected to find such a thing on any computer I might happen to encounter.

Yes, I was the stupid one. I had made a serious error, assuming that every computer would be like every other, or at least there would be comparable tools on each one.[141] I had not yet reached the philosophical development to understand the point I want to state here: the principle which I now call the "Little Red Hen Rule": **If you want something done, *do it yourself*.**

And so: once I got past my confusion about the lack of an editor at FEL, I decided I would begin work on my own editor: it would be a great project for helping me learn BASIC. And so it came to pass: not very long afterwards we had a general editing tool for storing text and altering it interactively. It wasn't very fast, but it had a nice selection of commands, and I could always add new ones as we recognized the need for them. And so those days of dreary tedium of manual alteration of paper-tapes were over.

---

[139] They had a third computer, much older and simpler, which we shall discuss in a future Case Study.

[140] The distinction I make is that an *editor* is a simple tool for producing a desired *file* of text (it makes a flat ASCII file, useful by almost any program) whereas a *word processor* produces a *printed* document in a desired format (it makes a special binary file, often proprietary, which cannot be used by any other software). Editors have no facilities for italics, margins, image insertion, or more sophisticated document formatting; their purpose is to make a file with the desired content, not a printout in the desired format. The common WINDOWS tool called NOTEPAD is the nearest approach to such a thing these days.

[141] This is a danger we must guard against. Computers are *not* as general as all that, especially when they are used in production settings. We shall consider this aspect at greater length in a future volume of this series.

Case Study: Debugging a Plot Program (Part 2)

Now we can proceed to the second topic. In those days, FEL had a number of customers who used our pair of HP 2116 computers, timesharing by telephone line [142] to run a set of BASIC programs specially written for that company. Some used business software, some used engineering software. By prior arrangement with them, the computers were "off-line" during the noon hour so we could do maintenance.

We could also use them to do FORTRAN, which was not possible on the time-shared BASIC system. (I know how odd this sounds, but it was long ago.)

Again, my previous experience got in the way. I write this paragraph forty years (and a week or two) after my first encounter with the CDC using FORTRAN, and there I used punch cards, which was somewhat less cumbersome than the paper-tape, since one could keep the "good" cards and only needed to revise the "bad" ones until one had the desired "deck" for the program at hand. I don't have a listing of my *very first* program, but I do have the second one, from September 12, 1973. It was in FORTRAN and performed the very simple computation of the volume of a cylinder of a given radius and height. From this perspective of forty years and five days, the code is trivial, but the interesting features of the listing have to do with the operating system. The last portion of the typical listing received by a user of the CDC 6400 was called the DAYFILE, in which appeared the various commands performed by the operating system, along with terse status information, and a summary of the computer usage, including the charge of $0.40 an external user would have to pay. We might discuss the DAYFILE another time; for now the important detail is the way in which one compiled and executed a FORTRAN program. The deck of cards had the following sequence:

```
PJF01,A1509,*FLORIANI.  (This was called the "job card. ")
RUNT.
LGO.
7-8-9 card. (This "end-of-record" indicates the end of SCOPE commands.)
xxx     (cards containing FORTRAN source)
7-8-9 card. (This "end-of-record" indicates the end of FORTRAN source.)
xxx     (cards containing input data for the program)
6-7-8-9 card. (The famous orange EOF (end-of-file); see the front cover.)
```

The "RUNT" statement invoked a version of a FORTRAN compiler, which produced a binary executable file called "LGO"; any such file could be executed by simply using its name. This command sequence was very easy for someone just beginning to learn programming, and was taken almost as "magic" without further discussion. Only later courses would explain the mysteries of the compiler and loader (sometimes called "linker") and the even darker and more esoteric matter of execution. But really, *none* of these things are truly mysterious at all, or no more so than the mystery of an internal combustion engine (Do *you* own a car? Do you *drive* it?) or baking cookies. (Have *you* ever baked cookies? Have you *eaten* cookies? Well?)

Now you may not even know what a compiler is, or why this is relevant to the matter of lunchtime at Frankel Engineering. But you are about to learn.

---

[142] No this was *not* any sort of "internet"; it was using a dial-up modem on a Teletype at 10 characters per second. Very slow, but it got the job done, and gobs faster than doing it by hand. Two companies had a "high-speed line" that went three times faster.

So... Tuesday September 20, 1977, at FEL. Charlie looked at his watch. "All right, Pete, we'll shut down System One and start compiling."

We went into the computer room – it was cold, due to the two big air conditioners churning away. Charlie went up to the closer of the two HP 2116 machines, checked that no users were still logged in, then shut it down. Then he went over to a stack of boxes full of paper-tapes, picked one up, and placed it by the front panel of the computer.

He opened the box and took out a fat roll of paper-tape. "All right, Pete – you got your FORTRAN source there?"

"Yeah," I responded a bit hesitantly, thinking of RUNT and wondering what was going to happen. "You want it now?"

"No, I've got to load the Pass One first."

(In order to keep things clear, I will tell you the steps as we go along.)

Step 1. Load Pass One of FORTRAN compiler

Charlie took that first roll of paper-tape and stuck it into the paper-tape reader on the front of the computer, flipped the front-panel switches to point to the paper-tape binary loader, and pressed the RUN button. "This loads Pass One," he explained. That tape began speeding through the reader, spewing down into a big pile on the floor.

Then he took this odd little thing, a bobbin with a crank like on a fishing reel, and wound up that tape. "We have to do this or the tapes will get all snarled," he told me. When he was finished he asked for my source tape.

Step 2. Execute Pass One of FORTRAN compiler

He put my source tape into the reader, changed the program start address by flipping switches, and pressed the RUN button to start the program running. My tape chugged slowly through the reader, while something began to grind, and from another place in the machine, a stream of black paper-tape spewed out onto the floor.

When the computer stopped, he rolled up my source tape, fastened it with a little circular paper clip, and handed it back to me.

Then he rolled up the newly punched tape. "This is the intermediate tape," he told me as he wrote a label on it with a white pencil in his tidy draftsman's hand. He handed that to me also.

Step 3. Load Pass Two of FORTRAN compiler

Then he reached into the box and took out another fat roll of paper-tape and loaded that into the computer. He reset the switches to the paper-tape loader, and pressed RUN. That tape spewed onto the floor and when it was done he rolled it up.

Step 4. Execute Pass Two of FORTRAN compiler

He asked me for the intermediate tape, and put it into the reader, then changed to the start address and pressed RUN. That tape chugged through the reader, and again grinding was heard as a new paper-tape was disgorged.

When the intermediate tape had been completely read in, he rolled up the intermediate tape and gave it to me, then he rolled up the newly punched tape and labelled it, remarking, "This is the relocatable binary."

Step 5. Load Relocating Loader (a.k.a. "Linker")

For the third time he took out a tape from the box; this wasn't very large. He changed the switches to run the loader, then rolled it up.

Step 6. Execute Relocating Loader

He asked for the relocatable binary, and put that into the reader, then started the program running. Once it was through, he wound it up and gave it back to me, then he took out another large roll and put it into the reader, stating: "This is the run-time library."

After that was read in, he rolled it up and resumed the program, at which point another paper-tape was produced. "This is the absolute binary," he told me as he rolled it up and labelled it. "I'll get the plotter set up. Get that Bridgeport part-program, then we'll try it out."

I vaguely seem to recall that we had to load perhaps three libraries in order to produce the absolute binary. Also, when we finally ran my program (the absolute binary) it read in just a snatch of the part-program, then the plotter drew a single line and nothing more happened... so I had to do some more work on the source. I omit further reminiscences – but the point of this extended and antiquated narrative is not that particular plot program I was working on.

No; my point is this. I began learning computing in 1973, and since then I have worked on compilers and gotten into many of the most internal and hidden details of operating systems; I have seen many different forms of graphical presentations about what goes on inside a computer, heard lectures and seen movies and animations attempting to present this in a clear and relevant manner. But nothing ever made the entire compile/link/execute operation – that operation which is the entire heart of all development of computer software – nothing has ever made this operation as radically dramatic and tactile and lucid as that experience in the frigid computer room back in 1977, with that oily black paper-tape spewing in heaps on the floor, and Charlie loading tape after tape, winding them up, and annotating them.

Of course there are varieties of compilers and linker/loaders, whole rafts of relocatable libraries, and even run-time libraries, depending upon the particulars of the operating system. But this object lesson (pun intended) is very useful for us to consider the serious limitations that *all* computers have, even if at this point we have long since relegated compile/link/load to the realms of magic. Let's just review:

Step	Load & Execute	Input	Output
1,2	Compiler pass one	Source code	Intermediate code
3,4	Compiler pass two	Intermediate code	Relocatable code
5,6	Relocating loader	Relocatable code, libraries	Absolute binary
7,8	Absolute binary	(user input)	(user output)

Thus, there are four different programs requiring execution, and at least five "files" (in this case, paper-tapes) of varying content: source, two intermediates, at least one library, and the final absolute binary.

If this was a course in introductory compiler design, machine architecture, or operating systems, I might elaborate on the topics of linking, libraries, and execution, but these fascinating topics are deferred. For now, you may be grateful that all those passes and intermediate files are hidden from you – but you ought to realize that the *same sort of work is occurring invisibly* – whether you know it or not. Moreover, and this is the really important thing:

Someone has to know and understand all these steps.

Someone has to grasp their Teleology: their ends, their reasons for occurring: *or they won't happen.* These things are not, emphatically *not*, magic. Arthur C. Clarke wrote a number of interesting stories, but he was quite wrong when he claimed that sufficiently advanced technology is indistinguishable from magic. As I wrote elsewhere:

"Any technology, no matter how advanced, possesses a well-known path leading from the purely sensory study of nature, by a series of completely rational –

moreover, completely teachable – steps, to that technical tool or mechanism or device or method. It is necessarily true – for technology is merely Greek for 'the study of art' – and art is a thing that is done by Man."[143]

Even more important is the fact that the ability to perform such things will be lost if those steps are not taught. They do not exist in nature, and hence are not re-discoverable, though they could readily be re-invented.[144] And the question of re-invention leads us into another fascinating puzzle.

Case Study: More About Compilers

Almost nine years after I started at Frankel I had obtained my M.S. and was working in Florida. I had to come up to speed quickly with this new PASCAL-like language called "C" (that was its name, not its designers' grade). Like PASCAL it had a horrible format, and so the first thing I wrote was a re-formatter to tidy it up and generate a usage list of variables, routines, and so on. Once I was competent in "C" I was assigned to alter their compiler to generate assembly language rather than produce the relocatable binary directly. This strategy would also enable symbolic debugging, which the entire department was eagerly awaiting.

The compiler group had two teams working on the "C" compiler: one handled the "front end" phase which performed the parsing of the source code, the other handled the "back end" phase which performed code generation and optimization. (These are the two fundamental phases of compilation; recall the "Pass One" and "Pass Two" paper-tapes of the old FORTRAN compiler at FEL.) Also there was a master controlling routine which oversaw everything, and a "no-man's-land" region where the transition from "front end" to "back end" occurred; neither of the teams wished to deal with those. Of course I needed to deal with:

(1) the front end, since I needed to know the symbol table and all its intricacies,

(2) the back end, since I had to alter the final output of the code-generation,

and also

(3) no-man's-land, since data had to be transferred between the two phases,

(4) and the master controlling routine which governed the phases, since this now had to invoke the assembler in order to complete the compilation.

That project was a lot of fun, actually, and of course everyone was always checking with me to see how it was going and how soon they would be able to take advantage of symbolic debugging in their own projects.

Now, this study is not about the compiler, or the alterations necessary to generate assembly code, or to accomplish symbolic debugging. Rather, it is about the very curious sort of testing which had to be performed in order to "validate" the new release of that compiler. Especially considering my work in molecular biology and the larger contact of computer science with philosophy, it is well worth examination.

---

[143] Floriani, *The Horrors in the Attic*, part 4 of the Saga *De Bellis Stellarum*.

[144] That is because all these tools, as technical as they are, are true artistic creations of Man, not mathematical formalisms or realities of nature: "You cannot finish a sum how you like. But you can finish a story how you like. When somebody discovered the Differential Calculus there was only one Differential Calculus he could discover. But when Shakespeare killed Romeo he might have married him to Juliet's old nurse if he had felt inclined." GKC, *Orthodoxy* CW1:342. Once the software and its documentation is gone, there cannot be any exploration of the details of its character. One might as well try completing Dickens' unfinished mystery of Edwin Drood – who, odd as it must sound, was an engineer.

There were two parts to the testing and validation for our compiler. The first was a suite of several hundred test programs, together with an invocation script and a verifier utility. In a huge repeat-loop for each of the entries in the test suite, the invocation script called the test-compiler to compile that entry and run it, all of which was stored onto a temporary output file. The verifier was then called to check that output against the "standard" result for that particular entry, and the status was recorded in a performance report. This took a long time, I seem to recall running it overnight. Afterwards, we checked the performance report: there were a handful of known and expected FAILs (these were options permissible to a given implementation); all the rest had to PASS.

Once that test suite had been passed in the acceptable manner, there was another test, and this one is the truly interesting thing about the project.

I had to use my test compiler to *re-compile the compiler itself* – and this had to be performed three times, each new compile using the result of the last compile.

Whoa. Do you understand that?

(Note: if you got lost when you read the study about all those paper-tapes, you might want to practice some more. Maybe get a mirror and try drawing a picture of yourself as you draw a picture of yourself... Ahem. Can you spell *Recursion?*)

Now, let us try this again. Here is the situation. We have a currently existing "good" compiler validated previously, which we shall call C_0. We also have my revised source code for a symbolic-debugging compiler, which we call S. For the sake of explanation, we shall define the compiler to be a function $\chi(\sigma) = \beta$ where χ is the compiler, σ is a source file, and β is its corresponding object (executable) file.

So here are the four steps I had to do:

1. $C_0(S) = C_1$ this was the initial project, producing a new compiler.
2. $C_1(S) = C_2$ the first testing step
3. $C_2(S) = C_3$ the second testing step
4. $C_3(S) = C_4$ the third testing step

Presumably, at this point C_3 and C_4 ought to be identical.

Well, the funny thing was that at step 2, something broke, and the compile failed. Of course since the symbolic debugging was already functional, I could take advantage of it, but here was the hard, hard, HARD thing about debugging.

I had to figure out where the problem was in *two* senses. One was where in the compiler (the C_1 program) things went wrong – which meant that C_1 was running. But it also meant that I had to figure out where *in the very same compiler* (that is, however, considered as the source code, S) the problem was arising.

Fascinating.

No, I don't recall exactly what the error was, and it's not really relevant to the matter anyway. And I did get it fixed, and validated, and there was joy. But the fun of all this was looking at the *same* piece of software in two *very different* ways.

Speaking of ways: there are several other ways of looking at this self-reflective topic...

So, did you get a mirror and try drawing a picture of yourself as you draw a picture of yourself?

Oh, you're not a very good artist? (Neither am I. All my humans look like comic-strip characters.) All right then, maybe you'd prefer a little assignment in programming. Then try this:

Assignment: Write a program which prints itself out.

While you think about that I will tell you about some others. Of course as a computer scientist the first thing which flies into the consciousness is *recursion*, a powerful tool which we have already discussed. But since you are valiantly trying to handle that little programming project, and we are trying to proceed according to the "doctrinal methods of the thirteenth century" (which means using any and every means, practical or theoretical, at our disposal) let's see some which come from other fields.

1. Perhaps the simplest is this:

abbr.

which is the abbreviation for "abbreviation."

2. In molecular biology we learn that the enzyme called "DNA polymerase" (which is the machine which replicates DNA) as well as all the machinery (the ribosome, transport RNA, and other components) can all be found coded within the DNA which they are called upon to replicate. This self-referential machinery is common to all living things, and indeed is the fundamental self-reference required for a thing to be able to grow and reproduce. (One needs to imagine a copier which can not only copy its own blueprints, but every part of its machinery...)

3. This is rather mystical, and yet I find it significant. When Christ is giving His final commands to the Apostles (see Matthew 28:18-20) He says this:

"Teaching them to observe all things whatsoever I have commanded you."

Which, since He is commanding them, clearly includes *that* command as well. Hence it is the fundamental self-reference by which the Church grows, just like the living things studied by biology.

All right, have you worked out your little project? Still staring at the blank screen, are you? Oh. Well, come on, just start, and maybe you'll see what's needed.

I'm aware that there are various schemes for doing this, though I've never bothered to look up how others do it. I've written it myself, and no doubt it could be shortened, or done with more style, but the fun of this is like any other solitaire game: it's so easy to state, one just wants to try working it out for one's self. One solution is in the samples at the end of this book, and on our website, though I do think you're missing out on a piece of fun if you don't try it for yourself.

Case Study: a Track Cam

Frankel Engineering was a small consulting house, and one of the best things about it was the extreme mixture of different sorts of problems we encountered from day to day. We might be working on a long-term project like the development of a software package for something, and meanwhile a customer would call or stop in with some short-term project. For example:

One day perhaps in 1980 Charlie and I were both busy with our own work when we heard the door open, and an older man came in together with a "grunt" worker who was carrying something large. They were, if I recall, from a company which made the machines to manufacture cigars.

"Hello, Ed," Charlie greeted him.

"Hello Charlie." The older man signalled to the grunt who placed the object on the desk in front of Charlie.

Charlie looked at it: a disk, a heavy chunk of metal maybe about a foot across and about two inches thick, in which was a central hole, say an inch in diameter, and a smaller one a couple inches away. Around these was gouged a deep channel about an inch wide and deep, but it was *not* perfectly circular: it wriggled smoothly but irregularly as it went around the disk.

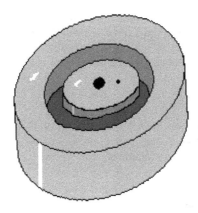

Charlie nodded. "A track cam."

"Yep."

"What do you need?"

"Another one."

"No blueprint, I guess?"

Ed shook his head. "Nope. Probably made by hand, maybe back at the turn of the century."

Charlie shrugged, then turned to me. "Pete? Any thoughts? Maybe we make a tracing, then digitize it?"

I came over and looked at it. "Sounds like an idea... hold on. We'll have to curve-fit the points, and..."

You may be wondering if I had forgotten my comments about our tour guide at Lehigh – since the curve of this track cam will not be a mathematical "function" – but that was not a problem. However there were other issues which we had to deal with.

So, while Charlie made a tracing of that track cam, I set up a list of the issues, and then we discussed them:

1. Assume the center of the central hole is the Cartesian origin. Get its diameter.

2. Assuming the center of the offset hole is on the x-axis, get its location and diameter.

3. Find out what diameter end-mill Ed wants to use for cutting the track.

4. Get a fairly dense collection of points along both edges of the track. Also obtain its depth.

5. Perform a curve-fit of that collection, making sure it is "smooth"; its smallest radius of curvature must not go below the size of the end-mill.

Once Charlie had a tracing, I took it to our plotter and began digitizing the curves. The plotter was a flatbed plotter, capable of handling paper about a foot or so by a foot and a half; it had a special sighting device which you put into its penholder instead of the usual felt-tip pens. There were four "steering" buttons to move the pen, and the plotter could "sense" its geometric position when one pressed a special key on its control panel – and we had a little utility which used this feature to collect a series of positions. This was a bit tedious, but not very difficult. Once we had a bunch of points, we plotted them, just to see how close we came to the actual cam.

As Charlie compared the plot with the actual cam we talked.

"So what is this thing for?" I asked.

"Well, this big hole is its turning axis, and the other hole is probably to get it aligned with the rest of the machinery. Then a roller rides inside that track, and as the cam turns, some lever moves up and down as the roller follows that track. Probably cuts off the tobacco leaf – they make machinery to produce cigars."

"Oh."

"So what about curve fitting? It's a closed curve, so it's not a function."

"Well, we handle that by using the parametric form: we let both x and y be a function of the point's index. Now, the trick is to get the thing to be just as smooth where the two ends meet as it is throughout the rest of the curve... and fortunately, our curve fit is almost tailor-made to handle it."

"How?"

"You know how two points determine a line, and three points a parabola. This technique takes every four points and fits a cubic equation to them. There's a few constants to be solved for, and we simply require the first derivatives to match at the junctions between intervals, which gives us a smooth curve as a result. So what we'll do is adjust what happens at the start and end of the four-point intervals, make the two curves link up so it's a closed loop."

"I see... so you'll change the program and then generate a series of points at an even increment..."

"Right. I've also got to check that the radius of curvature of the fitted curve doesn't get smaller than the tool size he's going to use, and then do the offset. And you're going to write up the rest of the stuff to drill those two holes and the starting and ending tool motions?"

"Right.... unless somebody comes in with another problem."

Now I don't have the code any more, and if you want to see how to compute cubic splines, you might try deriving it for yourself.[145] Then, if you are going to handle a track cam, you also must arrange things so that the curve for one group of four points unites correctly with the next group of four points, considering that the "last" group must mate with the "first" group. And don't forget you'll have to offset that curve once you have it, and that means you'll need the first derivative, since we're not going to attempt milling with a tool exactly as wide as the track!

The point here is not the elegant numerical method. It's cooperation between specialists and knowing your toolbox well enough that you can use them (with maybe some minor revisions) to deal with any odd problem that somebody brings in.

And yes: after a relatively short time, the program was changed, we computed the curve and evaluated it at a suitable interval, set up the part-program and ran off a test on our plotter, and then punched it onto paper-tape. Then Charlie called Ed who

---

[145] We are given four pairs of x-y coordinates and all four pairs must satisfy the cubic $y = Ax^3+Bx^2+Cx+D$ for some constants A, B, C, D, which is four equations in four unknowns. However, the method is a bit more involved as we need to manage the "smoothness"; see any numerical methods text for details on cubic splines and other curve fitting techniques.

came by and picked up the original cam, a paper-tape, a listing, and the plot. He was happy, and we went back to our other duties.

Case Study: About Multiplying

Some time later, I was working in Harrisburg when an industrial engineer came to my cubicle and said, "How good is your computer at multiplying?"

I shrugged. "What do you mean?"

"I can't get my calculator to handle this equation."

"What equation?"

"The hypergeometric probability equation. We're doing a sample from the run of a new product, and if we assume a given failure rate, we need to know the chances of finding failed components in our samples..." He handed me a sheet of paper on which was written:

$$p(x) = \frac{\binom{d}{x}\binom{N-d}{n-x}}{\binom{N}{n}}$$

Hypergeometric probability mass function [146]

I saw those combinatorics and suppressed a grimace. "All right, so what values do you have?"

He began: "N is 10,000..."[147]

Yes, well. Even 30 years later, there aren't any computers that can handle the general combination of 10,000 things directly.[148] So I asked him for the other parameters he was using, and told him I would write a program for him.

Here are the meanings of the variables in the above equation, and some example values:

N	total number of items (10,000)
d	total number of defective items (50)
N–d	total number of good items (9,950)
n	sample size selected *without* replacement (100)
x	number of defective items in the sample (explore between 0 and 50)

Obviously we have everything we need: the values and the equation. The problem is that the equation contains combinatorics which will require the factorial of 10,000.

---

[146] See (e.g.) *Modern Probability Theory and Its Applications*, 179.

[147] While I distinctly recall 10,000 was the total number, the rest of the values I have forgotten, but as you will see they are irrelevant to the issue to be discussed.

[148] On a typical 32-bit personal computer one can use floating-point to compute up to $\binom{10,000}{134}$ which is about 2.05e307, but after this the value goes out of range. (The upper limit of floating-point for the HP we used was 1e77.) Of course there are tools which transcend the limitations of the machinery by performing computations symbolically, but we had none at that time.

Recall that the combinatoric $\binom{n}{r}$ is the function which computes the number of combinations (*not* permutations) of n things taken r at a time:

$$\binom{n}{r} = \frac{n!}{r!(n-r)!}$$

So... Do *you* know how to help our colleague industrial engineer?

A Hint.
Remember that this has to compute a *probability*, which will be between zero and one – and since the equation is a fraction, somehow no matter how large the numerator gets, it's going to be compensated for by a large denominator.

An Answer.
The trick of course, is to expand the combinatorics then apply the algebraic properties of multiplication.

$$p(x) = \frac{\binom{d}{x}\binom{N-d}{n-x}}{\binom{N}{n}}$$

Expanding the combinatorics, we get:

$$p(x) = \frac{\dfrac{d!}{(d-x)!x!} \cdot \dfrac{(N-d)!}{((N-d)-(n-x))!(n-x)!}}{\dfrac{N!}{(N-n)!n!}}$$

After rearranging the fraction:

$$p(x) = \frac{d!\,(N-d)!\,(N-n)!\,n!}{(d-x)!\,(N-d-(n-x))!\,N!\,(n-x)!x!}$$

Arranging this so that each of the four factorials in the numerator has a similar factorial in the denominator, we have:

$$p(x)=\left(\frac{d!}{(d-x)!}\right)\left(\frac{(N-d)!}{(N-d-(n-x))!}\right)\left(\frac{n!}{(n-x)!}\right)\left(\frac{(N-n)!}{N!}\right)\left(\frac{1}{x!}\right)$$

We can write out these "upper factorials" like this:
$T_1 = d(d-1)(d-2) \dots (d-x+1)$
$T_2 = (N-d)(N-d-1)(N-d-2) \dots (N-d-(n-x)+1)$
$T_3 = n(n-1)(n-2) \dots (n-x+1)$

128

$$D_1 = 1/(N(N-1)(N-2) \ldots (N-n+1))$$
$$D_2 = 1/(x(x-1)(x-2) \ldots 2)$$

So that the original equation now looks like this:

$$p(x) = T_1 \cdot T_2 \cdot T_3 \cdot D_1 \cdot D_2$$

Now, we apply associativity and commutativity, arranging both numerator and denominator so as to deal with the largest terms first, thus keeping everything in bounds. We are thus able to compute a series of terms, one from the numerator and one from the denominator, divide just those terms, and produce a new running product by multiplying by that fraction. The code for one possible solution is available on the website, but you ought to try implementing it for yourself, just for fun. Here are the first few values from my code:

x	$p(x)$
1	0.306698
2	0.075507
3	0.012016
4	0.001390
5	0.000125

So if there are 50 defective items in a group of 10,000, there's just over a 30 percent chance that there will be one defective in a sample of 100.

Now that we have struggled through this example from the Real World, let's explore the factorial and see what we ought to expect.

Some Notes on the Factorial

The factorial comes up in many problems in which one desires to count the permutations or combinations of things. It is simply defined using the big-pi notation:

$$n! = \prod_{i=1}^{n} i \qquad \text{for } n > 0.$$

Usually we also extend the definition so that $0! = 1$. So, using this iterative definition, the code for factorial is remarkably easy to write:

```
int function factorial(int n)
{
    int i,p;
    p=1;
    for(i=1;i<=n;i=i+1)
        p=p*i;
    return p;
}
```

Another definition is also used in order to exemplify recursion:

$$n! = \begin{cases} 1 & n < 2 \\ n(n-1)! & \text{otherwise} \end{cases}$$

Which may be implemented in this manner:

```
int function factorial(int n)
{
    if(n<2)
        return 1;
    else
        return n*factorial(n-1);
}
```

While it may have some vague utility as an introduction to the idea, this sort of implementation, however, ought not be used in actual software. As we have seen, recursion is a very powerful idea, and it must be paid for: there is a fair amount of additional code (not to say *hidden* code), and that code uses both time and memory.

Moreover, the point of actually *writing* a function to implement the factorial is a bit wasteful, whether using a loop or recursion, since there are so few factorials which can actually be represented using the standard data-storage types: 32-bit, 64-bit, or even floating-point, and it's faster to look up the value in a table. While you might wish to work out these limits for yourself, this is a reference book, so here are the cut-off values:

type	n	value of n!
32-bit	12	479001600 (4e8)
64-bit	20	2432902008176640000 (over 2e20)
double	170	about 7.2574156e306

The integers may be either signed or unsigned, as the additional bit does not help. The "double" means the double-precision floating point type-declaration in "C" on a common x86-based personal computer.

If you need the actual values of factorial for a real program, see the website, or else compute the values into a table *once* at initialization time. Also see Appendix 3 for a table.

Finally, please remember that if you are aiming for a *probability* based upon factorials, you will probably want to do some manipulation of the equation to keep the intermediate results within bounds. The same trick can often be used in similar cases involving rapidly-growing functions.

Case Study: an Elementary Merge

This technique might be considered a sort of fond homage to the "three-way IF" of old FORTRAN, which enabled transfer of control based on whether a given value was less than zero, equal to zero, or greater than zero. In order to properly set the stage for this problem, I would like to sketch it with some visual aids, namely, a pack of standard playing cards. Choose just a few black cards and arrange them in two rows, side-by-side, but put each row into ascending order by the card rank: Ace, 2, 3, ..., 10, Jack, Queen, King, ignoring the difference in suits.
For example:

♣A♠4♣7♠7♣9♠Q   ♠3♣4♠5♠8♠K♣K

Now, we are going to *merge* these two rows so that the result is one row, and the cards are still sorted, so that we have:

♣A♠3♠4♣4♣5♣7♠7♠8♣9♠Q♠K♣K

We note that we ought to take advantage of the fact that the two original rows are already in sorted order: efficiency means that we can't merely append one row to the other and sort the result.

The technique is simple. We merely point to the first list with the left hand, and the second list with the right hand, and consider just those two cards: whichever is smaller goes next, and we shift that hand along. When there are no longer any cards in one of the lists, we proceed to handle the rest of the remaining list, and when both lists are gone, we're done.

Since the rows have a "handedness" (the left row and right row are equivalent from the routine's view) it has chiral symmetry. As noted in the code, other applications may demand special handling for the case when both lists contain identical items. Also, there are ways of simplifying the end-of-list cases, but these niceties are left as exercises for the reader.

Case Study: Arrowheads

Now let's go in a different direction and look at a simple piece of code which draws an arrowhead on a given vector. It comes in handy when you want to draw a graph (that is, a set of nodes and edges, not an x-y plot of an equation), or even if you are merely trying to debug some messy diagram, like the original polygon in the "island" example.

We are given:

(x_1, y_1)	the from-point
(x_2, y_2)	the to-point (where the arrowhead will go)
s	length of the arrowhead (constant)
β	angle between the arrowhead and the given vector (constant)

We will also need the library routine to draw a line segment, something like this:

```
void DrawSegment(xfrom, yfrom, xto, yto)
```

In order to draw an arrowhead, we have to determine two additional points (xa_1, ya_1) and (xa_2, ya_2) which are a distance s away from the to-point, such that the angle between the given vector and a line from each of them to the to-point is β. Like this:

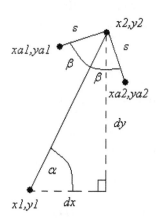

It's a very easy thing to do, providing one knows trigonometry: one simply determines α, the angle of the given vector, then adds or subtracts the arrow-angle β to determine the two endpoints of the arrowhead.

But in order to get the angle of the vector we would need to call an arctangent function, and then we'll have to compute a sine and a cosine for the sum and

131

difference... all this seems a bit over-complicated, and one wonders whether there isn't a more tidy way.

Well, of course there is – it's basic trig – and it is instructive to see how it is done. We can readily get the sine and cosine of α by the following. Let

$$dx = x_2 - x_1$$
$$dy = y_2 - y_1$$
$$d = (dx^2 + dy^2)^{1/2}$$

Then (assuming d is not zero) we can compute the cosine and sine of α easily:

$$\cos(\alpha) = dx/d$$
$$\sin(\alpha) = dy/d$$

Also, we can pre-compute the sine and cosine for the (constant) arrow angle. We're almost ready to proceed – we merely need to get the identities for sine and cosine of sums and differences of two angles, which look like this:

$$\sin(\alpha + \beta) = \sin(\alpha)\cos(\beta) + \cos(\alpha)\sin(\beta)$$
$$\cos(\alpha + \beta) = \cos(\alpha)\cos(\beta) - \sin(\alpha)\sin(\beta)$$
$$\sin(\alpha - \beta) = \sin(\alpha)\cos(\beta) - \cos(\alpha)\sin(\beta)$$
$$\cos(\alpha - \beta) = \cos(\alpha)\cos(\beta) + \sin(\alpha)\sin(\beta)$$

Now, in order to find (xa_1, ya_1), we simply compute the sine and cosine of $\alpha+180-\beta$. First, we observe that

$$\sin(\alpha + 180) = -\sin(\alpha)$$
$$\cos(\alpha + 180) = -\cos(\alpha)$$

Then:

$$\sin(\alpha+180-\beta) = - (\sin(\alpha)\cos(\beta) - \cos(\alpha)\sin(\beta))$$
$$\cos(\alpha+180-\beta) = - (\cos(\alpha)\cos(\beta) + \sin(\alpha)\sin(\beta))$$

So the desired coordinate is

$$xa_1 = x_2 - s \cdot (\cos(\alpha)\cos(\beta) + \sin(\alpha)\sin(\beta))$$
$$ya_1 = y_2 - s \cdot (\sin(\alpha)\cos(\beta) - \cos(\alpha)\sin(\beta))$$

To get the other point we perform the same computation for $\alpha+180+\beta$:

$$\sin(\alpha+180+\beta) = - (\sin(\alpha)\cos(\beta) + \cos(\alpha)\sin(\beta))$$
$$\cos(\alpha+180+\beta) = - (\cos(\alpha)\cos(\beta) - \sin(\alpha)\sin(\beta))$$

So the desired coordinate is

$$xa_2 = x_2 - s \cdot (\cos(\alpha)\cos(\beta) - \sin(\alpha)\sin(\beta))$$
$$ya_2 = y_2 - s \cdot (\sin(\alpha)\cos(\beta) + \cos(\alpha)\sin(\beta))$$

Granted the savings of avoiding an arctangent and another sine and cosine is relatively minimal, but this is a simple example of how the powerful tools available to us in algebra and trigonometry can be put to use when performance matters. You ought to think through the computation in any case, and be sure not to overlook special cases, such as the fact that tangent "goes to infinity" at the odd multiples of $\pi/4$. Be sure to consider trig identities before simply resorting to library routines like arctangent.

Case Study: Hypocycloids

Now, let us see a somewhat more sophisticated graphics problem, which will scare off a lot of readers if I say it treats of the representation of the two-dimensional curve called a *hypocycloid*, which is generated by having a smaller circle rotate within a larger one without slipping. It is a very elegant diagram, and one used to be able to buy a very cool toy made of plastic gears by which you could draw them yourself. It was called a SPIROGRAPH. I got one for Christmas sometime in the late 1960s, and had a lot of fun with it.

It was March 24, 1977. I was at Lehigh, and I had just helped a friend work out a messy problem in trigonometry which required handling a kind of double rotation, and to my surprise I suddenly realized that the math I had done would enable me to generate the same sorts of curves as that toy, but without the fuss. The next day, when I happened to visit the CDC (as I did very frequently those days), I peered in the window at the operations console and saw that those good old plotters were presently loaded with *liquid ink* which made the plots far nicer than the usual ballpoint pens, I decided to set up the program... and soon I had my own very elegant hypocycloids. The routine is easy to write, though the math is a bit tricky to set up. Like the arrowheads, it uses the sum-of-angles equations. You ought to try working out the mathematics for yourself, it's well worth the effort.

Incidentally, the designs are a lot more interesting when one uses a prime, and generates all the steps from 1 up to half that prime, like this one for 13:

Hypocycloids with ratios 1/13, 2/13, 3/13, 4/13, 5/13, 6/13.

Note that one can also make very nice figures merely using *straight* lines to link the vertices of a regular polygon. That program is quite simple to write and its results are satisfactory: you can admire them on the screen, or print them out and have fun making "extreme" stained glass windows. (That is why you should keep a box of crayons or colored pencils around; you never know when they will come in handy.)

Speaking of making things based on regular polygons, this is the best place to insert something which I had promised myself to include, simply because it happened while I was working on my doctorate – but also because it is so unusual.

Case Study: Seven-pointed Snowflakes.
Or, How I Got in Trouble in Grad School Making Christmas Decorations.

Not because they were religious. And not, like Calvin (of the famous "Calvin and Hobbes" comics) drawing his famous "stegosaurs in spaceships," because I was drawing them during class. I got in deep trouble by making *seven-pointed snowflakes* to help decorate the Computer Science office. Yes, you read that correctly. Snowflakes with *seven* points. But you can make them too. Here's what you need:

1. Sheet of white paper.
2. Circle-drawing tool (a compass, big dish (hee hee), or something round).
3. Protractor.
4. Pencil.
5. Scissors.
6. Ruler.

Instructions:

1. Use your circle drawing tool to draw a nice big circle on your white paper – however big a snowflake you want.

2. Cut along the circle, so you will have a nice round piece of paper. You can save the scraps for making "Who-ville" style zam-zoogles or pamfunals to pile on your floor or to hang on your Christmas Tree, or for writing notes, or chopping into confetti for New Year's or whatever other decoration you may need.

3. Take your round paper and fold it in half, then open it up and lay it with the fold vertical, like this:

(Yes, it's kind of like a Greek "Phi." And if I add a triangle we'd have the "deathly hallows" if you know what that is. But this is an even more fantastic use of magic.)

4. Using your protractor, mark off *six* ticks, each 25 and 5/7th degrees apart, or at:

    25.7 degrees
    51.4 degrees
    77.1 degrees
    102.8 degrees
    128.5 degrees
    154.3 degrees

or as close to these values as you can get. (You can probably estimate it by hand: just space *six* ticks evenly along the edge of the half-circle.) Now it should look like this:

5. Fold it along the seam. Then, using the ruler, draw very faint lines from each tick to the center, like this:

6. Now, this is the tricky part. You have to fold your half-circle into a kind of fan, along each of those six lines you have just drawn. BUT! You have to fold each successive line the *opposite* way from the previous fold, so you'll get a kind of fan. It will look like this:

Try it, it's not hard. You're almost there.

7. Now, make it nice and flat, so it looks like a long isosceles triangle with a curved base:

8. Using the scissors, clip out little triangles or other shapes along all the sides. I often trim off the point at a nicely skewed angle...

9. Now you will have a strange looking triangle full of holes, sort of like Charlie Brown's "ghost" costume. Here's what it will look like, still folded up:

10. Now for the fun part. Open it up, and lay it flat. Wow. You now have a snowflake with *seven* points! Wow.

I won't show you the final result, because you need to have the fun of doing it for yourself. No one will believe you, and if you are careful not to let your pencil marks show, no one will guess how you did it.

Here's what happened when I was in grad school. I hung mine up in the office and waited for one of my friends to come by. Then I said, "Hey what do you think of the snowflake I made?"

The friend, who found it hard to believe someone as old as me, who was working on a doctorate, would bother to make such a childish thing – but being courteous, would say, "Well, it's nice."

I kept staring at it – then I'd point at it and in a glum tone say, "*Oh, dear*. Look at what happened. I made it with *seven* points, not six!"

The friend would look – then look again, and count the points carefully and say, "What do you know! Sure it has seven! How did you do *that*?"

To which I'd reply, "Oh I must have folded it wrong or something..."

Of course some can tell right away, but others are glad to learn yet another cunning application of science.

Oh yes, there's a secret, which you may be able to figure out, even if you are not a grad student. But I am not going to tell you here, since it is rather obvious.

Case Study: An Early Plotter Problem and the Plot System

In a future volume you will hear about some of the fascinating problems one of FEL's customers brought to us back in the late 1970s. A local company, Reading Sheet Metal, had a CNC punch press, and one of their requests led to an important development in our software collection, one which became an industry standard. (Not due to our version, of course; others were working on this too.)

In a previous Study, I explained about Numerical Control of machine tools and how part-programs are developed from a blueprint by mathematics and engineering; the result was then punched into paper-tape for feeding into the automatic (NC) machine tool. Running a test of a part-program took time and materials, and kept the machine tool from making useful products – so most machine shops liked to have some sort of graphical verification of the part-programs. And so, it was either very late 1977 or early 1978, at a time when FEL had not yet bought the HP 3000 but was still using the two old workhorse HP 2116 machines, that Reading Sheet Metal decided to buy a small flat-bed plotter, and asked us to write a plot program to verify the part-programs for their CNC punch press which they generated using our software.

It was a fascinating problem to write the program, partly due to the horrible documentation, partly due to the even more horrible and strangely devised "coding" that plotter used – it was hard since the BASIC we then used had no facility to print any arbitrary ASCII character, and the plotter's codes required certain symbols we could not readily produce, such as the lower-case letters. That was settled by a very interesting technique, which is worth telling about.

I was looking into the question of printing arbitrary characters, and remembered that Charlie had a little program that could produce "man-readable" characters, and another which translated a part-program into the old EIA character set, which unlike ASCII was odd-parity. He had a file of "special symbols" which were read in by the program – and I asked how that file had been produced. He told me they had used a special low-level debugging tool which enabled display or alteration of individual sectors of the disk drive; they started with a file of plain ASCII, then altered the disk sector so it had the necessary characters. So I did the same thing, except that I put all 256 possible bytes into four strings, each 64 characters long. (That old BASIC we used had a string limit of 80, the size of the old punch-cards; a good bit shorter than that popular "Twit" thing.) And once we had all 256, everything was straightforward. We still had to work through the very unusual formatting of the plotter instructions, but it was done, and soon we were producing plots of punch press part-programs.

However, the project raised some important issues. First was the question of *mapping*: of deciding on how to scale or "project" the coordinates of a selected region of the part-program into a drawing area. Related to this was the issue of *clipping* –

handling the portions which were excluded from view. We also talked about what would happen if we had to control other plotters – we discussed the idea of having a library of routines to handle all this, but we held off further work since in the summer of 1978 we had our new HP 3000 installed, and the picture changed.

We decided to arrange a set of library routines which would handle general plotting tasks, beginning with mapping and clipping. We called this the "FEL Plot System" or PlotSys for short. The operating system of the HP had a facility to permit a running program to dynamically link to a selected routine in the system library, and we used that to enable the user to select the kind of plotter at run-time, thus making the Plot System device-independent. In following years we handled plotters and also graphics terminals from several different suppliers; these required dealing with several interesting riddles.

For example, drawing a line between two given coordinates using only the motions possible to a given plotter. Recall that the plotter I used for drawing music at Lehigh could only perform the moves of a chess king on a 0.01 inch grid. Another plotter was more like a queen, moving multiple steps in both x and y, but there was a small upper limit – suggesting a kind of quantum mechanics – and thus we had to arrange an interpolation mechanism to enable drawing lines of arbitrary slope. Arcs are frequently needed, and most plotters could not plot arcs, so these had to be arranged. Labels of printed characters were also needed, along with minor utilities such as dashed or dotted lines, and so on.

The ever-increasing growth of interaction (which would culminate some years later in the mousey color graphics of desktop computers) began tending towards what we now call "CAD" and "CAM" (computer-aided design and manufacturing), and we tried to explore the possibility of implementing a drawing editor (a simple version of a CAD system) on the HP 3000.

Alas, there was one serious difficulty here, one we knew about, and warned about – but... Ah well; let us not be concerned with such non-technical matters here. It was deemed necessary to have the ability to make "a free-hand sketch." Remember, there were no mouses (mice?) yet – so we got a "wand" (a kind of electronic pen).

However, the wand was only accessible through a regular terminal, and hence was handled by the system as if there was a *human user* at the other end, typing. As I discussed elsewhere, that system's I/O capabilities were intended for business-type data entry, not for device-intensive use – in particular there was no way of arranging to handle general "interrupts" from an external device. (Of course the machine detected them, but the operating system provided no way to use them.) The result was that the free-hand sketch would work up to a point – and then, when the system was busy capturing the fields from a data-entry screen, or locking some values in a database,[149] there would be gaps where the wand was ignored. The "smooth curve" we expected to draw had strange gaps where no data had been captured.

---

[149] Contrary to good design, and to their marketing proclamations, the database was intimately bound to that system, as has been the case ever since. Of course such design is a debatable topic: I once talked about "spooling" (i.e. background printing) with an operating system programmer at Harris. He was fervently opposed to including such an "application topic" in the purity of their operating system. I never learned what he considered the main purpose of the OS; perhaps it was only memory and process management, which to me seems to be a dangerously minimal view. Even worse is the maximal view taken by Dillinger and the MCP in "TRON": there ought not be *any* user applications at all; *everything* was the business of the System, which was therefore in sole control. This is deep metaphysics indeed. Recall *medio*

Alas-squared. That project was never brought to a satisfactory conclusion, but then that system was not appropriate for the problem.

But our Plot System was a true triumph in so many ways it is hard to recall specific examples. Every graphics program would work on any plotter for which we had written a driver; this pleased our customers and simplified our own work. It was easy to enlarge the driver collection, and it did not require alteration of the existing graphics applications. Also, strange to report, we had anticipated (or followed) the growing tendency of the industry, which had already begun standardizing device-independent graphics libraries in schemes like the SIGGraph "CORE" of the ACM. And though we never went very far with three-dimensional stuff, we did have some projection tools and used them to good effect on various difficult NC projects.

Case Study: Industrial-strength Simulation of an Old Computer

As I mentioned earlier the first computer I learned was the powerful CDC 6400. The second computer I encountered (meaning studied and programmed) was the famous little workhorse called the PDP-8, built by Digital Equipment Corporation. This had a 12-bit word, a very small instruction set, relatively limited I/O (paper-tape and Teletype; no disk drive), and while it had those much-desired blinking lights and a bunch of switches, it was in almost every way the polar opposite to the CDC. Small, single-use, extremely limited – and yet it was intimate, and so it permitted a degree of experimentation not possible with the large, expensive, multi-user machine. Moreover, since I had already learned the assembly language for the CDC, which requires learning a fair amount about the machine architecture, I found the assembly language and architecture for the PDP-8 almost trivial.

One curious detail about the machine I used at college: at some point someone had arranged a "tap" onto one of the bits of the accumulator, and sent that line into an amplifier attached to a small speaker. Thus, by appropriately flipping that bit in the accumulator at properly computed intervals, one could generate tones of various pitches. It didn't take me long to analyze this program and generalize it so as to play a specified "file" (actually a paper-tape) of coded music. Lots of fun.

I have decided to do a Case Study of this antique for a very funny reason: I encountered it again in my industrial experience, in a very curious situation. This occurred in October of 1982 when I worked at FEL: Grumman Aerospace had bought a new computer and was purchasing our punch press software. This was a user-oriented tool which would enable them to produce part-programs for their numerically controlled punch press: using the blueprints for a given part to be made from sheet metal, they would write instructions about the layout, cutout shapes, and repeating patterns to be punched, and submit these to our software. A plot was made of the work to be done, then a paper-tape for the part-program was punched. That tape would then be fed into the punch press in order to produce the part.[150]

---

tutissimus ibis = "you will go most safely in the middle"; also see the discussion on the "permissive blood pressure" of the heart in my *Subsidiarity*.

[150] This punch press software raises several interesting issues which will be explored in a future volume of this series. The plotter, incidentally, was controlled by our Plot System which we discussed earlier; moreover, it was a major difficulty for us when it was delivered, since the Hardware Manufacturer didn't provide *any* manuals for it, and the customer was there waiting to see it work. The sales rep was in a panic talking with the factory... let's just say it's a good thing we had the Plot System.

At some point they mentioned they had a large inventory of existing "programs" (the instructions regarding layout, etc.) which they had composed using an older punch press package, and they wanted to know how they could use them. We inquired about the software they were using, and were told it was a very old package that ran on a small machine known as a PDP-8... I smiled when I heard that.

So we discussed possibilities. They had the user manual and the binary for that old package, but no source code, and the company which wrote it had long since vanished. They didn't want to continue to maintain the old PDP-8, since they now had a new computer with our new software. The question was: how hard would it be to replicate that old package on the new computer?

After further discussion, we decided it would be easier and safer to implement a *simulator* of the PDP-8, which would then execute the *existing* program. This would preclude our overlooking any odd special cases in a new implementation.

Yes, you read that correctly. I "built" a PDP-8 *inside* our HP 3000, in software, and then ran the customer's *old existing* program on that simulator.

It sounds crazy, almost bizarre: but we got the job done and far more importantly, we satisfied the customer.

Now, I am not going to lecture about writing a simulator on one computer for *another* computer – not here and now, anyway. Rather I want to tell you something about the project which is of real technical interest, especially relative to machine efficiencies and planning for future machines.

Since the crucial limitation of this program would be *time*, I built into the simulator a performance-tracking facility to count how many times each of the machine instructions were performed. After the simulator was complete and we had tried it out with some of the customer's files, I examined the various rates of instruction use.

There wasn't much to be done to improve the major computational instructions, which had to perform their operation in the same manner as the original machine. But I wondered about the use of the old machine's "JMS" (jump-to-subroutine) instruction. We might see some speed improvement if we could somehow augment the simulator by determining what some of the routines were doing. So I changed the simulator to record the number of distinct subroutine addresses and tally those. Two routines were used exceedingly many times, so I examined the original binary to see what was going on there.

These proved to be multi-word bit shifters used for performing multiplication and division. After determining where the calling code left its arguments and where it expected the result, I added a new piece of "firmware" by substituting simulation of two new "multi-word shift" instructions for one of the unused I/O (opcode 6) instructions. I patched the original code to use these new instructions rather than performing the old JMS, then ran the test again. This gave an amazing improvement, on the order of thirty percent.

With these alterations of "firmware," our simulator was running at a speed comparable to that of the original machine. Moreover, the input and output was handled in files, not on paper-tapes (except at the final step, as these were required by the punch press). Thus, the user had a great deal of new flexibility to handle his work.

Another portion of the story came a decade later, when I taught two semesters of assembly language programming. I wrote an entirely new simulator to be a user-oriented "lab kit" sort of tool to run on a PC, added a miniature assembler, and provided these utilities for my class. They were a bit disappointed at having to learn the programming for such an obsolete machine, but as I explained, *all* the major topics of machine architecture and memory access would be encountered: indeed, the *entire* suite of machine instructions could be covered in detail – which would not be possible for an x86-based CPU. Moreover, the students could do some curious things as step through an interrupt, or see an animated display of the machine and memory, none of which could be done on a physical machine. Debugging in general is far easier on a machine simulator. (As a reward for their struggles with that antique, I had them write the recursive "mondrian" graphics program on the x86 machine, which they found enjoyable.)

Case Study: More About Simulation

That PDP-8 simulator was a lot of fun to work on, though of course only in rare cases will such an approach provide an acceptable solution to a real need. Simulation, however is a powerful technique, and can be used with profit in other situations. For example, in a graduate-level operating systems class, we had to simulate the various job and service queues of an imaginary operating system, then perform experiments using our simulator to see the effects on throughput of changes like adding another disk drive and so forth. As you may have expected, I approached this project with some delight, because it reminded me vividly of my experience with the Operating Console for the CDC 6400 – and since I had already done my Master's Thesis on the "animation of algorithms," I made the assignment a good deal more fun by *animating* it. The result was indeed similar to the amazing screens of SCOPE's DSD displays...

```
MPL  4 n 22 351.3970        C       P       I 22  5        JOBTABLE
                                                          1   637  -   1.4495
QUEUE   lopri  8 hipri   1   cpu  1  page  0  io  0        2   635  L   0.2320
                                                          3   656  L   0.4330
        15          6        13                           4
        12                                                5   659  I   0.2540
         1                                                6   666  H
         3                                                7
         2                                                8
        16                                                9
        17                                               10
        11                                               11   643  1   0.0400
                                                         12   644  -   0.5045
                                                         13   647  c   0.1170
                                                         14
                                                         15   629  -   2.4115
                                                         16   642  L   0.3090
                                                         17   661  L   0.9710
                                                         18
                                                         19
                                                         20
                                                         21
                                                         22   662  I   0.0030
345.0740 cp  7 J 657 START  0.1700                       23
345.1240 cp  1 J 637 START  1.9580                       24
345.8915 cp 19 J 649 START  0.0830                       25
345.9005 cp 22 J 638 END    0.9230   5.4355              26
346.5685 cp 16 J 642 START  0.7090                       27
346.5820 cp 19 J 649 END    0.0830   0.6905              28
346.6715 cp  7 J 657 END    0.1700   1.5975              29
346.7870 cp  2 J 635 START  0.6320                       30
347.2030 cp 19 J 663 START  0.2070
347.8030 cp 18 J 658 START  0.3120
347.8600 cp 17 J 661 START  1.3710
348.3865 cp  6 J 636 START  0.0530
348.5045 cp 19 J 663 END    0.2070   1.3015
348.8450 cp  6 J 636 END    0.0530   0.4585
348.9015 cp 18 J 658 END    0.3120   1.0985
349.6775 cp  5 J 659 START  0.5470
349.7015 cp 13 J 647 START  0.4150
```

Alas, the effect is lost since the above is a static monochrome image; the real running program is quite video-game-like in its dynamics as jobs enter and leave the various color-coded queues in the upper left. The right column shows the currently running jobs, the colors of which correspond to the several queues; the scrolling portion in the lower left shows a chronological trace of job activity.[151] Very cool to watch.

About that same time I was involved in helping another programmer optimize his program for scheduling pilots and flight-attendants; I applied ideas from my MS to animate his program, which enabled us to examine its algorithm in detail. I also recall attending a graduate seminar when one of the other students presented her animation of a very difficult parallel sorting algorithm – very fascinating.

Then there was another project a few years later when I had to write a device driver for a new ATM NIC.[152] I had little experience with that deep sort of networking, so I decided to build a simulator for that NIC as a method of getting into all the technical details quickly. I don't have any displays or code to explore, but the details of that project are not as important as the strategic approach I used.

As we have seen in other studies, we must begin by understanding the matter at hand: defining terms, using formalisms (whenever appropriate) such as mathematical objects or automata. Queues and probabilities may have to be stipulated as necessary if real data is not otherwise on hand: the technique is to create an accurate *model* of the thing being simulated, even if the simulated tests are not as realistic as one might like. (Besides, if you do your work well, you can always improve your test-bed as you acquire results from the thing you are modelling.)

The second principle to keep in mind is to *make visible* whatever you can, whether it be by some dynamic graphics as I did in my operating systems assignment, or by tracking instruction use as I did with the industrial PDP-8 project, or by other means. Your purpose is not only to understand the real thing, and somehow provide a mechanical analogy in software, but to "instrument" that model to provide visibility to its working, as well as the tracking of its performance.

Finally, you ought to keep in mind that you are not the only one for whom such an exhibit may be useful. When done well, your simulator can become a guide to further improvements of the real machine.

These things are not just speculative. There are many engineering disciplines which rely on such approaches. As far back as 1973 I saw the package called STRESS, which modelled static structures for applications in civil and mechanical engineering; somewhat later I saw ECAP and SPICE for electrical engineering, and there are many others. As an undergraduate I wrote a logic-gate simulator; later a friend used my re-implementation to test out his design of electronic dice for his senior electrical engineering project. Indeed, my first task at FEL in 1977 – that plot-program for the Bridgeport NC milling machine – was a simple and static form of simulation, which would read the part-program and generate a plot which reproduced the behavior of the machine tool.

---

[151] For computer archaeologists: yes, both the "A" and "B" displays of DSD are imitated here.
[152] These codes stand for "Asynchronous Transfer Mode" (which has nothing to do with banking) and "Network Interface Card."

Case Study: the Three-Line Crawl

For this study we'll visit November of 2000, during my work in cable television. Also, I warn you in advance this study contains some exploration of certain philosophical aspects of the matter in hand.

One of the various branches of our company maintained a sort of bulletin-board kind of TV network, on which would run a variety of advertisements for used cars, real estate, yard sales, personal items, and all sorts of things, along with periodic infomercials or cutting over to one of the other marketing/sales networks. This project is worth some study, which we shall cover in a separate volume; for now, we shall just consider one component of that project.

As usual we had a meeting, and Management explained some of the new features which were wanted for that network. Among others was a "crawl" to show the various stocks – lines of text which continually scroll across the bottom of the screen, such as can be seen on certain news/information networks. However, our Management wanted to have *three* independently scrolling lines, each from its own data source, were to move at different speeds, have independent colors, and so on.

My boss and I looked at each other, and the video expert stated that such equipment was available, but it cost around a quarter of a million dollars.

That was, as I recall, a Friday.

I came in again on the following Tuesday and showed them what I had done over the weekend. "It's called NUHERP," I said.[153]

It was exactly what they had described, though of course they immediately began to demand alterations, changes, and extensions.[154]

"I guess you just saved the company a quarter of a million dollars," my boss quipped later.

So what is the lesson here? And how did I manage it so fast?

Well, there were just two items I needed to solve. First, the tricks to enable control of the "full screen" of the PC in the way in which "screen savers" work. The second was to handle the "scrolling" of a rectangular portion of a given window. Once I found the appropriate library routines to call, the rest was easy. Each of the three scrolling lines had its own set of variables which managed its current status, including its color and formatting characteristics, its data source, and its scrolling rate. Then it was simply a matter of iterating through the display of these three items at a fixed rate, adjusting their position each time, dropping off a character at the left, and appending a character at the right as necessary.

This technique might be called "rapid prototyping" or "bread-boarding" – but the essential skill here is *not* being able to acquire all the trick codes or library routines, not being able to compose the code rapidly, and not even being fairly adept at typing.

No, there is a far more critical skill required in order to accomplish such things rapidly, and that skill is a harmony of more fundamental skills: for the pleasure of pedantry [155] we might call it *compositional teleology*.

What has to be done if one wants to do this?

---

[153] Greek ἑρπω (*herpô*) = "I crawl"; *serpo* in Latin, whence the English "serpent."

[154] As surprising as that may sound, I was used to such customer demands from my days at FEL. I expect it; it happens all the time, as you will hear in the volume about molecular biology. Besides the thing I had made was so simple it was easy to revise.

[155] As Chesterton says in *Orthodoxy* CW1:258.

At the risk of sounding recursive, one needs to ask: *What needs to be done?*

That is the essence of all development, but it is even more essential when one wants to perform the task as rapidly as possible.

That essential is simply stated: the problem must be stated as clearly and unambiguously as it can be, with all side issues and irrelevant details deferred for the moment. In our case, the one critical idea was to cause a line of text to appear to scroll from right to left, as if it were on a ribbon moving leftwards in front of the viewer... Once that was arranged, the matter of making multiple such lines, each independent of the others, with different formats, content, and speeds, was straightforward. Other aspects – the full-screen arrangements, the use of the remainder of the screen, the sources of the actual texts to be used, the way in which we might configure the colors, format, data-sources, and scrolling rates – and we must not overlook the *audio* component either – all those could be set aside, indeed, ignored or left hard-wired for the sake of the experiment. We didn't need any of those things to be handled *today*. The one thing which really needed to be demonstrated was those three lines, each moving at different rates.

To restate the skill another way: one needs to express the innermost kernel character of the problem, leaving aside all secondary matters for the time being, and considering only what is required to accomplish that task.

Strange to say, this skill correlates well to one of the Beatitudes: "Blessed are the clean of heart: they shall see God."[156] Another translation gives this as "pure of heart," and there are commentators who indicate this signifies the idea of single-mindedness. St. Thomas Aquinas correlates this Beatitude with the Gift of Understanding.[157]

Why do I bring up such an abstract philosophical and theological matter here?

Simply because as the Scholastics argued, God is our "End" – He is our purpose in being.[158] This is the core matter of the branch of Philosophy known as Teleology: the study of Ends, that is, of Purposes.[159] Granted, Purpose may be a difficult topic for some fields, but after more than thirty years of experience it's a bit hard to pretend it's irrelevant to computing.

So, according to this Beatitude, if one wants to see the Purpose, one needs to pursue it single-mindedly, avoiding all distractions.

Now, having said all that, I must remind you that I called this NuHerp project an experiment in the *paradox* of Compositional Teleology. I say it is a paradox since at the very moment you are striving to be "pure of heart," single-minded in pursuit of the Purpose, you must also "zoom out" your inner view to the widest possible scope, so as to take in the vastest possible collection of possible aids to achieving that goal.

The paradox (or challenge) is not to allow that huge array of very cool tricks and powerful tools now in your view to distract you from that Purpose!

What did *I* see when I wanted to solve this particular problem? Simply, the fact that for all the years I have been using any sort of video display to interact with computers, just about every single one of them was able to *scroll* the currently displayed text upwards, as if a vast roll of paper was shifting past my view from below

---

[156] Matthew 5:8. In his *Catena Aurea* St. Thomas Aquinas reports that St. Augustine links this verse to Wisdom 1:1: "Think of the Lord in goodness, and seek him in simplicity of heart."
[157] Aquinas, *Summa Theologica*, II-II, Q8 A7.
[158] "End" here does not mean a sort of destructive termination like the legendary bit-bucket, but the ultimate reason for being: the Purpose.
[159] Oddly enough, the *Dictionary of Philosophy* claims it to be opposed to Mechanism, but this is hardly the place to argue about that. Of course I did say there was a Paradox here...

to above. If a display could so readily scroll upwards, it ought not be very difficult to arrange it to scroll from right to left.[160] It only remained to find out whether the WINDOWS system libraries contained a procedure to accomplish this, or if I had to cobble it together from more fundamental routines.[161] Once I could make a portion of the screen scroll leftwards as I wished, I simply had to arrange the necessary mechanisms to make that inner core action into something useful.

Case Study: A Question of Qs (Part One)

Here is another three-part invention from the same cable TV company. Another volume in this series will present the entire ad insertion scheme in detail, but for the present we are only going to look at Qs.

English has two different words – queue and cue – both pronounced like the letter Q. Oddly enough, both came up in my work on local ad insertion. The word "queue" comes through the French from the Latin word *cauda* which means "tail" whereas "cue" is claimed [162] to derive from a variant spelling of Q, the initial letter of the Latin *quando* which means "when," being used to mark the point in playscripts *when* an actor is to speak, move, etc.

The first queue came up very early in my time there, when I was learning about ad insertion as accomplished by the existing software. The kernel of their system was the "ENGINE" which performed local ad insertion: it was reported to be unstable, failing frequently – far too frequently for a program which had to run round the clock, 24 hours a day, seven days a week. Not only that, it had been accepted as *policy* that all Field inserters running this ENGINE had to be shut down and rebooted once a day, due to – ahem – "memory leaks in WINDOWS." Now, that old version of the ENGINE used a set of library routines known as the "Standard Template Library" or STL, about which I had heard during my graduate work. The STL was claimed as a major advance in the profession: it was supposed to have been Tested with a capital T, and Proven Correct, so one did not have to worry about writing one's own code to do trivialities.

Oh yes, indeed.

But this is no place to be cynical, to grin with condescension, or to argue the fascinating topic of how proofs (be they abstract, spoken, or printed) relate to software (be it abstract, printed, or actually coded and implemented). No; this is a Case Study. (If you want the Scholastic view of the topic, I may provide it elsewhere eventually.)

I had never used the STL before, and I knew it would take some getting used to in order to work with. And so, regardless of my serious professional misgivings about their reliance on this library, I sat down and began to study how it was used. I investigated the old ENGINE and noted that it used a number of queues, the usual data structure used to manage items which must obey a first-in, first-out arrangement. These queues were implemented by the STL, and once you had called one into being, you could push things onto the queue or take things off, simply by calling one of the supplied library routines. All very nice, as one might expect from such a library.

---

[160] This is a classic paradoxical Chestertonian motif, a case of Things Which Are Too Big To Be Seen. See e.g. GKC's "The Three Tools of Death" in *The Innocence of Father Brown*, also his *The Everlasting Man* CW2:163.

[161] It's there; it's called ScrollDC.

[162] The *Oxford English Dictionary* states that this explanation is given by 17th century writers, though it also states that no supporting evidence has been found.

Therefore, I wrote a simple program to experiment with a queue, calling it into being, then pushing a handful of things onto it, and taking them off, displaying the work as it proceeded. It worked correctly, as one would expect.

I shrugged. Yeah, I seemed to have grasped the method of using the STL – but since the ENGINE had timing requirements which meant it had to be as efficient as possible, I decided to see how much time was consumed by the queue routines. I added the code to capture timing information, then, as is usual in such experiments, removed the displaying of the action, and stepped up the total number of repeats so as to get a decent measure from the instrumentation: instead of just pushing 3 or 5 items onto the queue, I pushed 1000.

To my surprise the program aborted.

Well, I said to myself: that's interesting. No doubt I did something wrong. I put the total item number back to 5 and replaced the display of the action: and the program worked just as expected.

Well-squared.

I commented out the display, put the number back to 1000, and ran it again. It aborted.

Then my eyes narrowed: is it me or is it the STL? *Let's try 500.*

And it worked. Ah...

All right, I better check powers of two – two-to-the-ninth is 512.

That worked also. Well, now...

How about one more than that – how about 513?

And it aborted!

So I went to my boss and he called the programmer who had written parts of that old ENGINE into his office to discuss the matter.

I told them about my findings then I asked, "Are either of you able to state an upper bound on the total number of items pushed onto these queues?"

They thought a little, and eventually answered, "No."

"Well then, I think I might have a guess as to why the ENGINE aborts sometimes..." Then I told them about my discovery, adding, "I think it would be worthwhile for me to replace all the uses of these queue library routines from the STL, which we *now know fails under certain conditions*, with calls to my own routines. It's just a queue, after all."

And the other programmer stared and said, "All those routines? *It would take a week!*"

Shaking my head I smirked at my boss – who had attended Lehigh University as I had. "I'll have it finished this afternoon."

And I did. Written *and* tested.

One final note: that old ad insertion system was completely replaced in 2000, [163] as you will learn in a future volume. The new ENGINE did *not* use the STL.

---

[163] The new system had some outstanding cases of very long up-times: the record was 790 continuous days for a machine in Harrisburg, PA, which stayed up and running our software from May 28, 2003 to July 25, 2005. This strongly indicated that those supposed memory leaks were not in the operating system. The machines at that site had an average up-time of almost 260 days (8.5 months).

Case Study: A Question of Qs (Part Two)

Now we shall talk about the other sort of cue: the signal known to cable television as the "cue-tone": a four-part DTMF [164] signal, which sounds like the touch-tone noises of modern telephones. These signals are sent on a secondary channel, and are not normally audible to ordinary viewers, though I recall hearing them on occasion during certain sports programs. They are sent a few seconds in advance, to signal an opportunity for playing a local commercial. This time interval (typically 5 to 7 seconds) is called the "preroll" since in older times, the playback was done by a VTR, the motors of which required a brief time to come up to speed, that is, to start *rolling*. This preroll is still needed, though there are no longer any motors, even software requires a brief lead time to perform its work. (We built controls into the ENGINE so the preroll could be adjusted to give acceptable performance.)

These cue-tones are of fundamental importance to ad insertion. If they do not come, no spots may play, even if everything else is correct. So we spent a lot of time discussing and planning the ways of reliably delivering the cues to our Field machines.

The primary arrangement for delivering cues to our machinery at a Field site was *local* cues: that is, we had an array of special devices to capture those signals from the various cable networks and provide them to the ENGINE. But this method, as good as it was, also had a number of difficulties, since it required additional equipment, and could be interfered with in various ways. We wanted to have an option which might unify the equipment and give us more control and more warning if things weren't working correctly.

As explained in the other volume, we changed our ad insertion system to use a networking scheme via satellite known as VSAT, since many of the headends where our inserters were located were not yet reached by land-based high-speed network lines. We were already receiving all the individual signals of the various cable networks at our headquarters, so we could readily capture their cue-tones. We would then need some way of sending those signals out over the satellite.

Of course that sounds odd, since things could go wrong at our headquarters, or our satellite signal could get blocked. Moreover, the usual understanding of network communications seemed at odds with the requirement, and the discussion seemed to revolve around ideas like:

"But how can you use a computer network (TCP/IP) to transport a *sound*?"

Or:

"How can a cue-tone be represented in a *file*?"

However, the point of the cue-tone is *not* the sound. It is the *Quando*, the When, the point in time which it marks by the moment of its appearance. Moreover, as long as we correctly adjust the preroll on the ENGINE, we should readily be able to perform the spots at the required moment, even if we have added some delay to the reception of those cues.

Then someone asked, "What happens when – say – a plane passes over our satellite dish?" Yes, our headquarters *was* on a flight path to the local airport, and this was likely to happen.

I recalled a class I had taken during my M.S., a rather difficult yet fascinating class on the theory of error-correcting codes. The first and simplest was mere

---

[164] DTMF stands for Dual-Tone Multi-Frequency, the method used for audio representation of telephone numbers.

repetition: any given signal σ is transmitted three times, which means the receiver will encounter one of the following cases, where τ represents an erroneous message:

σ σ σ	We assume the signal is σ.
σ σ τ	We assume the signal is σ.
σ τ σ	We assume the signal is σ.
τ σ σ	We assume the signal is σ.
σ τ τ	We assume the signal is τ.
τ τ σ	We assume the signal is τ.
τ σ τ	We assume the signal is τ.
τ τ τ	We assume the signal is τ.

This single-error-correcting code works by a simple majority vote. It may seem a bit dangerous, but it works provided that the probability of *multiple* errors is small. Moreover, the method provides us with a way of recovering the *correct* message, at least with a higher probability than if we only sent the message once.

And that is what we did. We sent each cue signal three times. [165]

But Doc (you say) you just told us the importance of the cue signal was in its *time*, not in its content!

Yes, that is correct. But what was in those messages, and how did we do it anyway?

The answer was we used UDP, the "User Datagram Protocol" which might also be called the "Unreliable Data Protocol" – the primitive mechanism on which all other IP machinery is based. It does *not* expect a reply, and in fact is one-directional. (Think of a lonesome DJ in a radio station late at night. He doesn't know if his monologues, his goofy intros, his hit-tunes – if *anything* – is getting out to his listening public. Unless someone happens to call in with a request – or a complaint. See the ad insertion volume for more on this topic.)

But as far as we were concerned, the significant point about this one-way UDP message was that it would introduce no additional time-lag while those to whom that message was addressed woke up from their other duties and replied, "Yeah, I got it." Yes, they still had to wake up and deal with that signal, but they didn't have to reply back to headquarters over the satellite.

We did protect that signal by various means, including a checksum. And, as I said, we also tripled it, sending out a total of three times, with a one-second delay between each.

And now I ought to tell you what was in that signal. The most critical of all was which network it was cueing, and this we represented by the actual network id. There was no point in attempting to represent the actual cue-tones by their touch-tone symbols; we performed that mapping once in our cue-detection machinery at headquarters, and from then on only used the network id. The date and time of the reception of the cue (at headquarters) was also recorded. Finally, we marked *which* of the triple repeats this particular signal arose from: a *zero* marked the packet sent upon the reception of the original signal, a *one* marked the repeat sent one second later, and a *two* marked that sent two seconds later.

---

[165] This is not a mystical "three" thing (e.g. the Hebrew superlative by triple-repeats as in Isaiah 6:3) but a real truth of information theory. For technical details, see any text on error correction such as Lin and Costello's *Error Control Coding*. I seem to recall this idea appears in Heinlein's *The Number of the Beast*, which had a spacecraft with a natural-language interface (think K.I.T.T. the talking car of the old TV show "Knight Rider"). The user could command the ship to store multiple copies of information for safety by saying: "I tell you three times."

That was the trick. And when the ENGINE received one of these cue-message UDP packets, it merely checked which of the three repeats it had caught, and adjusted its preroll to compensate for the lag. Of course once one signal had been received, the repeated signals were discarded.

Here is an example of the internal log entry for an actual inserter, 3CHES, from July 21, 2005, showing the content of the cue packet:

```
03:33:22.554 184 got AmDg18ffedf04c20050721033323569 0 SCFI from 10.9.1.12
```

This packet contains a 14-byte prefix followed by the message:

AmDg	validation symbol
18	message length in hex
ffedf04c	checksum of the message

Then comes the message, which has the following components:

2005	year in timestamp of original cue
07	month in timestamp of original cue
21	day in timestamp of original cue
03	hour in timestamp of original cue
33	minute in timestamp of original cue
23	second in timestamp of original cue
569	millisecond in timestamp of original cue
0	origin-code
SCFI	cable network this cue came from

The origin-code was 0, 1, or 2, indicating this message's position in the triple repeats. Here, the zero indicates this particular message was sent immediately upon reception of the cue at headquarters. The blank after that digit indicates that this message originated from the cue-detection machinery, and was sent via satellite; we shall consider the alternatives in a later case.

Yes, this method worked – it worked very well, and Comcast relied upon it for over five years. According to the logs which were still available near the end of that period, covering 1,616 days, we received a total of 3,468,278 cues, averaging one every 50 seconds; the run rate of spots played was 97.69 percent.[166]

Case Study: A Question of Qs (Part Three)

We have just considered the method of transmitting cue-tones to the Field by tripled one-directional UDP packets sent via satellite. The purpose of our ad insertion system, of course, was to play as many spots as possible, given the schedules and other criteria governing such playback, so we had a number of monitoring and reporting tools to track performance. We did note, however, that despite this "I tell you three times" approach, there were times when cues did not arrive at given remote sites: solar conjunctions, rain fade, snow in the remote dishes, misalignments and even human interference could cause such things. Our customer, therefore, insisted that we

---

[166] The records cover 4/5 of the total 5.5 years this system was in use, including that day on which nearly every network ceased regular programming as they "went live" with coverage on September 11, 2001. That was the date of our lowest run rate, 70.6 percent.

make alternative pathways available [167] – these alternatives, however required augmentations which had to be enabled by the customer. There were two other methods of delivering cue-tones to our ad inserters: (1) by direct reception of the original DTMF cues from the cable networks, which required additional hardware and wiring at each headend, or (2) by delivery via the land-based network, which required that the headend be connected to the INTERNET. Direct reception required augmentation of the ENGINE to query the various playback cards, which had an option to receive the cue-tones directly; this method is straightforward. The other method has some points worth further study.

In order to consider the matter, we shall present a diagram for part of our system layout at headquarters:

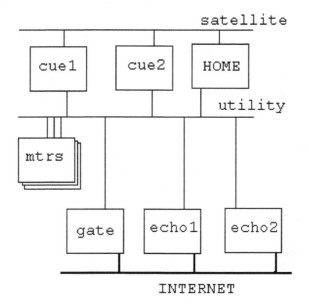

Ad Insertion System
Network Diagram for Headquarters (partial)

The pair of cue machines (cue1 and cue2) receive the cue-tones from the various cable-networks, and transmit the appropriate trio of UDP packets onto both the satellite network and the utility network. A number of dedicated computers (mtrs) running WATCHER, our monitoring program, listened to the signals on the utility network and displayed them on the four big screens in our Control Room. File transport was performed by HOME, and software running on GATE handled input and output for our Traffic Department.[168] When the system went live on March 2, 2000, there was no arrangement for cue packets to become visible to anyone (whether employees or others) via the INTERNET. Furthermore, at that time only a small handful of headends were wired to the INTERNET. But in June of 2001 it was decided to make arrangements to transmit the cue packets over the INTERNET as well.

---

[167] This strategy of multiple pathways (denoted by the anatomical term "anastomosis") is discussed in my *Subsidiary*; we shall hear more on it in a future volume.
[168] A future volume will explore that local ad insertion system for cable TV.

This required a pair of machines which would listen for cue-packets on our utility network and "echo" them onto the INTERNET. The ENGINE would also have to be augmented to provide a secondary way of receiving these packets. (I should mention that we could set prerolls independently for each form of cue-reception.)

An interesting thing occurred relating to the way in which these packets went out over the INTERNET, since we were using several subnets arranged by our customer in order to reach their headends.

The ever-alert Control Room Guy noticed that WATCHER was reporting a problem: the disks of many Field machines were filling. We traced the problem to the logging of *tens of thousands* of repeated instances of cue packets being received.

But where were they coming from?

The first time this happened, in 2001, near the time that this was being implemented, the problem was traced to an old version of the ENGINE which was running on a pair of special-purpose inserters connected on the Utility network. They shouldn't have been repeating the cues, since they had no leaves and in fact didn't use cues at all, but they were, and the echo machines were dutifully repeating the cue packets out to the Field. We upgraded the software for that pair of special inserters and then cleared up the mess, then I altered the echoing programs to ignore any "stale" cue packets – those which had been received "too long" ago. That, I felt, was sufficient.

But it wasn't. In 2004 it happened again. As I was writing this study, I looked through my scanty records, and browsed my even scantier recollections, and was not able to find a conclusive explanation for this bizarre replication of the cue packets. My guess is that it was related to a change in the Field, possibly on the network router(s) involved. Or, perhaps, there was some rewiring by which the private network used only by the inserters at a given headend was cross-linked to the "distribution" network (a subnet of the "INTERNET") by which the cues were being distributed. But I don't really know what it was, and don't recall that we ever learned what had happened. The decision was simply to protect the ENGINE from spurious repeated cues.

Therefore I altered the ENGINE itself to track whether or not a given packet had already been received. Any replications were reported only at one-minute intervals,[169] so there would no longer be any filling of disk space due to immense internal logs.

As far as I recall, we didn't see any other odd occurrences in the final year of that system's use.

Case Study: A Question of Qs (Part Four)

I will tell you about one other little cue-related project. As you will learn in another volume of this series, the machinery of local ad insertion requires a schedule: this is a file which specifies, for a given headend, date, and cable network, a series of time intervals. With each interval is associated a list of one or more "spots" (identifiers for the actual commercials, stored in MPEG form). The meaning of such an entry is very simple: if a cue from that cable network is received at that headend on that date in that interval, those particular spots are to be played.[170] These intervals are

---

[169] There are 1,440 minutes in a day. See Appendix 1 for useful facts like that.

[170] There are a number of additional restrictions about these things which are not relevant to our discussion; they are necessary to the rules of ad insertion by which the Traffic Department makes the schedules.

dictated to a large extent by the policies of each given cable network regarding when they send the cues.

Now, in general, it is desired that we play as many of those scheduled spots as possible: this depends on things our company can control, like making sure the schedule is as full as possible, and that all the spots have been received by the customer, encoded by Operations, and delivered by the file transport machinery (of which you will learn far more elsewhere). As we have just discussed, we have some control over reception and delivery of the cues. But we cannot control when the cues are sent – the most we might be able to do is adjust the alignment of the intervals.

As part of our machinery to deliver the cue packets, we kept a permanent record of all cues received at Headquarters. This was initially a kind of check of our cue-reception machinery, and for study of performance by the Field – but it was obvious that the growing archive of cue-logs could have other purposes.

One day (when I had a few spare minutes) I decided to whip up a little "user tool" which could present in one display all the cues received on a given day: it would have user-controls to select from the various cable networks, and a little calendar with tricky buttons to choose a single day, a day-of-the-week, weekday or weekend, or all cues for selected dates. It had 24 horizontal lines for the 24 hours, and marked the time of each logged cue with a short vertical line. Then I also built in a way of showing the intervals from the relevant schedules, marked as horizontal colored lines. I called it "QANAL" for cue-analysis.

I showed the result to a couple of co-workers, and you would have thought I had just given them a box of donuts... As I shall report in another case study, there is a lot to be said for such simple tools, and the users will probably say it: "Hey, could you add something that will show me...?" And so on.

Sample screen shot from QANAL

QANAL was just a simple thing, but Traffic found it useful to improve their performance – and yet, when our customer decided to discontinue their use of our ad-insertion system, this useful tool got canned like the rest of it. (That sort of problem, however, is beyond the scope of our study.)

Case Study: a User Tool for Shirt Design

Here's another minor-key tale. It was Thursday August 10, 1983. I was working at FEL, and I had arranged to take my vacation the following week.

Sam came back to the NC department and told us he'd like to have a nice little user-oriented program to help one of our customers design new shirts.

We looked at each other. This wasn't the usual sort of numerical control engineering project we got. We asked whether this was a problem of laying out the various parts of the shirt on a roll of cloth, akin to the Shearing Problem we shall consider in a future volume.

No, Sam explained: they had seen our color graphics terminal, and thought maybe they could use that to get an idea of what various designs might look like. "Just a background color, and then two or three or four horizontal stripes, maybe narrow, maybe broad, of different colors," Sam told us. "But these folks aren't knowledgeable about computers, so it has to be *very* easy to use. Something it would take about five minutes to explain."

We looked at each other and shrugged. Another crazy project – not only that, I had today and tomorrow to do it.

Now, there weren't any PCs with fun drawing editors... I don't mean something sophisticated like AUTOCAD or even PHOTOSHOP: I mean that fun little thing called PAINT. The program would run on our HP 3000, and use the color graphics monitor we had. So we talked about the project – the one thing I recall mentioning was that the effect of an image made by light-emitting display would probably not be the same as the equivalent image on any light-*reflecting* surface, especially a textile, and they certainly wouldn't be able to print the image... at that time the only device capable of producing a color image on paper was the plotter, which was not adept at filling regions nor mixing colors. But Sam said they understood; the point was just to enable them to concoct ideas about possible schemes...

So we collected some ideas about it: we would permit the creation, storage and retrieval of a "project," to consist of a background color, a number of horizontal bars, each with its own position, width, and color, and a "palette" of colors.

Then I went home, had dinner, got a six-pack of beer (yeah, the same substance which once stimulated a certain physicist to envision the "cloud chamber" used in the study of nuclear reactions), and walked back to work.

It was about 2 AM when I finished. It was a nice little tool: except for the place where the user gave the project a name, there was almost no keyboard use, except for the function keys, which were used for everything, including placement and alteration of the horizontal bars.[171]

The next day I showed Sam, Charlie and the others how it worked. They thought it would be easy to use, and very suitable for the desired purpose. I left for vacation with a feeling of accomplishment.

---

[171] Recall that this was in the days before mouses, or maybe I mean mice.

What was the outcome? Well... I am not sure, that was over thirty years ago. I seem to recall that the customer liked it, but somehow I think they changed their mind about buying it. My guess is that they really wanted something they could print, and not just look at on the screen.

Case Study: CDC 160 to the Rescue

All right, enough of the minor; let's add three sharps and move on. In May of 1979 when I was working at FEL, one of our customers came to us with a question. They had a large number of part-program tapes for a Wiedemann NC punch press, and they had just purchased an Amada punch press, but they wanted to continue to make those parts on their new press. They had all the manuals and relevant documentation, so what could we do to help them?

We asked if the tapes were in ASCII, but the answer was no. They were in EIA, a different character set used on many numerically controlled machine tools: it was odd-parity and used a number of special binary (non-ASCII) sequences: for example, the EIA "carriage return" was 1000 0000 binary, which is 200 octal, or 80 in hex.

"Paper-tapes in EIA," I moaned to Charlie as we discussed the matter. "You know how much trouble we have trying to read them into the HP."

Huh! (You exclaim, some thirty-odd years later.) You have a powerful, modern computer (modern for 1979, anyway) – how come you can't use it to do such a thing?

Well... earlier I mentioned how important it is to understand the abilities and limitations of the tools you have at your disposal. One of the frustrations for users, managers, and programmers, is in continually over-estimating the amazing powers of the computer. Sometimes the problem seems to arise from the popular culture: like my expectation that a COMPUTER ought to have loads of flashing lights and an array of switches and dials and all that. But sometimes it arises from the operation of what we might dignify by the word "marketing." Even the salesmen from computer companies don't grasp that the typical "general-purpose" machine they sell – like that PC you can buy these days in a department store, or over the net – is *not* really all that general-purpose. It was made to satisfy what its builders envisioned as a particular kind of need, and even if it is formally "capable" in some sense, it will probably not succeed at accomplishing functions which are beyond that vision. For example, as we shall see in greater detail in a future volume, we did not use a typical off-the-shelf "consumer" kind of PC to perform local ad insertion: we needed a robust "industrial" sort of machine with hefty redundant power supplies, a large bay for hard drives, and a generous number of expansion slots. But that was simply a matter of knowing where to buy the right sort of thing. What if there wasn't any "right sort"?

At Frankel Engineering we had a HP 3000 "minicomputer" which provided time-sharing services for multiple users. It was quite an impressive piece of equipment, and I learned a lot working with it. It was a 32-bit machine, and it had a robust multi-tasking system with a powerful array of features, including the usual system-embedded database everybody has had for the last thirty-odd years... Ahem. But when it came to certain kinds of technical needs it had a severe limitation, almost invisible to many, including some who perhaps should have known better.

That limitation was that its operating system was intended for what we could call the Business User, and not for the Technical Specialist. The operating system limited user input (from the programmer's perspective) to relatively short sequences of standard characters, and it balked at esoteric things like binary and parity and dedicated special-use peripheral hardware. I am not going to explain why, or guess what was going on; these things no longer matter since I don't think HP 3000s exist these days. (Incidentally I can make an almost identical complaint about the typical personal computer of the 2010s, which is now even more limited. Even with its gaudy system-embedded databases and spiffy web browsers. What a shame. *Dic cur hic* is not just a slogan, even if it is in an obsolete language.)

The point about that system's input/output facilities came down to this. At that time we were doing all our programming on the HP 3000. We had talked about handling paper-tapes on the 3000 previously, and had banged our heads against the HP wall for some time. But now we had a customer who needed our help, and it was up to us to think of a way to supply that need.

"Too bad we can't use that CDC," Charlie said, glancing into the computer room with a kind of nostalgic grin. "It's got the fastest tape reader and punch in the place."

Wait, you exclaim. Wasn't the CDC at Lehigh? Do you mean FEL had one also?

Yes, there was a CDC at FEL. It is an amazing story, a piece of local high-tech history – though it was a CDC 160, an ancient predecessor of the CDC 6400.[172]

In 1960 Sam Frankel was approached by Carpenter Steel in Reading, PA, to work out some thermodynamics for their new furnace. After some discussion, Sam reported that he would probably need to resort to numerical methods to obtain a solution, and proposed taking advantage of that new tool, the Electronic Computer.

It was an amazing step for him to take. This was over 50 years ago; one could not go into a 5-and-10 and buy a computer. He had to take out a major loan.

And then there it was: a CDC 160, designed by no less than Seymour Cray:

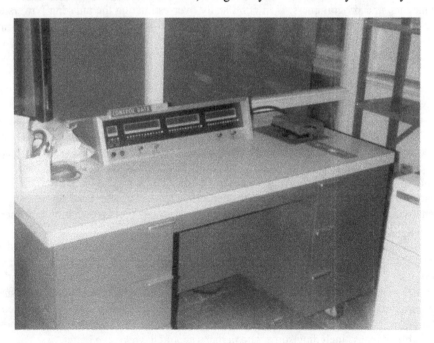

---

[172] Indeed, the instructions of the CDC 160 are extremely similar to those of the Peripheral Processors (PPs) of the CDC 6400. I have heard the design of the PPs were indeed based on that of the 160; both were the work of that master-craftsman, Seymour Cray.

As you can see, it looked like a professional desk, maybe six feet long by three feet wide, and 30 inches high, and you could sit at it. It had 4K of core. Yes, that's right: 4096 words, each with 12 bits, and it was made with real "core" memory, that is tiny iron rings through each of which coursed three very fine wires... There was no disk drive, no video display, no keyboard, no mouse; there was, however a very speedy paper-tape reader and paper-tape punch – and directly in front of the operator was its little control panel, with a power switch and three little four-place digit lamps, under each of which were a row of tiny buttons. That was all.

It came with a FORTRAN compiler (FORTRAN II, if you are curious) which of course was on paper-tape. It also included an odd device called a Flexowriter, which was a typewriter joined with a paper-tape reader and punch. You used that to prepare your program, or to make your listing. It was put into use then, sometime in 1960, and in 1983 it was still being used, some *twenty-three* years later. (Quite a life, but then it really was an impressive machine.)

Now let us return to 1979. Charlie and I went into the computer room and peered down at the nearly twenty-year-old CDC with its fast paper-tape reader and punch. How could we use it?

We still had all the manuals for the CDC 160, including its instruction set... so I wrote a cross-assembler – a program which ran on the HP 3000, yet generated binary for the CDC. (This of course would be punched on paper-tape, as the CDC had no other I/O device.)

We had already discussed the transformation from Wiedemann to Amada; some reformatting was necessary, and the customer had a few additional requirements. The only complexity would be the tooling assignments, which the Wiedemann specified with two digits, and the Amada with three; moreover, the actual shapes of those tools had to agree between the two machines. Fortunately, our customer had been using a standard tooling arrangement for their parts, and they could adapt a similar arrangement for the new punch press. (You may think of these "tools" as having shapes sort of like cookie-cutters; rounds, squares, rectangles, and so on.)

So, by relying on the CDC, the project consisted of a fairly straight transformation of one paper-tape into another.

It was a fairly short assembly program, with just a few special cases to handle, including the lookup table to translate from the two-digit Wiedemann tool numbers to three-digit Amada tool numbers. But the result was sufficiently easy for our summer workers to use.

And so the large batch of tapes were converted, and the customer was happy.

As was once said in a similar context: "Well done, good and faithful servant."[173]

Case Study: CDC 160 to the Rescue, Again!

As FEL slowly phased out the use of the old HP 2116 machines, more and more of our engineering work was being performed on the HP 3000, which included punching paper-tapes. We wrote PUNCH, a general program to make paper-tapes, which would handle generic stuff like leaders and trailers, conversion to oddball formats, and even the famous "man-readable" headers, which Charlie had devised on the old systems some time ago. I ought to show you what such things look like...

---

[173] See Matthew 25:21.

```
oooooo  oooooo  o        ooooo   oooo    ooooo   oooooo
o       o       o          o      o      o   o      o   o
o       o       o          o      o      o   o      o   o
. . . . . . . . . . . . . . . . . . . . . . . . . . . . . .
oooo    oooo    o           o     oooooo  ooooo   oooo
o   o   o       o           o     o    o  o   o       o
o   o   o       o           o     o    o  o   o       o
o   o   o       o           o     o    o  o   o       o
o       oooooo  oooooo      o     o    o  o   o   oooooo
```

You have to imagine this as an inch-wide strip of thickish black paper which smells of oil, with a row of tiny holes running along it, not quite in the middle, and various larger holes punched in transverse rows. In the above example, we're actually looking at the tape from the back: it starts on the *left* and proceeds to the *right*, and the lowest order bit is at the *top*. The small dots are the feed-holes which were engaged by the sprocket (a small toothed gear) in the reader or punch to pull the tape along.

Now, there were no real difficulties *generating* paper-tapes. The HP 3000 could produce any desired sequence of the full range of 256 possible eight-bit characters.

But the paper-tape punch (being mechanical, not purely electronic) would sometimes leave a tiny fragment of paper jammed in a hole. (Behold, the famous "dangling chad. ") Such things could (and did) occur, and would cause real troubles for our customers.

We wanted to have a way of verifying that the newly-punched tape was correct according to the file from whence it had come. This should have been an easy project: just read that tape back in, and compare it to its source file.

But the difficulty was that on the HP 3000 we could not *in general* read in any sort of tape. Its system didn't like to read in arbitrarily long sequences of binary, which would be essential to such a verification.

So, once we had that Wiedemann-to-Amada translation tool for the CDC 160 completed, we discussed the matter again, and I wrote a "checker" program using our cross-assembler.

This program would scan a paper-tape and produce a series of checksums. I altered PUNCH, the HP 3000 program which produced our paper-tapes, to generate the same checksums and produce them as a report.

Here's an example of the PUNCH checksum report, with the user's inputs underlined. We would print these out (you could get the report without making a new tape, if necessary) and take them to the CDC along with the paper-tapes. You will note that the program requests a title: this would be punched in "man-readable" characters, so that the tape would be accurately identified.

```
:RUN PUNCH.PUB
F.E.L. PUNCH UTILITY    VERSION 2.1
FRI, JUL  1, 1983,  2:39 PM

USE PUNCHDEF-Y,N,L ?Y
USING PUNCHDEF.
FILE?DEMOFILE
OUTPUT: PUN=DEV31,NEW;DEV=31;CCTL;ACC=OUT;REC=-72,,F,ASCII
CODE= EIA
ENTER $TITLE:DEMO PART 123
TURN ON PUNCH?
TURN OFF PUNCH?CHK
```

156

```
FILE DEMOFILE   FRI, JUL  1, 1983,  2:50 PM

CHECKSUM DATA:

# FRAMES: 16754
( 139 FEET,  7.4 INCHES)
HIGH %0004
LOW  %0562


CHKSUM: %2014

LATERAL:
WRD 1 :   %0427
WRD 2 :   %7104
WRD 3 :   %7237
WRD 4 :   %1302
WRD 5 :   %1516

LONGITUDINAL:
CHN 8 :   %1353
CHN 7 :   %7701
CHN 6 :   %4664
CHN 5 :   %0244
CHN 4 :   %6576
CHN 3 :   %0540
CHN 2 :   %3076
CHN 1 :   %7455

END OF PROGRAM
:
```

So, when we wanted to verify a given paper-tape, we took that report along with the tape to the CDC and ran the checker program. After the tape was scanned, the machine displayed a series of numbers in the "Accumulator" display on its console, in the same order as those on the report. If they all agreed, it was extremely likely that the paper-tape had been accurately punched.

And just to demonstrate the wisdom of our efforts, one day the checksum did *not* agree! So we merely punched the tape again, verified it, and threw out the bad one. We were glad we could still take advantage of that old CDC.

Case Study: Transcending the Limits of the Operating System

For a few years our corner of Western Europe has had a fancy for this thing we call fiction; that is, for writing down our own lives or similar lives in order to look at them. But though we call it fiction, it differs from older literatures chiefly in being less fictitious. It imitates not only life, but the limitations of life; it not only reproduces life, it reproduces death. But outside us, in every other country, in every other age, there has been going on from the beginning a more fictitious kind of fiction. I mean the kind now called folklore, the literature of the people. Our modern novels, which deal with men as they are, are chiefly produced by a small and educated section of the society. But this other literature deals with men greater than they are – with demi-gods and heroes; and that is far too important a matter to be trusted to the educated classes. The fashioning of these portents is a popular trade, like ploughing or bricklaying; the men who made hedges, the men who made ditches, were the men who made deities. Men could not elect their kings, but they could elect their gods. So we find ourselves faced with a fundamental contrast between what is called fiction and what is called folklore. The one exhibits an abnormal degree of dexterity operating within our daily limitations; the other exhibits quite normal desires extended beyond those limitations. Fiction means the

157

common things as seen by the uncommon people. Fairy tales mean the uncommon things as seen by the common people.

– GKC, Charles Dickens, CW15:85-6

This study will sound so unreal you may think it is a fairy tale. In some ways, this is the most bizarre of our studies; it certainly was one of the most difficult. Once upon a time, a customer had over ten thousand parts, each with its own special identifier and each part had some text information associated with it – this information had to be maintained in its own individual file for processing by our software. Not only that, this Customer demanded that these entities be referred to not by a file name, but by part id, which could contain spaces, dashes, slashes, quotes, colons – any sort of punctuation symbol, and might be 30 or 40 characters in length.

However, the Operating System in question had a rather unusual file system which had only two levels: a "root" directory which could contain a number of "leaf" directories – and those "leaf" directories could contain no more than some relatively small number of files, somewhere near 1,100 as I recall. But the real challenge was that this operating system required file names to start with a letter, followed by zero to seven letters or digits – no special characters were permitted.

(Just in case you are wondering whether life might have been easier for us on your favorite Operating System: you had better investigate the real limits of *your* system before getting too cocky. You may be very unpleasantly surprised about what is permitted – and what *isn't* permitted. Try naming a file ".." on UNIX or WINDOWS.)

That Customer was expecting all our software to be altered to accommodate their part numbers. It was not possible to suggest another computer – they had just bought that one. It was not possible to violate the very famous "pigeonhole principle" by wedging 10,000 files into a directory which could only hold 1,100. Requesting revisions of the operating system was not an option, nor acquiring the relevant source code to do the work ourselves. It seemed to be an utterly hopeless situation.

What, then, was the answer?

Since we could not alter the *existing* file system of that operating system, we just built another one on top of it.[174]

What does this mean? It meant we had to build our own file directory structure, which is merely a simple form of a database, mapping a given part identifier into an actual file name (a real name, made according to the rules of the system), which of course had to be in two pieces, a subdirectory name and a file name, in order to hide the limitation of files in a single directory. Those names were formed in a serial fashion, something like this:

part id	subdir	file
X 374554, sect II (4")	D01	A001
X 374554, sect II (3.5")	D02	B001
6.3 fender J238/5 top	D01	C024
6.3 fender J238 /5 bottom	D03	A052

---

[174] If you have never looked under the hood of your computer, you ought to know that a "file system" is merely a formal *mapping* which relates the file name (the name you give it) to a particular location on the disk drive, usually what is called a logical sector address, just like a latitude and longitude on the globe. That pair <*filename, location*> is stored along with other information (current length, date/time, security data, etc) in the *directory entry* for that file. Yeah, that's all it is, very simple – and all the grunt work is arranged by the operating system.

(Oh yeah, we had a list of the parts, and I remember warning them about the inconsistent spaces, but they wanted it *exactly as it had been specified...*)

It was a horrible amount of very annoying work, requiring alteration of all code which requested a file name from the user, which now asked for the "part id." This string was passed to a new routine which returned the "real" filename corresponding to that part id, either verifying it as an existing part and returning the corresponding "real" file, or generating a new internal file name when ordered. This routine was used whenever the standard "file open" routine of the operating system had to be called, and every place where there was a reference to a file name.

We also wrote a utility program, rather like a primitive form of the popular file "explorer" tool, which enabled the users to examine the "Parts Directory," produce lists and other reports, and perform basic operations like renaming or deleting parts. Some programs were altered to operate so as to "perform process X on the *current part*" – thus we avoided handling of part-id-based intermediate files. We also had to build a "system load" tool which brought in the existing parts.

It was not pretty, and there were some nasty liabilities: they still had to know the "real" file name if they had to recover a file from a backup. (Those were still on magnetic tape, and done by the Operating System, we had no way of revising that.) But we managed to complete the project, and in the end, it did get accepted by that Customer.

Case Study: On Having Nothing To Do

> There are some who complain of a man for doing nothing; there are some, still more mysterious and amazing, who complain of having nothing to do. When actually presented with some beautiful blank hours or days, they will grumble at their blankness. When given the gift of loneliness, which is the gift of liberty, they will cast it away; they will destroy it deliberately with some dreadful game with cards or a little ball. I speak only for myself, I know it takes all sorts to make a world; but I cannot repress a shudder when I see them throwing away their hard-won holidays by doing something. For my own part, I never can get enough Nothing to do. I feel as if I had never had leisure to unpack a tenth part of the luggage of my life and thoughts.
>
> – GKC, *Autobiography*, CW16:202

In our exploration of the *real* Problem-Solving Skills of Computer Science, I mentioned how I learned to rein in my youthful excitement to attack problems at the keyboard, and direct it to more fruitful uses by inserting strategic pauses to consider the matter at hand more carefully. This idea of having Nothing To Do is not really as absurd as it sounds. There are plenty of instances we might provide. Very early in their training, visual artists learn to appreciate the use of contrasts and especially the use of "space"; there is a parallel in the brief but perceptible silence between spoken words, or in the switch between up-bow and down-bow on a stringed instrument, at which it produces no sound;[175] we have already mentioned the almost invisible but terribly useful "white space" which ancient writers did not use. All these, however, seem to be traits of purely human actions, if not actually matters of Art.

It is therefore surprising to find out that there are *practical* uses for such "void" things. It will be even more surprising for you to hear that I used it in one of the most

---

[175] See Forsyth, *Orchestration*, 337 ff.

time-critical pieces of code I have ever written: the innermost routine which played spots for local ad insertion: the routine which fed the MPEG data to the special video playback card. Picture the good guys on the steam locomotive engine trying to catch the bad guys, frantically shoveling coal to keep the wheels cranking... Time was of the essence: once I started playing the spot, I had to keep feeding MPEG to the card as it re-synthesized the audio and video. (Yeah it had buffers, but that playback chip was as voracious for MPEG as the steam engine for coal.) Anyway, the routine was very simple, something like this:

```
repeat
        Read a block of MPEG from the spotfile
        Send the block to the playback card
        Sleep for 0.002 seconds
        Ask the playback card for its status
until we've sent out the entire spotfile
```

Now you will wonder what on earth that instruction "sleep for 0.002 seconds" could possibly mean, given that this is an incredibly critical routine, and if my constant supplying of MPEG falters, the playback card will "starve" and the viewing public will see a pixelated image, or (even worse) a BLANK SCREEN.

(You mean during our spot? Yeah. NO WAY we can let *that* happen, Doc.)

Well... you see, there is a reason for that absurd pause, and it's the sort of thing where one needs to be paying attention to the *whole problem*, and not just trying to play selfish "peephole optimization" games. The fact is that this routine is used within a *playback thread*, of which there were typically *eight* on any given inserter. At any given time, especially at what we called the "witching hours" (the times when commercials are most often played: 28 minutes after the hour, or 2 minutes before the hour; see the sample screen from QANAL a few pages back!) *several* of these threads might be playing simultaneously. Of course this is a single-CPU machine performing time-slicing (multi-tasking) so its Operating System must stop one of the running threads in order to permit another to execute, alternating them in a round-robin fashion. By using this very curious pause, I arranged to demarcate the execution of the routine so as to *give up* the CPU at a point I have selected, rather than take the risk that one playback thread might *starve* another. This is akin to a trick of musicianship worth recounting:

> The extreme shortness of the Bass bow as compared with the length of the string which it has to set in vibration makes a long *tenuto* an impossibility. Even in the *piano* the bow must be changed [in its direction of movement] every three or four seconds. That is not a caution against writing a single long-held note *piano*, for the players will change their bows at discretion, and so secure the *tenuto* effect. **But in the case of a long *legato* phrase it is absolutely essential that the bowing should be broken up.** [that is, arranged in the score *by the composer*.] If this is not done, each player will phrase his part for himself, and places may occur where the whole of the players will accidentally give an undesired prominence to an unintended phraseology.[176]

"Undesired prominence" sounds nicer than *starving*. Indeed, if one is going to deal with any sort of serious work in concurrent programming, it is most advisable for one to investigate a field where such things have been going on – and dealt with – for centuries. Bear in mind that the music does not need to be formally contrapuntal,

---

[176] Forsyth, *Orchestration*, 445, emphasis added.

though that surely sheds remarkable insights upon important topics. But as soon as one has more than one performer, or, as in the case of an organist, or even a violinist, can control the sounding of more than one note simultaneously, one has *concurrency* and must be able to deal with all its complexities. No wonder the First Great Rule of Organ-Playing is "Consonance is always just a half-step away."

Ahem. To resume our main topic of Doing Nothing: I wish to mention one other curious fact from a completely different field, which is no less concurrent: the field of molecular biology. Of course the living cell is awesomely fascinating and contains machinery of extremely concurrent activity: one reference contains an electron micrograph for which the associated text states: "...some genes may have bound up to 70 active transcription complexes at any one time..."[177] Another notes that the human cell contains 100 copies of the 45S pre-rRNA genes, enabling parallel action at a one-hundred-fold rate, necessary for supplying the 5 to 10 million ribosomes required for the cell to divide every 24 hours.[178]

My point, however, has to do with another sort of Nothing, which is suggested by the matter of the secondary structures of RNA as it forms the backbone of the ribosome, or of transfer RNA molecules. It appears that certain portions of the RNA sequence of bases work in tandem, forming what is called a Watson-Crick palindrome, since the two portions of the molecule will form a double helix with each other. The precise character of the sequence does not seem to be relevant, ah, let us say, in the sense that it spells out some "word," but only in the sense that those two portions must correspond, and moreover, *be of the correct length*. I am not speaking from any deep knowledge of molecular biology, but the idea I get is that these things are forming *spacers* which will hold *other parts* of the sequence (that is, the "active" parts) at the appropriate distance. This insight arises directly from computing, as attested even from the most formal treatment of Turing Machines, or by any programmer who has had to manipulate text in any way: there is nothing "different" about a space, or indeed about any character, since there aren't "characters" inside the computer, only representations of small integers. And since RNA contains only the four bases A, C, G, U, and a given sequence is to form a "backbone" to some larger structure, then some portions of that sequence are being used as mere spacing, and not for the sake of what they may be "spelling" out. We are too used to reading, and we naturally see the spaces by a radically different mechanism. Or rather we don't see them at all. But inside the machine, the space " " is just another character like "A" or "0" or "+" or "a" – and 32 is much like 65 or 48 or 43 or 97.

> I have one last comment to make about Nothing, curiously linked to biology: Water is the phantom ingredient in much Italian cooking. One of my students once protested, "When you add water, *you add nothing!*" But that is precisely why we use it. Italian cooking is the art of giving expression to the undisguised flavors of its ingredients. In many circumstances, an over-indulgence in stock, wine, or other flavored liquids would tinge the complexion of a dish with an artificial glow. That is why some recipes will direct that if the quantity of broth used is not sufficient, you should continue cooking with water, as needed. ... Whenever broth or wine has a part in developing the flavor of a dish, it is in the recipe. Otherwise use water.[179]

---

[177] Rawn, *Biochemistry*, 753.

[178] See Darnell, *et al.*, *Molecular Cell Biology*, 357.

[179] Hazan, *The Classic Italian Cookbook*, 18, emphasis added.

Case Study: Cancer Research

There are two kinds of evils which some would call necessary evils. The first kind are those which, necessary or not, are so poignantly and unmistakably evil that no repetition could reconcile us to them; they are obvious, abnormal, inimical to man. Mad dogs, cancer, cruelty to children, innocent men in penal servitude, slicing a man to death in China, or starving a man to death in Hammersmith – these things are unbearable. They should be called unbearable, even while they have to be borne. Even if they were eternal evils, we must still confront them with an eternal impatience. We must be like hounds in leash; sane dogs tugging at our collars to get at the mad dogs and destroy them.
> – GKC, *Illustrated London News*, Nov. 25, 1911 CW29:193

As you will learn in a future volume of this series, my doctoral work was in aid of the work of molecular biologists who were trying to take advantage of the large and growing collection of prokaryotic rRNA sequences. I have been interested in molecular biology for some time, and it has long been apparent to me that there needs to be a unification of our field with theirs, akin to that made between theirs and chemistry almost two centuries ago.[180] But that issue is a large one, and this is not a suitable place for beginning that discussion. I do, however, want to tell you about what was the real beginning of my own work in computational biology (or whatever the appropriate term for the new sub-discipline might be).

It occurred in the fall of 1989, when a friend and erstwhile fellow student from Lehigh called me. He was then doing postdoctoral work at the National Institute of Health, working on an investigation of a certain protein called *p53*, then suspected to be what is termed an *oncogene*: a piece of the cellular machinery which, when operating correctly, tends to prevent cancer.

My friend had performed the sequencing of the relevant gene from samples of two different cancer victims, and had transcribed the sequences. He was trying to bring them into alignment with the "wild" sequence – that is, the equivalent portion of DNA from a non-cancerous human.

You may think this is easy, and it is, relatively – until you actually try it. The intellectual efforts of dealing with these collections of sequences can be very tedious... those same four letters, in seemingly random order... one way is to write them on slips of paper, and then try sliding them back and forth, looking for the place where they are almost the same... It gets dull very quickly.

(People wonder why I dislike playing chess – it's like the most dull sort of debugging, trying to trace hexadecimal values all over memory. Something you almost naturally expect that a machine ought to be doing for you.)

But my friend is a truly scholarly scientist, wise in the manner of classical scientists since he was humble enough to know when to appeal to someone for assistance. He asked me what he ought to do so that he could learn programming.

A fascinating topic, I said; it depends on why you want to learn: was there some particular puzzle you are dealing with, or do you want to extend your knowledge?

We discussed the topic at length over beers, and he showed me the two mutant sequences and the wild sequence – and it was quickly apparent: as good as it would be for him to learn programming, he really needed the answer to his riddle.

So I wrote a program to align the sequences, right there in his apartment.

---

[180] One might date the authentic beginnings of biochemistry to Wöhler's synthesis of an organic compound called urea from inorganic substances in 1828.

Just in case you are wondering, I didn't have to "consult the literature"; this problem is almost as trivial a task as one might find in elementary programming. There were only two aspects of the job which presented even the slightest effort: (1) manage the raw data, since there were *six* experimental fragments, three portions from one sample and three from another, which were to be aligned with the wild *p53* sequence; (2) how to format the output in a tidy and useful way. But neither of these took very long to surmount. My friend read the sequences to me as I typed them, each into its own file, and we ran the program. The result was more than satisfactory: it revealed what he suspected: that the two different cancers arose from two different alterations in the wild sequence.

Here is a portion of the result. Each row has five lines:
 (1) the position
 (2) the amino acid code for the triple in the wild sequence
 (3) the wild sequence for *p53*
 (4) the sequence from the first experimental sample, *test1*
 (5) the sequence from the second experimental sample, *test2*
The dots indicate positions where the experimental sequences agree with the wild sequence. Note that test1 has a mutation T→C at 310, test2 has C→G at 430.

```
              310       320       330       340       350
           N  V  L  S  P  L  P  S  Q  A  M  D  D  L  M  L
p53        CAACGTTCTGTCCCCCTTGCCGTCCCAAGCAATGGATGATTTGATGCTGT
test1      .......C..........................................
test2      ..................................................

              360       370       380       390       400
           S  P  D  D  I  E  Q  W  F  T  E  D  P  G  P  D  E
p53        CCCCGGACGATATTGAACAATGGTTCACTGAAGACCCAGGTCCAGATGAA
test1      ..................................................
test2      ..................................................

              410       420       430       440       450
           A  P  R  M  P  E  A  A  P  V  A  P  A  P  A  A
p53        GCTCCCAGAATGCCAGAGGCTGCTCCCCCCGTGGCCCCTGCACCAGCAGC
test1      ..................................................
test2      ............................G.....................
```

Yes, as you can see, I really did work on cancer. In some small way I helped with the study of the *p53* oncogene.

Remember: this tool was not going to be a major for-sale multiple user application, something where an elegant user interface was needed, or demanding extreme performance. It was the construction of an *ad hoc* piece of lab equipment in the classic mode. The files were typed in by hand from lab notes; the algorithm was as simple as it could be; the result was formatted just enough to be readable by the researcher. There was no need for sophistication... sure there might have been, and there are plenty of opportunities for generalization and extension to make this tool a bit more useful. But the result was good enough for the work of a mere lab assistant, considering it was a very simple little task. Sometimes such little things are needed in order to make real advances.

Case Study: an Unexpected, Eerie, and Powerful Trick

> ...this strangeness of life, this unexpected and even perverse element of things as they fall out, remains incurably interesting.
>
> – GKC, *Heretics*, CW1:143

One of the coolest things I ever learned came from my exploring the run-time libraries of the CDC 6400. I won't give you the original machine instructions, but simply state the effect in pseudo-code. Assume we have two integer values, A and B, and let the operation $\oplus$ represent XOR (pronounced "ex-or"), the Boolean "exclusive OR" operator. Then consider the effect of the following three assignments:

$$A \leftarrow A \oplus B$$
$$B \leftarrow A \oplus B$$
$$A \leftarrow A \oplus B$$

You got that? Ever see it before? Know what it does? Any guess?

All right, don't struggle over it. I didn't think you'd know. I didn't know either.

Well... isn't this an *experimental* science? Aren't we going to try applying our reason to solving it? (If you want to work it out as an exercise, stop reading *now*.)

Let's just see what might possibly happen, given all the possibilities for A and B. Since these things are "words" it hardly matters how many bits they have, as long as we know what happens to each individual bit. Let's rewrite the three steps so we can talk about the intermediate stages without confusion:

$$A_1 \leftarrow A \oplus B$$
$$B_1 \leftarrow A_1 \oplus B$$
$$A_2 \leftarrow A_1 \oplus B_1$$

A	B	A_1	B_1	A_2
0	0	0	0	0
0	1	1	0	1
1	0	1	1	0
1	1	0	1	1

All right – what is this strange thing doing? Can you tell?

Yeah, you got it: B_1 is now A, and A_2 is now B. They have been *swapped*.

So these three strange, almost absurd-looking lines of code *interchange* the values of A and B *without the use of additional storage*.

Wow.

Our author is easily impressed, you are saying. Yeah, I guess so. But I think you'd be hard pressed to work out such a cool trick for yourself.

What do we learn from such things? One is the power of Authority: of those who have already experienced something, and are able to communicate it. Another is the power of "experiment" – even a simply "reasoned" experiment like the above truth-table.[181]

Such clever things can be very impressive, *providing* one gives an adequate explanation in the documentation. Otherwise, they can leave one gasping for air: *this looks so odd – can it mean anything reasonable?* But one needs to trust, even as one uses one's reason. There is no conflict here: in Greek, "trust" and "faith" are the same word. Reason is by no means excluded; rather, it is *expected*.

Of course I cannot pass by this mention of XOR without citing what I call the *locus classicus* of that most curious operator:

Mom: Johnny, do you want ice cream or cake?
Johnny: YES!

In other contexts I call this the Boolean Yes: that is, when "yes" is given as an answer to a question containing an implicit XOR,[182] intended to be responded to by a choice of one or the other.

---

[181] Without venturing into more complex realms, such things hint at what St. Paul calls λογικη λατρεια (*logikê latreia*) = "reasoned service (worship)." See Romans 12:1.

[182] English doesn't have such a thing, except by the unwieldy circumlocution "but not both." Thank God most programming languages do. I wonder if tech mothers say XOR in such cases.

Some Metaphysics and a Conclusion

I have two other case studies to present, though they are rather esoteric, discussing strange matters of mathematics as they enter into computing.

Case Study: One Zero, or Two?

Zero is a marvellous idea, and there has been a lot of interesting material written about what so many people think of as "nothing"; but then so is ε, which is how the theoreticians write the idea called the "empty string" which holds the same place for strings as zero holds for numbers. The other famous symbol like these is ∅, which stands for the empty set.

Now, when I first began learning about the inside workings of computers with respect to that magnificent example called the CDC 6400, I found that the integers were represented in base two and stored in a memory unit containing 60 bits. However, that did not mean such values represented the 2^{60} possible integers from zero to $2^{60}-1$, since one bit was reserved: the topmost bit was called the "sign bit" and indicated whether the number was positive or negative.

To my surprise, the computer had *two* ways of representing zero: the "positive zero" which was 60 zeros, and the "negative zero" which was 60 ones. This sounds strange, and maybe even creepy, but these two zeros behaved just like the mathematical zero when you added them, or did any other sort of arithmetic operation with them. This strange situation was the result of the designers choosing to use what is called One's Complement for the representation of signed integers. That means you could produce the mathematical "negative" of a given integer by performing the Boolean NOT operation on all 60 bits. For example, positive one and negative one are:

+1 = 0000000000 0000000000 0000000000 0000000000 0000000000 0000000001

and

−1 = 1111111111 1111111111 1111111111 1111111111 1111111111 1111111110

Thus, there had to be both a "positive zero" and "negative zero":

+0 = 0000000000 0000000000 0000000000 0000000000 0000000000 0000000000

and

−0 = 1111111111 1111111111 1111111111 1111111111 1111111111 1111111111

So the range of integers which the CDC 6400 could perform computation was from $-2^{59}+1$ to -0, and $+0$ to $+2^{59}-1$. The limit of negatives matched the limit of positives, but elegant tidiness came with the oddity of a "second" zero.

The second computer I studied was the PDP-8. Besides the fact that its memory unit had only 12 bits, and again its topmost bit was used to represent the sign, it used another form of representing signed integers, known as Two's Complement. In order to perform the mathematical "negative" one had to do two steps: first, the Boolean NOT operation, and then *add one*.

Now, let's see how zero is handled when we compute its negative by this means:

0000 0000 0000	zero
1111 1111 1111	result of performing the Boolean NOT
0000 0000 0000	result of adding one (there is also an overflow)

Hence, the negative of zero is indeed zero! There is no odd "second" zero.

166

Just to help you understand what's going on, I'll show two more values:

```
0000 0000 0001    positive one
1111 1111 1110    result of performing the Boolean NOT
1111 1111 1111    result of adding one
```

Hence negative one is represented by 1111 1111 1111.

```
0000 0000 0010    positive two
1111 1111 1101    result of performing the Boolean NOT
1111 1111 1110    result of adding one
```

Hence negative two is represented by 1111 1111 1110.

However this arrangement has a rather different anomaly. Since we use one bit for the sign, we can have any of 2^{11} = 2048 possible values in the remaining eleven bits. That means there are just as many negative numbers as positives – *but* though zero is not "signed" algebraically, it uses up one of those 2048 possible patterns with a positive sign bit. So that means the ah, let us call them "non-negative" numbers are:

0, 1, 2, ... up to 2047,

for a total of 2048, but there are the same quantity of negative numbers, so if we start at –1 and count downwards, we can reach –2048. Thus the range of the negatives is:

–2048, –2047, ... –3, –2, –1

All right, that's not the worst of it. Here's what –2048 looks like in binary:

```
1000 0000 0000
```

Let's see what happens when we try to get its negative:

```
1000 0000 0000    which is –2048
0111 1111 1111    result of performing the Boolean NOT
1000 0000 0000    result of adding one
```

Which means, to our surprise and chagrin, that the negative of –2048 is *itself!* There is no *positive* representation for 2048, not using signed 12-bit two's complement.

So, which is worse? Having two zeros to manage, or an integer which cannot be negated? The designers of a machine have to make some sort of choice, and the only alternative is to not have a signed value at all. (Those "unsigned" integers are convenient to have, but not to the exclusion of the signed kinds!)

This riddle serves to remind us that these things are not really integers at all, but *representations*, and so they require our attention, or at least our continual awareness that they have limits and anomalies.

Case Study: Infinity

Now, having been pestered by zero, let us go to the other end of things and contemplate infinity. There is a famous bit in Chesterton about this:

> To accept everything is an exercise, to understand everything a strain. The poet only desires exaltation and expansion, a world to stretch himself in. The poet only asks to get his head into the heavens. It is the logician who seeks to get the heavens into his head. And it is his head that splits.[183]

In his book on computers Father Jaki has this quote: "That queer quantity 'infinity'is the very mischief and no rational physicist should have anything to do with it." then

---

[183] GKC, *Orthodoxy*, CW1:220

adds, "Wise programmers take note!"[184] At first I was not quite sure what he meant, since (as we have just seen) just trying to manage negation of simple integers can give us a rough time, and there are other riddles we've seen earlier. Certainly no reasonably competent programmer has any difficulty handling infinity. For example:

```
// print out the result of dividing x by y
if(y==0.0)
    printf("%f over %f is Infinity!\n",x,y);
else
    printf("%f over %f is %f\n",x,y,x/y);
```

It's not as if we take literally that famous advertising encomium about the mighty Cray supercomputer:

"It's so fast it can do the infinite loop in a second and a half."[185]

Since even the simplest integers (like zero, or one) are merely *representations* of things which are formally abstract, there is no additional difficulty in handling the representation of the equally abstract "infinity" as well. Indeed, since I have in this very line typed the word "infinity" into my computer and the Universe has not ended, nor has my computer crashed, there is nothing very special about having a representation of INFINITY in a computer. In fact, the CDC 6400 had two representations for floating-point infinity, one positive, one negative:

$+\infty$ = 3777 xxxx xxxx xxxx xxxx (octal)

$-\infty$ = 4000 xxxx xxxx xxxx xxxx (octal)

Only the top 12 bits indicated the condition; the lower 48 bits were irrelevant. And even the x86 family (the chips used by many commercially available personal computers) also have two infinities for floating-point:

$+\infty$ = 7F 80 00 00 (hex)

$-\infty$ = FF 80 00 00 (hex)

Why do these exist, and what role do they play?

Very simply, let us say we attempt the division of one by zero, which, people think is called "infinite" by the mathematicians. I could try to yell and rant and dance (though I do not dance) an explanation why this is NOT true. Mathematicians know better: they know "infinity" is not the name of a "number." (They sometimes commit heresy, just as astronomers who – in weak moments – declare their admiration for a gorgeous *sunset*.)

Then again, I've seen electrical engineers do an equivalent kind of rant (and dance) to compute the "derivative" of the unit step function, and explain why they pretend infinity "is" a number, and then play with it. Thank God their "zero" isn't zero, or their first "short circuit" would have long since melted the universe, hee hee.

But to give just the slightest explanation: the idea of infinity comes down to *ideas*, not numbers. A typical mathematician trying to speak precisely will say something like: "As x decreases towards zero, the value of $1/x$ increases without

---

[184] Jaki, *Brain, Mind, and Computers*, 281-2 quoting Eddington, *New Pathways in Science*, 217.

[185] I can't give a citation for this. I heard it long ago, and it's still awesomely funny. It's worth mentioning that it has a "negative" something like this: "That company times their benchmarks with a sundial." But then you should see the discussion on timing earlier in this book.

bound." That is what is meant; nothing more. (The missing word in such discussions is "limit"; see any introduction to Calculus for a full and rigorous treatment.)

The issue of those representations of floating-point infinity doesn't simply have to do with setting up the mechanics of what ought to get produced when one divides by *zero* precisely. The issue has to do with difficulties in the representations of floating-point numbers. You might *not* really be dividing by zero, but by a very small number, and because there are some peculiarities about the range – that is, not every "very small" number has a corresponding "very large" number as an inverse, just as two's complement integers have a negative which has no corresponding positive. So it would be best to produce some rational result (no pun intended) which the programmer can handle appropriately. Yes, attempting admittedly forbidden computations is clearly an error, if it is not just a joke or a test, but it does not *always* mean the program should "abort" and just "go away"; sometimes the computation is not formally forbidden, it is merely beyond the machine's range, so special action has to be taken.

No, on second thought, Father Jaki was right: *Wise programmers take note.*

A Conclusion

So, what is the conclusion? First, we are merely concluding this volume; there are three others planned which will investigate three interesting topics in somewhat greater detail:

(1) string theory and the "wildcard" alphabet used in DNA sequence analysis;

(2) a local ad insertion system, including monitoring and file transport;

(3) two difficult problems arising from the needs of the users of a numerically controlled punch press.

There may be more beyond these three; certainly there are many other strange and interesting stories to tell, and further insights to be explored.

But also we have tried to spend a little time exploring our discipline, giving it a very casual sort of organization, and drawing links from a variety of sources and disciplines. Some of these suggest material for other monographs: an exploration of the history of computing, with attention to the ideas explored here; more on the metaphysics and on the philosophy of the discipline, with attention to the very deep hints which have been raised; a mini-reference of some major characters of the field, with their dates, tiny biographies and especially their role in advancing the work; it should include a chronology showing major milestones. Whether I write these or someone else does is not of issue; the point is to write them eventually.

And there's always room for more real programming: reference books, annotated examples, and all that. Real code can be just as useful as an algorithm even when the theorems are proven in the accompanying paper; sometimes the code itself helps explain more than the theorems do. It's lots harder to overlook special cases when you have to get the program running.

Sure, it sounds like a lot of work, and probably hard work too. But then as a young friend of mine said at a moment like this:

"Somebody has to do the hard jobs."

Appendix 1 – Some Useful Values

(See Appendix 2 for the powers of two, which are also useful.)

The Metric Prefixes

kilo = thousand (10^3 or 1e3)   milli = thousandth (10^{-3} or 1e–3)

mega = million (10^6 or 1e6)   micro = millionth (10^{-6} or 1e–6)

giga = billion (10^9 or 1e9)   nano = billionth (10^{-9} or 1e–9)

tera = trillion (10^{12} or 1e12)   pico = trillionth (10^{-12} or 1e–12)

peta = quadrillion (10^{15} or 1e15)   femto = quadrillionth (10^{-15} or 1e–15)

exa = quintillion (10^{18} or 1e18)   atto = quintillionth (10^{-18} or 1e–18)

Some Constants [186]

π = 3.14159 26535 89793 23846 26433 83279 50288 41971 69399...

e = 2.71828 18284 59045 23536 02874 71352 66249 77572 47093...

ϕ = 1.61803 39887 49894 84820 45868 34365 63811 77203 09180...

$\sqrt{2}$ = 1.41421 35623 73095 04880 16887 24209 69807 85696 71875...

$\log_{10} 2$ = 0.30102 99956 63981 19521 37388 94724 49302 67681 89881...

Some notes about these:

• π is the ratio of the circumference to the diameter for any circle. It was apparently called that since the word *perimeter* begins with p. In the Bible, when the Temple equipment was being arranged, π was estimated to be *three*:

> He made also a molten sea, of ten cubits, from brim to brim, round all about; the
> height of it was five cubits, and a line of thirty cubits compassed it round about.
>
> 1 Kings (3Kings) 7:23

π was proven to be transcendental by Lindemann in 1882, thus finally answering the over 2000-year-old question about "squaring the circle." The decimal expansion of π does not repeat, nor is it the root of any polynomial with integer coefficients.

In 1897 Edwin J. Goodwin, M.D. tried to the get Indiana General Assembly to pass a bill (#246) which would have enacted the "value" of π to be 3.2; it would have also altered $\sqrt{2}$ to be 10/7 = 1.428571 428571...

Some people still persist in using 22/7 as an approximation to π, which ought to be reserved only for rough back-of-envelope computations, since it is off in the third decimal place:

22/7 = 3.14285 71428 57142...

π = 3.14159 26535 89793...

A somewhat better fraction is 355/113, which is only wrong by about 2.66e–7:

355/113 = 3.14159 29203 5398...

π = 3.14159 26535 89793...

---

[186] From *CRC Standard Mathematical Tables*. The given values are truncated, not rounded.

Note: a programmer ought *never* "compute" π by relying on a built-in function such as arctangent.[187] When you need π in a program, determine what sort of computational error you can tolerate and then code the constant explicitly, stating that error limit.

● e is the base of the natural logarithms, and was devised by Euler. It is the area under the infinitely long curve $y = 1/x$, starting at 1 and proceeding to the right forever:

$$e = \int_1^\infty \frac{1}{x} \cdot dx$$

● $\sqrt{2}$ While it's not possible to "square the circle" it is quite easy to construct a line segment with an irrational length: in the right isosceles triangle with legs of unit length, the hypotenuse has length $\sqrt{2}$.

● $\log_{10} 2$ is a number to have in your bag-of-tricks for quick computations. You can divide any power of ten by 0.3 to approximate the power of two nearest it. Or multiply the power of two by 0.3 for the power of ten nearest it. For example:
  (1) What power of two is near $1000 = 10^3$?
      Divide 3 by 0.3 to get 10.
      Thus 10^3 is about 2^{10}. Actually $2^{10} = 1024$.
  (2) What power of ten is near 2^{20}?
      Multiply 20 by 0.3 to get 6.
      Thus 2^{20} is about 10^6. Actually $2^{20} = 1048576$.

● ϕ is also called the Golden Number. It is simply $\phi = \dfrac{1+\sqrt{5}}{2}$. Among other things, it is the limit of the ratio of adjacent Fibonacci numbers: 3/2, 5/3, 8/5, 13/8, 21/13, ...

Recall that Fibonacci numbers are defined recursively:
    F(0)=1,
    F(1)=1,
and for $n>1$,
    F(n)=F(n–1)+F(n–2).

---

[187] Because $\pi/4 = \tan^{-1}(1)$.

Time

1,000 seconds	= 16 minutes 40 seconds
1,000,000 seconds	= 11 days 13 hours 46 minutes 40 seconds
1,000,000,000 seconds	= 11,574 days 1 hour 46 minutes 40 seconds
	= 31 years [188] 259 days 1 hour 46 minutes 40 seconds
	(259 days is about eight and a half months)

1 day (24 hours)	= 1,440 minutes
	= 86,400 seconds
1 week (7 days)	= 168 hours
	= 10,080 minutes
	= 604,800 seconds
1 standard year	= 365 days
	= 8,760 hours
	= 525,600 minutes
	= 31,536,000 seconds

(Hence, π seconds is just short of 1 nanocentury.)

A useful power-of-two rule about music

Middle A is 440 Hz. Assuming equal temperament, Middle C is 261.63 Hz. Also, the 60Hz "hum" of standard AC line current is almost exactly the quarter-sharp between A# and B in the 16-foot octave (between the second A#/B on a piano).

Organ techs know a handy way of using the powers of two as a shorthand for the foot-lengths of organ pipes. Middle C is about $256 = 2^8$ Hz, produced by a (nominal) 2-foot open pipe, and since pitch is inversely related to pipe length, we may write:

$$9 = L + f$$

where $L = \log_2(\text{pipe length})$ and $f = \log_2(\text{frequency})$. Hence a 16-foot pipe sounds at 32 Hz, which is the lowest C on the piano. The top C on the piano is produced by a open pipe of length 1.5 inches or 2^{-3} feet, so its frequency is about $2^{12} = 4096$ Hz (4186.01 Hz in equal temperament based on A=440).

---

[188] In this equivalence "one year" is defined as 365 days exactly, so an adjustment for leap years must be made when an actual interval of time (between real dates) is being determined.

A Few Useful Equations

Trigonometry:

Sum and difference of angles

$$\sin(\alpha + \beta) = \sin(\alpha)\cos(\beta) + \cos(\alpha)\sin(\beta)$$
$$\cos(\alpha + \beta) = \cos(\alpha)\cos(\beta) - \sin(\alpha)\sin(\beta)$$
$$\sin(\alpha - \beta) = \sin(\alpha)\cos(\beta) - \cos(\alpha)\sin(\beta)$$
$$\cos(\alpha - \beta) = \cos(\alpha)\cos(\beta) + \sin(\alpha)\sin(\beta)$$

Combinatorics:

Permutations (where order matters)

The number of permutations of n things taken r at a time is given by:

$$P_{n,r} = \frac{n!}{(n-r)!}$$

Combinations (where order does *not* matter)

The number of combinations of n things taken r at a time is given by:

$$C_{n,r} = \binom{n}{r} = \frac{n!}{r!(n-r)!}$$

which is also item r in row n of Pascal's Triangle.

Sums of series:

$$1 + 2 + 3 + \ldots + n = \sum_{i=1}^{n} i = \frac{n(n+1)}{2}$$

$$1 + 2^2 + 3^2 + \ldots + n^2 = \sum_{i=1}^{n} i^2 = \frac{n(n+1)(2n+1)}{6}$$

$$1 + 2^3 + 3^3 + \ldots + n^3 = \sum_{i=1}^{n} i^3 = \frac{n^2(n+1)^2}{4}$$

$$1 + 2 + 4 + 8 + \ldots + 2^n = \sum_{i=0}^{n} 2^i = 2^{n+1} - 1$$

$$d^0 + d^1 + d^2 + d^3 + d^4 + \ldots + d^n = \sum_{i=0}^{n} d^i = \frac{d^{n+1} - 1}{d - 1} \qquad \text{(for an integer } d > 1\text{)}$$

Appendix 2 – Two and its Powers

Two is a curious old thing. No doubt you know about the grammatical term *number*, which describes a word as being *singular* or *plural*. Some ancient human languages like ancient Egyptian,[189] ancient Greek, and Old English also had the *dual*, which is special endings for things which come in pairs; there are even traces of it in Latin.

n	2^n	n	2^n	
0	1	33	8589934592	8.5e9
1	2	34	17179869184	1.7e10
2	4	35	34359738368	3.4e10
3	8	36	68719476736	6.8e10
4	16	37	137438953472	1.3e11
5	32	38	274877906944	2.7e11
6	64	39	549755813888	5.4e11
7	128	40	1099511627776	1.0e12
8	256	41	2199023255552	2.1e12
9	512	42	4398046511104	4.3e12
10	1024	43	8796093022208	8.7e12
11	2048	44	17592186044416	1.7e13
12	4096	45	35184372088832	3.5e13
13	8192	46	70368744177664	7.0e13
14	16384	47	140737488355328	1.4e14
15	32768	48	281474976710656	2.8e14
16	65536	49	562949953421312	5.6e14
17	131072	50	1125899906842624	1.1e15
18	262144	51	2251799813685248	2.2e15
19	524288	52	4503599627370496	4.5e15
20	1048576	53	9007199254740992	9.0e15
21	2097152	54	18014398509481984	1.8e16
22	4194304	55	36028797018963968	3.6e16
23	8388608	56	72057594037927936	7.2e16
24	16777216	57	144115188075855872	1.4e17
25	33554432	58	288230376151711744	2.8e17
26	67108864	59	576460752303423488	5.7e17
27	134217728	60	1152921504606846976	1.1e18
28	268435456	61	2305843009213693952	2.3e18
29	536870912	62	4611686018427387904	4.6e18
30	1073741824	63	9223372036854775808	9.2e18
31	2147483648	64	18446744073709551616	1.8e19
32	4294967296	65	36893488147419103232	3.6e19

Note: computer scientists should know by heart up to 2^{16}, as well as 2^{20} and 2^{32}.

Some observations:

2^{10} is 1,024. In the old days the epigram said "A picture is worth a thousand words." In this base-two era we might say it's worth 1,024 words. (No doubt the increase is due to inflation.)

2^{20} is 1,048,576. Hence the game of "Twenty Questions" (answered "yes" or "no") permits selection among more than a million items.

---

[189] The dual was represented by repeating a hieroglyph twice, and the plural three times; later this was abbreviated by a pair or triple of vertical strokes.

2^{30} is 1,073,741,824 – just past one billion. To help gauge the size, a billion seconds is over thirty-one years, and the circumference of the Earth is about 1.5 billion inches, or 4 billion centimeters.

2^{64} is 18,446,744,073,709,551,616 – a handy approximation to remember is 18e18. A Coulomb is about 6e18 electrons, so 2^{64} is about 3 Coulombs. Hence, if you let a 100-watt light burn for a little over 3 seconds, 2^{64} electrons will pass through it. Also, 2^{64} is approximately 9·20!, hence factorials past 20 don't fit into 64 bit integers.

It's not in this table, but 2^{79} = 604,462,909,807,314,587,353,088, which is very close to Avogadro's Number, 6.023e23, the number of atoms/molecules in one mole of a chemical substance.

Negative powers of two

Fractions have always seemed to be a difficulty. Often there was a simple idiom which suggested a fraction having *one* in the numerator, which may account for the English convention of using the ordinal terms (i.e., "third" or "fifth") in our formula for fractions. It's an ancient technique: typically the fractions in Egyptian hieroglyphics always had a one in the numerator, and any others occurring in problems had to be represented as sums: for example, 4/7 was written as 1/2 + 1/14. A curious story relates to the Egyptian hieroglyphics (called "the corn measure") for the first six negative powers of two. As Sir Alan Gardiner reports:

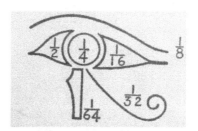

> In their measures for corn and for land, the Egyptians appear to have preserved a more primitive kind of fractions obtained by halving. ... The symbols employed in this, as shown in the accompanying cut, are derived from the ancient myth according to which the eye of the falcon-god Horus... was torn into fragments by the wicked god Seth. Later the ibis-god Thoth miraculously "filled" or "completed" the eye, joining together the parts, whereby the eye regained its title to be called "the sound eye." ... These fractions together add up to 63/64; presumably the missing 1/64 was supplied magically by Thoth.[190]

Which may suggest that the Egyptians guessed that the infinite sum of negative powers of two converges to unity:

$$1 = \frac{1}{2} + \frac{1}{4} + \frac{1}{8} + \frac{1}{16} + \frac{1}{32} + \frac{1}{64} + \sum_{i=7}^{\infty} \frac{1}{2^i}$$

---

[190] Gardiner, *Egyptian Grammar*, § 266.

n	2^n
-1	0.5
-2	0.25
-3	0.125
-4	0.0625
-5	0.03125
-6	0.015625
-7	0.0078125
-8	0.00390625
-9	0.001953125
-10	0.0009765625
-11	0.00048828125
-12	0.000244140625
-13	0.0001220703125
-14	0.00006103515625
-15	0.000030517578125
-16	0.0000152587890625
-17	0.00000762939453125
-18	0.000003814697265625
-19	0.0000019073486328125
-20	0.00000095367431640625
-21	0.000000476837158203125
-22	0.0000002384185791015625
-23	0.00000011920928955078125
-24	0.000000059604644775390625
-25	0.0000000298023223876953125
-26	0.00000001490116119384765625
-27	0.000000007450580596923828125
-28	0.0000000037252902984619140625
-29	0.00000000186264514923095703125
-30	0.000000000931322574615478515625
-31	0.0000000004656612873077392578125
-32	0.00000000023283064365386962890625
-33	0.000000000116415321826934814453125
-34	0.0000000000582076609134674072265625
-35	0.00000000002910383045673370361328125
-36	0.000000000014551915228366851806640625
-37	0.0000000000072759576141834259033203125
-38	0.00000000000363797880709171295166015625
-39	0.000000000001818989403545856475830078125
-40	0.0000000000009094947017729282379150390625
-41	0.00000000000045474735088646411895751953125
-42	0.000000000000227373675443232059478759765625
-43	0.0000000000001136868377216160297393798828125
-44	0.00000000000005684341886080801486968994140625
-45	0.000000000000028421709430404007434844970703125
-46	0.0000000000000142108547152020037174224853515625
-47	0.00000000000000710542735760100185871124267578125
-48	0.000000000000003552713678800500929355621337890625
-49	0.0000000000000017763568394002504646778106689453125
-50	0.00000000000000088817841970012523233890533447265625

The last primes which need to be tested as possible factors for integers stored as signed 32 and 64 bit values:

$$46{,}340 < (2^{31})^{1/2} < 46{,}341 \qquad \text{(last prime is 46,337)}$$
$$3{,}037{,}000{,}499 < (2^{63})^{1/2} < 3{,}037{,}000{,}500 \qquad \text{(last prime is 3,037,000,493)}$$

What Fits into *One* Byte, or *Eight* Bits

The 256 possible eight-bit values, written in binary, octal, hexadecimal, and decimal:

binary	oct	hx	dec	binary	oct	hx	dec	binary	oct	hx	dec	binary	oct	hx	dec
0	000	00	0	1000000	100	40	64	10000000	200	80	128	11000000	300	c0	192
1	001	01	1	1000001	101	41	65	10000001	201	81	129	11000001	301	c1	193
10	002	02	2	1000010	102	42	66	10000010	202	82	130	11000010	302	c2	194
11	003	03	3	1000011	103	43	67	10000011	203	83	131	11000011	303	c3	195
100	004	04	4	1000100	104	44	68	10000100	204	84	132	11000100	304	c4	196
101	005	05	5	1000101	105	45	69	10000101	205	85	133	11000101	305	c5	197
110	006	06	6	1000110	106	46	70	10000110	206	86	134	11000110	306	c6	198
111	007	07	7	1000111	107	47	71	10000111	207	87	135	11000111	307	c7	199
1000	010	08	8	1001000	110	48	72	10001000	210	88	136	11001000	310	c8	200
1001	011	09	9	1001001	111	49	73	10001001	211	89	137	11001001	311	c9	201
1010	012	0a	10	1001010	112	4a	74	10001010	212	8a	138	11001010	312	ca	202
1011	013	0b	11	1001011	113	4b	75	10001011	213	8b	139	11001011	313	cb	203
1100	014	0c	12	1001100	114	4c	76	10001100	214	8c	140	11001100	314	cc	204
1101	015	0d	13	1001101	115	4d	77	10001101	215	8d	141	11001101	315	cd	205
1110	016	0e	14	1001110	116	4e	78	10001110	216	8e	142	11001110	316	ce	206
1111	017	0f	15	1001111	117	4f	79	10001111	217	8f	143	11001111	317	cf	207
10000	020	10	16	1010000	120	50	80	10010000	220	90	144	11010000	320	d0	208
10001	021	11	17	1010001	121	51	81	10010001	221	91	145	11010001	321	d1	209
10010	022	12	18	1010010	122	52	82	10010010	222	92	146	11010010	322	d2	210
10011	023	13	19	1010011	123	53	83	10010011	223	93	147	11010011	323	d3	211
10100	024	14	20	1010100	124	54	84	10010100	224	94	148	11010100	324	d4	212
10101	025	15	21	1010101	125	55	85	10010101	225	95	149	11010101	325	d5	213
10110	026	16	22	1010110	126	56	86	10010110	226	96	150	11010110	326	d6	214
10111	027	17	23	1010111	127	57	87	10010111	227	97	151	11010111	327	d7	215
11000	030	18	24	1011000	130	58	88	10011000	230	98	152	11011000	330	d8	216
11001	031	19	25	1011001	131	59	89	10011001	231	99	153	11011001	331	d9	217
11010	032	1a	26	1011010	132	5a	90	10011010	232	9a	154	11011010	332	da	218
11011	033	1b	27	1011011	133	5b	91	10011011	233	9b	155	11011011	333	db	219
11100	034	1c	28	1011100	134	5c	92	10011100	234	9c	156	11011100	334	dc	220
11101	035	1d	29	1011101	135	5d	93	10011101	235	9d	157	11011101	335	dd	221
11110	036	1e	30	1011110	136	5e	94	10011110	236	9e	158	11011110	336	de	222
11111	037	1f	31	1011111	137	5f	95	10011111	237	9f	159	11011111	337	df	223
100000	040	20	32	1100000	140	60	96	10100000	240	a0	160	11100000	340	e0	224
100001	041	21	33	1100001	141	61	97	10100001	241	a1	161	11100001	341	e1	225
100010	042	22	34	1100010	142	62	98	10100010	242	a2	162	11100010	342	e2	226
100011	043	23	35	1100011	143	63	99	10100011	243	a3	163	11100011	343	e3	227
100100	044	24	36	1100100	144	64	100	10100100	244	a4	164	11100100	344	e4	228
100101	045	25	37	1100101	145	65	101	10100101	245	a5	165	11100101	345	e5	229
100110	046	26	38	1100110	146	66	102	10100110	246	a6	166	11100110	346	e6	230
100111	047	27	39	1100111	147	67	103	10100111	247	a7	167	11100111	347	e7	231
101000	050	28	40	1101000	150	68	104	10101000	250	a8	168	11101000	350	e8	232
101001	051	29	41	1101001	151	69	105	10101001	251	a9	169	11101001	351	e9	233
101010	052	2a	42	1101010	152	6a	106	10101010	252	aa	170	11101010	352	ea	234
101011	053	2b	43	1101011	153	6b	107	10101011	253	ab	171	11101011	353	eb	235
101100	054	2c	44	1101100	154	6c	108	10101100	254	ac	172	11101100	354	ec	236
101101	055	2d	45	1101101	155	6d	109	10101101	255	ad	173	11101101	355	ed	237
101110	056	2e	46	1101110	156	6e	110	10101110	256	ae	174	11101110	356	ee	238
101111	057	2f	47	1101111	157	6f	111	10101111	257	af	175	11101111	357	ef	239
110000	060	30	48	1110000	160	70	112	10110000	260	b0	176	11110000	360	f0	240
110001	061	31	49	1110001	161	71	113	10110001	261	b1	177	11110001	361	f1	241
110010	062	32	50	1110010	162	72	114	10110010	262	b2	178	11110010	362	f2	242
110011	063	33	51	1110011	163	73	115	10110011	263	b3	179	11110011	363	f3	243
110100	064	34	52	1110100	164	74	116	10110100	264	b4	180	11110100	364	f4	244
110101	065	35	53	1110101	165	75	117	10110101	265	b5	181	11110101	365	f5	245
110110	066	36	54	1110110	166	76	118	10110110	266	b6	182	11110110	366	f6	246
110111	067	37	55	1110111	167	77	119	10110111	267	b7	183	11110111	367	f7	247
111000	070	38	56	1111000	170	78	120	10111000	270	b8	184	11111000	370	f8	248
111001	071	39	57	1111001	171	79	121	10111001	271	b9	185	11111001	371	f9	249
111010	072	3a	58	1111010	172	7a	122	10111010	272	ba	186	11111010	372	fa	250
111011	073	3b	59	1111011	173	7b	123	10111011	273	bb	187	11111011	373	fb	251
111100	074	3c	60	1111100	174	7c	124	10111100	274	bc	188	11111100	374	fc	252
111101	075	3d	61	1111101	175	7d	125	10111101	275	bd	189	11111101	375	fd	253
111110	076	3e	62	1111110	176	7e	126	10111110	276	be	190	11111110	376	fe	254
111111	077	3f	63	1111111	177	7f	127	10111111	277	bf	191	11111111	377	ff	255

Appendix 3 – Factorials

n	n!		
1	1		
2	2		
3	6		
4	24		
5	120		
6	720		
7	5040		
8	40320		
9	362880		
10	3628800	3e6	(over 3 million)
11	39916800	3e7	
12	479001600	4e8	
13	6227020800	6e9	(exceeds 2^{32})
14	87178291200	8e10	
15	1307674368000	1e12	(over a trillion)
16	20922789888000	2e13	
17	355687428096000	3e14	
18	6402373705728000	6e15	
19	121645100408832000	1e17	
20	2432902008176640000	2e18	(about a third of a coulomb)
21	51090942171709440000	5e19	(exceeds 2^{64})
22	1124000727777607680000	1e21	
23	25852016738884976640000	2e22	
24	620448401733239439360000	6e23	(about a mole)
25	15511210043330985984000000	1e25	
52	about 8e67	(possible shuffles of a standard 52-card deck)	
170	about 7e306	(maximum in the 8-byte floating point x86 format)	

Stirling's approximation [191] for factorial:

$$n! = \left(\frac{n}{e}\right)^n \sqrt{2\pi \cdot n} + h \text{ for } n > 0, \text{ where } h \text{ is such that } 0 < \frac{h}{n!} < \frac{1}{12n} \ .$$

Limits for binary representations:

The 32-bit (four-byte) limit is 12 since $12! < 2^{32} < 13!$

$$12! = 479{,}001{,}600$$
$$2^{32} = 4{,}294{,}967{,}296$$
$$13! = 6{,}227{,}020{,}800$$

The 64-bit (eight-byte) limit is 20 since $20! < 2^{64} < 21!$

$$20! = 2{,}432{,}902{,}008{,}176{,}640{,}000$$
$$2^{64} = 18{,}446{,}744{,}073{,}709{,}551{,}616$$
$$21! = 51{,}090{,}942{,}171{,}709{,}440{,}000$$

---

[191] See *CRC Standard Mathematical Tables*, 49.

Appendix 4 – Pascal's Triangle

Some notes about this useful tool.

For non-negative integers n and r, the r-th entry in the n-th row of the triangle is the combinatoric:

$$P(n, r) = \binom{n}{r} = \frac{n!}{r!(n-r)!}$$

$P(n, r)$ can also be defined recursively:
  $P(n, 0) = 1$ for any $n \geq 0$
  $P(n, n) = 1$ for any $n \geq 0$
  $P(n, r) = P(n-1, r-1) + P(n-1, r)$
This means
  $P(n, 1) = P(n, n-1) = n$ for $n>0$
  $P(n, r) = P(n, n-r)$ for $n>0$, $0 \leq r \leq n$
Hence, every row is a palindrome, term-wise.

Even-numbered rows have an *odd* number of terms, in which the central member $P(n, n/2)$ is maximal for that row.
Odd-numbered rows have an *even* number of terms, in which the central members $P(n, (n-1)/2)$ and $P(n, (n-1)/2 + 1)$ are maximal for that row.

The sum of all the terms in a given row n is $\sum_{r=0}^{n} \binom{n}{r} = 2^n$

Some values for handling the range of integers

n	r	P(n,r)	comments
32	16	601080390	max in that row
33	16	1166803110	max for signed 32-bit
		2147483648	$= 2^{31}$
34	16	2203961430	overflow for signed 32-bit
34	17	2333606220	max for unsigned 32-bit (max in that row)
		4294967296	$= 2^{32}$
35	17	4537567650	overflow for unsigned 32-bit (max in that row)

All values of $P(n,r)$ for $n \leq 34$ except $n = 34$ and $r = 16, 17, 18$ are within range of a *signed* 32-bit integer.
All values of $P(n,r)$ for $n \leq 35$ except $n = 35$ and $r = 17, 18$ are within range of an *unsigned* 32-bit integer.

n	r	P(n,r)	comments
64	32	1832624140942590534	
66	33	7219428434016265740	max in that row
67	29	7886597962249166160	max for signed 64-bit
		9223372036854775808	$= 2^{63}$
67	30	9989690752182277136	overflow for signed 64-bit
67	33	14226520737620288370	max in that row
68	30	17876288714431443296	max for unsigned 64-bit
		18446744073709551616	$= 2^{64}$
68	31	21912870037044995008	overflow for unsigned 64-bit
68	34	28453041475240576740	max in that row

All values of $P(n,r)$ for $n \leq 67$ except $n=67$ and $30 \leq r \leq 37$ are within range of a *signed* 64-bit integer.
All values of $P(n,r)$ for $n \leq 68$ except $n=68$ and $31 \leq r \leq 37$ are within range of an *unsigned* 64-bit integer.

Appendix 5 – The ASCII Character Set

(ASCII = American Standard Code for Information Interchange)

	0	1	2	3	4	5	6	7		8	9	a	b	c	d	e	f
2		!	"	#	$	%	&	'		(	)	*	+	,	-	.	/
3	0	1	2	3	4	5	6	7		8	9	:	;	<	=	>	?
4	@	A	B	C	D	E	F	G		H	I	J	K	L	M	N	O
5	P	Q	R	S	T	U	V	W		X	Y	Z	[	\	]	^	_
6	`	a	b	c	d	e	f	g		h	i	j	k	l	m	n	o
7	p	q	r	s	t	u	v	w		x	y	z	{			}	~	µ

Note: An eight-bit byte provides 256 possible representations. However, ASCII was originally a *seven* bit code, with the eighth (topmost) bit used for parity: it was set so that every pattern contained an *even* number of bits which were one. Any character containing an *odd* number was deemed in error. It was not until later (maybe in the 1980s) that the above table became the usual representation, which relies on a "zero" parity. That is, the topmost bit is always zero, and no test for parity is performed. This presumably enabled another 128 characters, but of course there was no standard for what they are; now there are even larger encoding schemes, and the slow en-Babel-ing of the field creeps onwards, alas.

Also note that rows 0 and 1 were assigned to non-printing "control characters" such as 0001101, hex 0d is the "carriage return"; 0001010, hex 0a is "line feed"; the "ESCAPE" symbol is 0011011, hex 1b. (Note I have used the classic seven bits here.) The "carriage return" comes from the antecedent manual printing devices called "typewriters" as it "returned" the "carriage," effectively bringing the printhead back to the leftmost point in preparation for a new line of output; the "line-feed" ratcheted the carriage so that the paper advanced by one line. The "carriage return" is sometimes called the "Enter" key, though that may also be the "line-feed" depending; but it often has the effect of both, as some old-timers recall writing 13 and 10 (or 15, 12 in octal or 0xd, 0xa in hex).

Appendix 6 – Equipping Your Lab or Office

There are a number of useful items you ought to have at your disposal. I also include several titles "for further reading,"

Reference Works
   a. CRC *Handbook of Chemistry and Physics*, and *Standard Mathematical Tables*
   b. *The World of Mathematics* (4 volumes).
   c. Knuth, *The Art of Computer Programming* (multiple volumes).
   d. *Gray's Anatomy*.
   e. Wall chart of the Metabolic Processes.
   f. Latin/English dictionary. (Yeah, but you might be surprised.)
   g. Newman, *The Idea of a University*.

You should also have a good dictionary or two (sometimes older editions are more useful than newer ones!), an atlas, a thesaurus, and standard texts on algebra, logic, algorithms, automata theory, molecular biology, developmental anatomy, and any texts relevant to your specialty, as well as others which are irrelevant. Star charts, mineral samples, and other exhibits are up to you.

Lab Equipment
   a. notebook(s) and writing implements
   b. graph paper
   c. plenty of scrap paper
   d. set of colored pencils *and* a box of crayons
   e. ruler, protractor, compass, 30-60-90 triangle, scissors, etc.

Demonstration Tools
   a. SCRABBLE board game.
   b. 2 or 3 decks of standard playing cards, preferably all the same design.
   c. several dice (including the so-called "D&D" geometric dice, if possible).
   d. a standard (3x3x3, six-color) Rubik's Cube
   e. a ball of string (for demonstrating "string" theory, hee hee.)
   f. "Towers of Brahma/Hanoi." (If you are a woodworker, make this yourself.)
   h. a set of nesting "Russian Dolls" (*Matryoshka*).

For Further Reading (several of these are available on the web)
   a. Carroll, Lewis. *Alice's Adventures In Wonderland*.
      —. *Through the Looking Glass*.
   b. Juster, Norton. *The Phantom Tollbooth*.
   c. Sayers, Dorothy L. "The Lost Tools of Learning" (essay)
   d. Tolkien, J.R.R. "On Fairy-Stories" in *The Tolkien Reader*. (essay)
   e. E.E. "Doc" Smith. *Spacehounds of IPC*, and the Skylark series: *The Skylark of Space, Skylark Three, Skylark of Valeron, Skylark Duquesne*.
   f. GKC, "The Mistake of the Machine" in *The Wisdom of Father Brown*. (short story)

Have These Around Somewhere for Poking Into:
a. Babbage, Charles. *The Ninth Bridgewater Treatise*.
b. Boole, George. *The Laws of Thought*.
c. Peter of Spain (Pope John XXI), *Summulae Logicales*.
d. Euclid, *The Elements*.
e. Boethius. *The Consolation of Philosophy*. (available in English translation)

For Further Watching
a. *Desk Set* (with Spencer Tracy and Kathryn Hepburn).
b. *TRON*.

Utilities You Should Have (even if you have to write them yourself)
dump dumps the raw contents of a file in both hex and ASCII
sock listens to a specified UDP port and IP address (and also one for TCP)
base converts numbers between specified bases

Here is a sample output from sock, showing a cue packet:

```
F:\>sock r 5501 127.0.0.1
Host name: MyComputer
Official name MyComputer
Network interface  1: 127.  0.  0.  1
Receiving from 5501 on 127.0.0.1
..........
09/23/2013 11:45:14.453  rcv from 127.0.0.1 port 49156
Packet Length: 37
   0 41 6d 44 67 31 37 66 66 65 63 64 38 31 32 32 30 AmDg17ffecd81220
  10 31 33 30 39 32 33 31 31 34 35 31 34 34 35 33 20 130923114514453
  20 30 20 4f 4c 4e                                  0 OLN
```

Appendix 7 – Some Quotes, Maxims, and Epigrams
(collected here for convenience)

I revert to the doctrinal methods of the thirteenth century, inspired by the general hope of getting something done. – GKC, *Heretics*, CW1:46.

Divide et impera = "Divide and rule" – in *Bartlett's* ("ancient political maxim cited by Machiavelli")

Dic Cur Hic = "Tell Why You Are Here." (I learned this saying from my mother.)

A thing is more perfect as it is more perfectly one. – Kreyche, *First Philosophy*, where it is called a "principle of overwhelming practical application."

Quis custodiet ipsos custodes? = "Who will watch the watchers themselves?" – Juvenal, Satire VI.

The machinery of the world has been built for us by the Best and Most Orderly Workman of all. – Copernicus, in the Dedication to Pope Paul III of his *De Revolutionibus* (*On the Revolutions of the Heavenly Spheres*), quoted in Jaki, *The Road of Science and the Ways to God*, ch. 3 note 60.

The purpose of computing is insight not numbers. – Hamming, quoted in *Numerical Recipes* 241.

Those who devote themselves to the purpose of proving that there is no purpose constitute an interesting subject for study. – A. N. Whitehead, *The Function of Reason*, 12, quoted in Jaki, *The Purpose of It All*, 57.

He alone is capable of carrying out a rational work, who is able to give a complete account of the why and wherefore of every detail from its conception to its completion. – Theobald Boehm, *The Flute and Flute-Playing*, xxv.

"Never forget that it is a waste of energy to do the same thing twice, and that if you know precisely what is to be done, you need not do it personally at all." – Rovol of Norlamin to Richard Seaton, in E.E. "Doc" Smith, *Skylark Three*.

"No machine can lie," said Father Brown, "nor can it tell the truth." – GKC, "The Mistake of the Machine" in *The Wisdom of Father Brown*.

Nemo dat quod non habet = "Nobody gives what he does not have." – an epigram of Scholastic Philosophy.

Quidquid recipitur secundum modum recipientis recipitur = "Whatever is received is received according to the mode of the receiver." – an epigram of Scholastic Philosophy.

If you drop any science out of the circle of knowledge, you cannot keep its place vacant for it; that science is forgotten; the other sciences close up; they exceed their proper bounds, and intrude where they have no right. – Newman, *The Idea of a University*, Discourse IV § 2.

One of the severest tests of the scientific mind is to know the limits of the legitimate application of the scientific method. – Maxwell, *The Scientific Papers of James Clerk Maxwell*, quoted in Jaki, *The Relevance of Physics*, 382.

"Begin at the beginning," the King said gravely, "and go on till you come to the end: then stop." Lewis Carroll, *Alice's Adventures in Wonderland*, chapter 12.

Medio tutissimus ibis = "You will go most safely in the middle." Ovid, *Metamorphoses* 2, 137.

Gratis asseritur, gratis negatur = "Freely asserted [is] freely denied." An ancient maxim.

Felix qui potuit cognoscere causas rerum = "Happy is he who is able to know the causes of things." Virgil, *Georgics*, II, 490.

Everything that is in the intellect has been in the senses. – GKC, *St. Thomas Aquinas*, CW2:525.

You can only find truth with logic if you have already found truth without it. GKC, *Daily News*, Feb 25, 1905 in Maycock 103-4.

The function of every program is to contact and serve its User. Daley, *TRON*, 125.

Know your tool: have some sense of what's under your hood!

If you want something done, do it yourself. (the "Little Red Hen Rule")

The First Problem-Solving Skill: Follow the Directions.

Appendix 8 – An Unexpected Addition

"I often stare at windows."

GKC, "The Crime of Gabriel Gale"
in *The Poet and the Lunatics*

But there was a much keener stroke of mediaeval irony earlier in the play. ["Faust"] The learned doctor has been ransacking all the libraries of the earth to find a certain rare formula, now almost unknown, by which he can control the infernal deities. At last he procures the one precious volume, opens it at the proper page, and leaves it on the table while he seeks some other part of his magic equipment. The servant comes in, reads off the formula, and immediately becomes an emperor of the spirits. He gives them a horrible time. He summons and dismisses them alternately with the rapidity of a piston-rod working at high speed; he keeps them flying between the doctor's house and their own more unmentionable residences till they faint with rage and fatigue. There is all the best of the Middle Ages in that; the idea of the great levellers, luck and laughter; the idea of a sense of humour defying and dominating hell.

GKC "A Drama of Dolls" in *Alarms and Discursions*

There are a number of other things I would like to tell you: things which ought not be lost, but do not seem to fit readily into any of the other parts of this book. So I am sticking them in here, as an appendix. Many of these come from notes I took during my graduate work; I tried to be meticulous about this sort of thing, since you can always find all the serious tech stuff in books, but these topics are far more elusive. I am hardly out of line [192] in this effort: the flagship journal of the Association for Computing Machinery published a special section [193] devoted to this very important part of our work. There was also a paper called "Pessimal Algorithms and Simplexity Theory"[194] – the only paper I have seen so far to cite both Homer's *Odyssey* and Verne's *Journey to the Center of the Earth*: the author claimed the former was the first published example of *breadth-first* search, while the latter was the first of *depth-first* search. Which is very important for us to know.

Q. What is purple and commutes?
A. An Abelian grape.

"We approximate infinity by a terabyte."

"Now is the time to search your virtual memories."

"The blackboard looked like sky on a dark night."

"When somebody says it's clear, it's not clear."

"You really have to believe there is a difference between PASCAL and sorting."

"Rings always have an identity, otherwise it's a 'RNG'."

"Computer Science is not only about managing a data base."

"A little bird called SORTING. You take an M16 and blow it away."

"I should criticize no answer, no matter how wrong."

"You cannot afford to build a different computer for each different algorithm."

---

[192] I have an excellent little book, Traynham's *Essays on the History of Organic Chemistry*, which concludes with a chapter similar to this.
[193] In *Communications of the ACM*, Vol. 27, No. 4, April 1984.
[194] In *SIGACT News*, Vol. 16. No. 3, Fall 1984.

"You can't add a hundredth of a number."

"We reduced the problem of solving a linear system to solving a linear system."

"W comes before X, despite the fact that it's a larger letter."

Solve 50,000 variables in a 10^6 x 10^6 linear system. It's a large system. Not something you do for linear algebra homework.

"Once you sort it what do you do? You write it out."

"That problem is NP-stupid."

"The chloroplasts are always greener in the other petri dish"

"In addition to being obvious, it's true always."

"Sorting by polar coordinates" (This is how Santa packs his sleigh.)

"We worked on it until it ran faster. That's why most people won't publish their data sets."

"Suppose I have 20 workstations available. I don't, but suppose I do."

Aristotle was a biologist. Philosophers hide this. He once dissected an elephant.

It's done by a computer (so) it must be right. The general public doesn't realize that it's just as easy to lie with a computer.

Q: (Gasp) "Can we do that?"
A: (Gasp) "No."

"Never use scientists as actors."

"All graphs of size thirty are trivial... I don't want to say I know all of them personally."

"How do we know birds fly? It's not dead; it's not a penguin; its feet aren't in concrete. They're 'normal' if they fly."

"Even though it's the most amazing subject in the whole world, you're not all organic chemists."

"Dump" is different if it's a core dump or a dump truck.

Parsing is the kind of thing you do in grade school.

"Prime beef" – it has no factors.

"There's this feeling you get when you play around with graphs: there are a *lot* of graphs."

On Parallel Architectures: "You don't want to know about things being done out of order, or you'll never get a good night's sleep again."

"It's hard to avoid making the same mistake once."

"I was a graduate student, and tired."

Oh, no! The system's dead!
(sung to the tune of "Ding, Dong the Witch Is Dead")

Oh, no! The system's dead!
Close your eyes, go back to bed!
Tell the users: "System's down again!"
Reload the system file,
Phones are ringing all the while,
All proclaiming "system's down again!"
It's down now, a tale of woe
Oh, no, oh no – oh no!
So push, oh push the button,
Then, oh then we'll go – oh!
Up! Up! the system's up!
But every file is now corrupt!
Time to take the system down again!!!

From "Frankel-etto: an eight-bit opera"
Peter J. Floriani
December, 1981

Bibliography

Note: All Bible quotes are from the Douay-Rheims version.

Aho, Alfred V. & Ullmann, Jeffrey D. *Principles of Compiler Design*. (Reading, MA: Addison-Wesley, 1977).

Aquinas, St. Thomas. *Catena Aurea*. (Albany, NY: Preserving Christian Publications, Inc., 2000).

—. *The Division and Methods of the Sciences*. Translated by Armand Maurer. (Toronto: Pontifical Institute of Medieval Studies, 1986).

—. *Summa Theologica*. Translated by Fathers of the English Dominican Province. (Allen, Texas: Christian Classics, 1948).

—. *The Three Greatest Prayers*. (Manchester, NH: Sophia Institute Press, 1990).

Babbage, Charles. *The Ninth Bridgewater Treatise: A Fragment*. (London: Frank Cass & Co., Ltd. 1967).

Boethius. *The Consolation of Philosophy*. Translated by W. V. Cooper. (Chicago: Regnery Gateway, 1981).

Boehm, Theobold. *The Flute and Flute Playing*. (New York: Dover Publications, Inc., 1964).

Brinley, Bertrand R. *The Mad Scientists' Club*. (Cynthiana, KY: Purple House Press, 2001).

Burnham, Robert, Jr. *Burnham's Celestial Handbook*. (New York: Dover Publications, Inc., 1978).

Cajori, Florian. *A History of Mathematical Notations*. (New York: Dover Publications, Inc., 1993).

Cardwell, Donald. *The Norton History of Technology*. (New York: W. W. Norton & Co., 1995).

Carroll, Lewis. *Alice in Wonderland and Other Favorites*. (New York: Washington Square Press, 1960). (The pen name of C. L. Dodgson; this volume includes *Alice's Adventures in Wonderland*, *Through the Looking-Glass*, and *The Hunting of the Snark*.)

Chesterton, G. K. His collected works (CW) are published by Ignatius Press in San Francisco.

—. *Alarms and Discursions*.

—. *The Apostle and the Wild Ducks*.

—. *Autobiography*. (In CW16)

—. *Charles Dickens*. (In CW15)

—. *The Club of Queer Trades*. (In CW6)

—. *The Common Man*.

—. *The Everlasting Man*. (In CW2)

—. *Heretics*. (In CW1)

—. *Lunacy and Letters*.

—. *Illustrated London News* essays (In CW27-36.)

—. *Orthodoxy*. (In CW1)

—. *The Poet and the Lunatics*. (In CW9.)

—. *Robert Browning*.

—. *St. Thomas Aquinas*. (In CW2)

—. *The Innocence of Father Brown*. (In CW11/12)

—. *The Wisdom of Father Brown*. (In CW11/12)

—. *What's Wrong With the World*. (In CW4)

Daley, Brian. *TRON*. (New York: Ballantine Books, 1982).

Darnell, J., Lodish, H., and Baltimore, D. *Molecular Cell Biology*. (New York: Scientific American Books, 1990).

Forsyth, Cecil. *Orchestration*. (New York: The Macmillan Company, 1949).

Foster, Kenelm. O.P. (translator and editor). *The Life of St. Thomas Aquinas. Biographical Documents*. (London: Longmans, Green and Co. 1959).

Gaskell, Philip. *A New Introduction to Bibliography*. (Oxford: At the Clarendon Press, 1972).

Gardiner, Sir Alan. *Egyptian Grammar*. (London: Oxford University Press, 1969).

Gellert, W., Küstner H., Hellwich, M., Kästner, H. (eds.) *The VNR Concise Encyclopedia of Mathematics*. (New York: Van Nostrand Reinhold Co. 1975).

Gerald, Curtis E. *Applied Numerical Analysis*. (Reading, MA: Addison-Wesley Publishing Co., 1978.).

Gilson, Etienne. *The Spirit of Medieval Philosophy*. (New York: Charles Scribner's Sons, 1949).

Gilluly, James, Waters, Aaron C., and Woodford, A. O. *Principles of Geology*. (San Francisco: W. H. Freeman and Company, 1975).

Gray, Henry. *Gray's Anatomy*. (New York: Bounty Books, 1977).

Harrow, Benjamin. *Eminent Chemists of Our Time*. (New York: D. Van Nostrand Company, Inc. 1927).

Hayes, William. *Project: Genius*. (New York: Atheneum, 1967).

Hazan, Marcella. *The Classic Italian Cookbook*. (New York: Ballantine Books, 1973).

Hellemans, Alexander, and Bunch, Bryan. *The Timetables of Science*. (New York: Simon and Schuster, 1988).

Jaki. S. L. *Brain, Mind, and Computers*. (South Bend, IN: Gateway Editions, 1978).

—. *The Limits of a Limitless Science*. (Wilmington, DE: ISI Books, 2000).

—. *Numbers Decide and Other Essays*. (Pinckney, MI: Real View Books, 2003).

—. *Patterns or Principles and Other Essays*. (Wilmington, DE: ISI Publications, 1995)

—. *The Purpose of It All*. (Washington, D.C.: Regnery Gateway, 1990).

—. *The Relevance of Physics*. (Edinburgh: Scottish Academic Press, 1992).

—. *The Road of Science and the Ways to God*. The Gifford Lectures 1975 and 1976. (Chicago: University of Chicago Press; Edinburgh: Scottish Academic Press, 1978)

—. *Science and Creation*. (Edinburgh: Scottish Academic Press, 1986).

Juster, Norton. *The Phantom Tollbooth*. (New York: Random House, 1961).

Kreyche, Robert J. *First Philosophy*. (New York: Holt, Rhinehart and Winston, Inc., 1959).

Knuth. Donald A. *The Art of Computer Programming*. 3 vols. (Reading, MA: Addison-Wesley, 1973).

Lebrecht, Norman. *The Book of Musical Anecdotes*. (New York: The Free Press, 1985).

Lin, Shu, and Costello, Daniel J., Jr. *Error Control Coding*. (Englewood Cliffs, NJ: Prentice-Hall, Inc., 1983).

Maycock, A. L. *The Man Who Was Orthodox*. A Selection from the Uncollected Writings of G. K. Chesterton. (London: Dennis Dobson, 1963).

Newman, James R., ed. *The World of Mathematics*. 4 vols. (New York: Simon and Schuster, 1956).

Newman, John Henry. *The Idea of a University*. (New York: Doubleday Image, 1959).

Parzen, Emanuel. *Modern Probability Theory and Its Applications*. (New York: John Wiley & Sons, Inc., 1960).

Petri Hispani. (Peter of Spain, Pope John XXI). *Summulae Logicales*. (Rome: Domus Editorialis Marietti, 1947).

Pieper, Josef. *In Defense of Philosophy*. (San Francisco: Ignatius Press, 1992).

Press, William H., Flannery, Brian P., Teukolsky, Saul A., and Wetterling, William T. *Numerical Recipes*. (Cambridge: Cambridge University Press, 1986).

Rawn, *Biochemistry*. (Burlington, NC: Neil Patterson Publishers, 1989).

Roberts, Fred S. *Applied Combinatorics*. (Englewood Cliffs, NJ: Prentice-Hall, Inc., 1984).

Rodgers, R. and Hammerstein II, O. *The King and I*, (NY: Williamson Music Inc., 1951).

Runes, Dagobert. D., *et al. Dictionary of Philosophy*. (Totowa, New Jersey: Littlefield, Adams & Co., 1976).

Sedgewick, *Algorithms*. (Reading, MA: Addison-Wesley, 1983).

Shallo, Michael W. *Scholastic Philosophy*. (Philadelphia: The Peter Reilly Company, 1944).

Shiva, Sajjon G. *Computer Design and Architecture*. (Little, Brown & Co., 1985).

Sidgwick, J. B. *Amateur Astronomer's Handbook*. (New York: Dover Publications, Inc., 1971).

Smith, E.E. "Doc." *Skylark Three*. (Pyramid Books, 1930).

Steneck, Nicholas H. "A Late Medieval Arbor Scientiarum" in *Speculum*, Vol. 50, No.2 (Apr. 1975) pp. 245-269.

—. *Science and Creation in the Middle Ages*. (Notre Dame, Indiana: University of Notre Dame Press, 1976).

Stone, Harold S. *Discrete Mathematical Structures and Their Applications*. (Chicago: Science Research Associates, Inc., 1973).

Tarjan, Robert E. *Data Structures and Network Algorithms*. (Philadelphia: Society for Industrial and Applied Mathematics, 1983).

Taylor, Jerome. *The Didascalicon of Hugh of St. Victor*. (New York: Columbia University Press, 1961).

Traynham, James G. *Essays on the History of Organic Chemistry*. (Baton Rouge: Louisiana State University Press, 1987).

Ullman, B.L. and Henry, Norman E.. *Latin for Americans*. Second Book. (New York: The Macmillan Company, 1950).

Usher, Abbott Payson. *A History of Mechanical Inventions*. (New York: Dover Publications, Inc. 1988).

van Delft, Pieter and Botermans, Jack. *Creative Puzzles of the World*. (New York: Henry N. Abrams, Inc. 1978).

Van Nostrand's Scientific Encyclopedia. (New York: D. Van Nostrand Co., 1938).

Walsh, James, J., M.D. *The Popes and Science*. (New York: Fordham University Press, 1908).

Ward, Maisie. *Gilbert Keith Chesterton*. (New York: Sheed and Ward, 1943).

—. *Return to Chesterton*. (New York: Sheed and Ward, 1943).

Williams, J. and Abrashkin, W. *Danny Dunn on a Desert Island*. (New York: Pocket Books, 1957).

Windle, Bertram C. A. *The Catholic Church and its Reactions with Science*. (New York: The Macmillan Co., 1927).

Sample Code

The following samples (and others) will also be found on the website:

`http://www.DeBellisStellarum.com/cscs/cscs.htm`

Code for a self-reproducing program

```
/* Self-reproducing program  PJF 9/9/1990 */
void main() {
#define nl '\n'
#define max 18
int head=7,i;
char txt[max][80] = {
 {"%s%c"}
,{"%c{%c%s%c}%c"}
,{"/* Self-reproducing program  PJF 9/9/1990 */"}
,{"void main() {"}
,{"#define nl '~n'"}
,{"#define max 18"}
,{"int head=7,i;"}
,{"char txt[max][80] = {"}
,{"};"}
,{"    txt[4][12]=92;"}
,{"    for(i=2;i<=head;i=i+1)"}
,{"        printf(txt[0],txt[i],nl);"}
,{"    txt[4][12]=126;"}
,{"    for(i=0;i<max;i=i+1)"}
,{"        printf(txt[1],(i==0?' ':','),34,txt[i],34,nl);"}
,{"    for(i=head+1;i<max;i=i+1)"}
,{"        printf(txt[0],txt[i],nl);"}
,{"}"}
};
    txt[4][12]=92;
    for(i=2;i<=head;i=i+1)
        printf(txt[0],txt[i],nl);
    txt[4][12]=126;
    for(i=0;i<max;i=i+1)
        printf(txt[1],(i==0?' ':','),34,txt[i],34,nl);
    for(i=head+1;i<max;i=i+1)
        printf(txt[0],txt[i],nl);
}
```

Code for Non-recursive Traversal of a Binary Tree

```
// original Feb 19, 1984 in BASIC
// converted into "C" Sept 9, 2013
// TreeType has lft, rgt, dad pointers besides its data
// returns the maximum depth of the tree
// note three "Visit" routines to be used as desired

#define TRUE  (1)
#define FALSE (0)

int NonrecursiveTreeWalk(TreeType * root)
{
  TreeType * thisnode;
  TreeType * child;
  int done,descending,ascending,maxdepth,depth;

  if(root==NULL)return 0;
  descending=TRUE;
  thisnode=root;
  done=FALSE;
  maxdepth=0;
```

```
depth=1;
while(!done)
    {
    if(descending)
        {
        // descend to the left until we're at
        // the leftmost leaf of the subtree
        VisitPrefix(thisnode);
        while(thisnode->lft!=NULL)
            {
            VisitPrefix(thisnode->lft);
            thisnode=thisnode->lft;
            depth=depth+1;
            }//end while not-at-leftmost
        }
    VisitInfix(thisnode);
    if(depth>maxdepth)maxdepth=depth;
    // now see if there's anything to our right...
    if(thisnode->rgt==NULL)
        {
        // nothing on the right - ascend until we find
        // a left-branch we came down, or ar done
        VisitPostfix(thisnode);
        // just in case the root has an empty right-branch
        if(thisnode->dad==NULL)
            {
            done=TRUE;
            }
        else
            {
            // there's stuff on the right...
            ascending=TRUE;
            while(ascending)
                {
                // see if we had come left to get here...
                child=thisnode;
                thisnode=thisnode->dad;
                depth=depth-1;
                if(thisnode->lft==child)
                    {
                    // we came from the left - there's more to do
                    ascending=FALSE;
                    }
                else
                    {
                    // came from the right - see if we're done
                    if(thisnode==root)
                        {
                        VisitPostfix(thisnode);
                        done=TRUE;
                        ascending=FALSE;
                        }
                    else
                        {
                        VisitPostfix(thisnode);
                        }
                    }
                }//end while ascending
            descending=FALSE;
            }
        }
    else
        {
        // stuff on the right, go down that subtree
        thisnode=thisnode->rgt;
        depth=depth+1;
        descending=TRUE;
        }
    }//end while not-done
```

```
        return maxdepth;
    }
```

Code for non-recursive addition of a node to a binary tree

```
TreeType * AddToTree(int key,TreeType ** root)
{
  TreeType * n;
  TreeType * p;
  TreeType * q;
  int k,wentleft;

  // is the tree empty?
  if((*root)==NULL)
      {
      // yes it is empty
      wentleft=0;
      }
  else
      {
      // the tree isn't empty - find where this key goes...
      q=NULL;
      p=(*root);
      while(p!=NULL)
          {
          k=KeyCompare(key,p);
          if(k<0)
              {
              q=p;
              p=p->lft;
              wentleft=1;
              }
          else if(k>0)
              {
              q=p;
              p=p->rgt;
              wentleft=2;
              }
          else
              {
              // it was already there, we won't add it again.
              return p;
              }
          }//end while
      }
  // add a new item to the tree
  n=malloc(sizeof(TreeType));
  n->value=key;
  n->lft=NULL;
  n->rgt=NULL;
  if(wentleft==1)
      q->lft=n;
  else if(wentleft==2)
      q->rgt=n;
  else
      (*root)=n;
  return n;
}
```

Code for Merge

```
typedef struct CardType_
  {
  int suit; // 1=club 2=diamond 3=heart 4=spade
  int rank; // 1=ace 11=jack 12=queen 13=king
  }
CardType;
```

191

```
typedef struct CardListType_
  {
  int count;
  CardType list[52];
  }
CardListType;

void MergeCards(CardListType * lft, CardListType * rgt,
                        CardListType * result)
{
  int L,R,done,k;

  L=0;
  R=0;
  result->count=0;
  done=0;
  while(!done)
      {
      if(L<lft->count)
          {
          // still have some on left
          if(R<rgt->count)
              {
              // still have some on right
              k=lft->list[L].rank-rgt->list[R].rank;
              if(k<0)
                  {
                  // left side smaller, add that one
                  result->list[result->count]=lft->list[L];
                  result->count=result->count+1;
                  L=L+1;
                  }
              else if(k>0)
                  {
                  // right side smaller, add that one
                  result->list[result->count]=rgt->list[R];
                  result->count=result->count+1;
                  R=R+1;
                  }
              else
                  {
                  // the cards match, do both...
                  // (other uses might handle this case
differently)
                  result->list[result->count]=lft->list[L];
                  result->count=result->count+1;
                  L=L+1;
                  result->list[result->count]=rgt->list[R];
                  result->count=result->count+1;
                  R=R+1;
                  }
              }
          else
              {
              // right list is finished, but not left
              result->list[result->count]=lft->list[L];
              result->count=result->count+1;
              L=L+1;
              }
          }
      else
          {
          // left list is finished, see about right list
          if(R<rgt->count)
              {
              // left list is finished, but not right
              result->list[result->count]=rgt->list[R];
              result->count=result->count+1;
              R=R+1;
```

```
                      }
            else
                {
                // both are finished
                done=1;
                }
            }
        }//end while
}
```

Code for drawing an arrowhead on a line segment

```
//these values may be whatever you like...
#define ARROW_ANGLE (pi*25.0/180.0)
#define ARROW_HEAD 15.0

void Arrow(x1, y1, x2, y2)
{
  REAL d,dx,dy,vx,vy,ax,ay,bx,by;
  REAL xa1,ya1,xa2,ya2;
// draw the vector itself
  DrawSegment(x1,y1,x2,y2);
  dx=x2-x1;
  dy=y2-y1;
  d=sqrt(dx*dx+dy*dy);
  if(d<ARROW_HEAD)return;
  ax=dx/d;
  ay=dy/d;
  bx=cos(ARROW_ANGLE);
  by=sin(ARROW_ANGLE);
// draw the arrowhead on the left side
  xa1=x2-ARROW_HEAD*(ax*bx+ay*by);
  ya1=y2-ARROW_HEAD*(ay*bx-ax*by);
  DrawSegment(x2,y2,xa1,ya1);
// draw the arrowhead on the right side
  xa2=x2-ARROW_HEAD*(ax*bx-ay*by);
  ya2=y2-ARROW_HEAD*(ay*bx+ax*by);
  DrawSegment(x2,y2,xa2,ya2);
}
```

Code for drawing a hypocycloid

```
void HypoCycloid(int K,int L,double radius,double penfrac,double
start)
{
  double delta = 10.0;
  int i;
  double z,b,c,angle,startangle,maxangle,incangle;
  double r,zb,zc,rb,r_yt,t,xt,x,y,cosa,sina,ratio;

  if(K<L) {i=K; K=L; L=i; }

  if(radius<0)
      {
      z=-1.0;
      radius=-radius;
      }
  else
      z=1.0;

  ratio=(double)L/(double)K;
  b=radius*ratio;
  if(penfrac==0)penfrac=1.0;
  c=penfrac*b;
  startangle=(start*pi/180.0);
  maxangle=startangle+2.0*pi*L;
  incangle=delta*(pi/180.0)*b*ratio;
```

```
    angle=startangle;
    r=radius-z*(b-c);
    MovePenUp(r*cos(angle),r*sin(angle));

    zb=z*b;
    zc=z*c;
    rb=radius/b;
    do
        {
        t=(angle-startangle)*rb;
        xt=-c*sin(t);
        r_yt=radius-(zb-zc*cos(t));
        sina=sin(angle);
        cosa=cos(angle);
        x=-xt*sina+cosa*(r_yt);
        y= xt*cosa+sina*(r_yt);
        MovePenDown(x,y);
        angle=angle+incangle;
        }
    while(angle<=maxangle);

    MovePenDown(r*cos(startangle),r*sin(startangle));
}
```

Code for printing the actual value of a floating-point number

```
void ShowFloat(float num)
{
  int k;
  float whole,frac,next;
  int n,i,j;
  int bits[512];
  int pwr2[512];
  int acc[512];
  union
        {
        float f;
        unsigned char m[4];
        } q;

  printf("%26.20f = ",num);
  q.f=num;
  printf("[%02x%02x%02x%02x] ",q.m[0],q.m[1],q.m[2],q.m[3]);

  // deal with the sign first...
  if(num<0)
        {
        printf("-");
        num=-num;
        }
  whole=floor(num);
  frac=num-whole;

  // show the whole portion...
  i=0;
  do
        {
        next=floor(whole/10.0);
        acc[i]=whole-next*10.0;
        whole=next;
        i=i+1;
        }
  while(whole!=0);
  i=i-1;
  while(i>=0)
        {
        printf("%d",acc[i]);
        i=i-1;
```

```
            }//end while

        // show the fractional portion...
        printf(".");
        j=0;
        n=1;
        memset(pwr2,0,sizeof(pwr2));
        memset(acc,0,sizeof(acc));
        pwr2[0]=5;
        while(frac!=0)
            {
            frac=2.0*frac;
            k=(int)frac;
            bits[j]=k;
            j=j+1;
            frac=frac-(float)k;
            if(k==1)
                {
                // add the current power of two to the accumulator
                for(i=n-1;i>=0;i=i-1)
                    {
                    acc[i]=acc[i]+pwr2[i];
                    if(acc[i]>9)
                        {
                        acc[i]=acc[i]-10;
                        acc[i-1]=acc[i-1]+1;
                        }
                    }//end for i
                }

            // compute the next power of two
            for(i=0;i<=n;i=i+1)
                {
                if(pwr2[i]&1)
                    {
                    pwr2[i+1]=pwr2[i+1]+10;
                    }
                pwr2[i]=pwr2[i]>>1;
                }//end for i
            if(pwr2[n]>0)n=n+1;
            }//end while

    for(i=0;i<j;i=i+1)
        printf("%d",acc[i]);
    printf("\n");
}
```

Code for attempting to find a perfect hash

```
int hashcheck(char * buf,int p,int q)
{
  int i,h;
  h=0;
  i=0;
  while(buf[i]!=0)
      {
      h=(h*p+buf[i]);
      i=i+1;
      }//end while
  return h%q;
}

#define hashmax 500
#define hashpmax 1000
#define hashqmax 500

void PerfectHash(char * fname)
{
```

```
typedef char StringType[80];
StringType Table[hashmax];
int hash[hashqmax];
FILE * f;
char buf[512];
int i,j,m,smax,n,p,q,h,k;

f=fopen(fname,"rt");
if(f==NULL)exit(1);

n=0;
smax=0;
do
    {
    fgets(buf,511,f);
    if(!feof(f))
        {
        k=strlen(buf);
        buf[k-1]=0;
        strcpy(Table[n],buf);
        n=n+1;
        if(k>smax)smax=k;
        }
    }
while(!feof(f));
fclose(f);

q=n;
m=0;
do
    {
    p=1;
    do
        {
        for(i=0;i<=q;i=i+1)
            hash[i]=-1;

        for(i=0;i<n;i=i+1)
            {
            // generate the hash of the i-th table entry
            h=0;
            j=0;
            while(Table[i][j]!=0)
                {
                h=(h*p+Table[i][j]);
                j=j+1;
                }//end while
            h=h%q;
            if(hash[h]>=0)
                {
                if(i>m)
                  m=i;
                goto next;
                }
            else
                hash[h]=i;
            }//end for

        // SUCCESS! we found a pair which gives a perfect hash
        printf("p=%d q=%d\n",p,q);
        printf("\nhash table:\n");

        for(i=0;i<q;i=i+1)
            {
            if(hash[i]<0)
                printf("%3d\n",i);
            else
                printf("%3d %s\n",i,Table[hash[i]]);
            }//end for
```

```
                printf("\ncheck:\n");
                for(i=0;i<n;i=i+1)
                    printf("%3d %s\n",hashcheck(Table[i],p,q),Table[i]);
                exit(0);
next:;
            p=p+1;
            }
    while(p<hashpmax);
    q=q+1;
    }
    while(q<hashqmax);
}
```

Index

Note: the symbol *p†n* indicates that the given term can be found in note *n* on page *p*.

valine 80
vamp until ready 73
vector 46, 70, 131
Verne, Jules 184
video playback 39, 160
violinist 161
Von Neumann Principle 10, 26
Von Neumann, John 10, 26
vortices 91
VSAT 87, 146
VTR 146

Waclawik, James M. vi, 33, 55
walk-and-chew-gum 107
Ward, Maisie 6†14, 27†44, 107†124, 188
washing machines 81
WATCHER 31, 115†133, 149-150
water 112, 161
Watson, John H. vii
Watson-Crick 161
weed-whacker 31
wheel 41, 112, 160
white paper 23, 29, 32, 36-37, 134
White Rabbit 73
white space 43, 159
Whitehead, Alfred N. 29†47, 183
whitespacematters 89
Who-ville 134
Wiedemann 153, 155-156
wildcard 18†34, 95, 169
willingness to learn 89
willingness to teach 89
Willson, Meredith 31
Windle, Bertram 39, 188
windows 11, 14, 75, 83-84, 118†140, 133, 144, 158,
    184
wine 88, 161
Wolfe, Nero 71
word processor 118†140
Wöhler, Friedrich 162†180

x-86 130, 140
xor 9, 164-165
xyzzy 75

zam-zoogles 134
zed 43†63
zee 43†63
Zeus 88

www.ingramcontent.com/pod-product-compliance
Lightning Source LLC
Chambersburg PA
CBHW071146050326
40689CB00011B/2003